Malcolm H. H

The Wolverines

A Story of Michigan Football

The Wolverines

A Story of Michigan Football

by

Will Perry

THE STRODE PUBLISHERS
HUNTSVILLE, ALABAMA 35802

To My Mom And Dad,
Two Special Persons

We would like to thank the following for their cooperation in supplying pictures for this book:

Bob Kalmbach and John Hayfield of The University of Michigan, The *Michigan Daily, Ann Arbor News, Midland Daily News, Flint Journal, Detroit Free Press, Detroit News, Minneapolis Tribune,* Rentschler Studios, *Grand Rapids Press,* Eck Stanger, Jack Stubbs, Cecil Lockard, Stuart Abbey, Joe Arcure, and the Michigan Athletic Department. We are especially appreciative to Bill LaCrosse of the U. of M. Television Department for his color picture on the cover.

Contents

Foreword

Introduction

1. The Meaning Of Michigan Football 11
2. The Man From Shanghai...Or Anyone For Rugby? ... 20
3. "Pond Forever" 23
4. From Freight Trains To Dining Cars 28
5. The Big Seven Arrives 35
6. A Toast From Coast-To-Coast Or...
    Here Comes Mr. Yost 41
7. "We Want Heston" 48
8. The Rose Bowl 55
9. A Water Jug Becomes Famous 64
10. An Era Ends...Barely 69
11. "Then There Were Seven" 74
12. The Forward Pass Comes Of Age 78
13. Of Men And Spirit 82
14. A "Loser" Wins 89
15. A Call For Help Answered 92
16. "Kipke's Dedication" 98
17. A Ghost Gallops 104
18. The Benny-To-Bennie Show 109
19. Mr. Brown "Meets" Mr. Grange 113
20. "It's Touchdowns That Count" 118
21. Michigan Gains A Stadium, Loses An All-American ...127
22. The "Golden Years" Return 133
23. Rose Bowl? No, Thanks 137

24.	A Touch Of Class	142
25.	No Cheers From The Alumni	150
26.	A Touch Of The Ivy League	156
27.	A Near Miss	162
28.	Harmon Of Michigan	167
29.	A Birthday Present On The Coast	175
30.	A Trip To South Bend	182
31.	The Years Of Lend-Lease	192
32.	"M" Platoon Meets Army	200
33.	The Year Of People	205
34.	The Perfect Season	212
35.	Recount After The Roses	223
36.	Crisler Retires, The Single Wing Remains	228
37.	Ben's National Champions	232
38.	A Premature Burial	239
39.	The "Snow Bowl"	249
40.	"Victory Is Still Ours"	253
41.	The Changing World Of Football	259
42.	No Titles, But Compassion	264
43.	A Season For Upsets	271
44.	Fifteen-And-Six, Just Not Enough	280
45.	A Definition Of Victory	291
46.	The Formative Years	298
47.	"Woody Cut The Connection...50-20"	303
48.	You Have To Start Somewhere	307
49.	Bump's Finest Moment	310
50.	Rose Bowl IV	318
51.	One Pass Too Many	322
52.	Ron Johnson...Halfback	329
53.	Canham—The Guy From Madison Avenue	337
54.	Hamburgers And Road Maps	340
55.	"The Fire Had Gone Out"	346
56.	A Winter Of Wondering	352
57.	The Title Arrives Early	356
58.	Rain And Roses	364
59.	Not Enough Touchdowns	369
60.	A Long Ride Home	375
61.	The Tie Game	384
	Epilogue	389
	Appendix	391

Foreword

To be part of college football is to be part of more than an athletic contest. There is a special feeling involved in the spectacle of precision marching bands, the enthusiasm of the cheerleaders, the pageantry of a homecoming or a high school band day, the atmosphere that surrounds the campus. We know the elation of victory, the despair of defeat—then realize there is another game, another season. You feel the traditions that can spring only from a college campus, each unique, each special.

The Wolverines is a story of more than ninety-four years of football. It is, in a sense, the story of all college football. It is a positive story, one of accomplishment, of success, and of disappointment. It is the story of thousands of Michigan students waiting at a train station for a defeated team to return home from a crucial game with Minnesota, waiting to show they cared about their team. It is a story of 10,000 students following their team to the Rose Bowl, of pep rallies, of that one magic moment when their team rises to unexpected heights and victory follows.

We are proud of our football tradition at Michigan and honored to be part of it.

Don Canham
Director of Intercollegiate Athletics
and Physical Education
The University of Michigan

Introduction

Hail to the Victors valiant,
Hail to the conquering heroes,
Hail, hail to Michigan
The leaders and best;

Hail to the Victors valiant
Hail to the conquering heroes,
Hail, hail to Michigan
The Champions of the West.

Those eight lines, written seventy-six years ago, expressed the feelings of one young Michigan student inspired by victory on the football field. They also represent part of a tradition that is uniquely Michigan's. This is a story of that tradition; how it was built and how it is sustained. It is the story of Michigan football.

Durable, depending not on momentary brilliance, it was built patiently through time, to be shared by all ages. Perhaps the first threads of Michigan's tradition were woven on a Thanksgiving Day of 1898 in Chicago when the Wolverines, trailing the powerful Maroons of Amos Alonzo Stagg by five points and heading for defeat, produced a special *deus ex machina*. Michigan had possession of the ball late in the game when Charlie Widman ran sixty-five yards for a touchdown and a 12-11 Wolverine victory.

It was an important victory. It meant the first of twenty-five Western Conference championships for Michigan. But it meant something, too, for Louis Elbel, a music student who joined in a victory dance with hundreds of other Michigan students who had traveled to Chicago for that game.

Years later, Elbel recalled, "There was never a more enthusiastic Michigan student than I, but that team and that Chicago game pushed me way up in the clouds, and all I had to do was fill in the notes, and there was *The Victors*."

So Michigan had its first football championship and a fight song. In the decades to follow there would be more victories and more championships and defeats as the Michigan tradition added layer upon layer of substance. Yost, Heston, Kipke, Oosterbaan, Crisler, Harmon, Chappuis, the Elliotts, the Wisterts, Canham and Schembechler, and hundreds of others would add their special greatness to that tradition.

Before recounting their story let us replay just one Saturday in 1969, and therein lies the meaning of Michigan football. It is, indeed, the story of men.

The Meaning of Michigan Football

Don Canham stood next to the rail on the photo deck of Michigan's mammoth press box. Giant cameras with ABC stamped in red, blue, and green pointed silently downward toward the artificial grass field. The deck was overly crowded, and in the giant bowl below more than 100,000 committed fans offered a panorama of color.

"This is what it's all about," Canham offered, completely absorbed in the tenseness which somehow grips all great athletic events. He was completing his second football season as Michigan's athletic director. As a track coach for nineteen years, football had not particularly excited him, but that had changed. Michigan now was playing for the Big Ten championship before the largest audience ever assembled in modern-day football. The game was scheduled for television on a regional basis, but one-by-one stations across the nation plugged into the massive ABC network.

It was Michigan against Ohio State. The Buckeyes of 1969 were undefeated and acclaimed the finest college football team of the day; some said the best of all-time. There were suggestions that a proper match for Ohio State would be the Minnesota Vikings.

The staunchest of Michigan fans held thin hopes of victory. More realistically, most would settle for a close game. The nagging thought of an Ohio State rout could not be shaken, and such a one-sided outcome could ruin Michigan's chances for a trip to the Rose Bowl.

Going into this crisp, November Saturday, Michigan rated

11

as the prime choice to play Southern Cal on New Year's Day. Ohio State was the final victim of the Big Ten's long-standing "no repeat" rule which prohibited a team from successive appearances in the Rose Bowl. The Buckeyes played in the Rose Bowl the previous year, defeating Southern Cal, 27-16.

Coach Woody Hayes of Ohio State during the week offered his case to the press. He strongly urged reconsideration of this policy, pointing out the unusual competence of his team. There was strong support for his arguments. West Coast writers again were attacking the Big Ten's "no repeat" rule, but this time in greater strength. Michigan had lost once in the conference, a stinging defeat to arch-rival Michigan State in East Lansing. A loss to Ohio State would give the Wolverines a second place finish, a position they possibly would share with onrushing Purdue. And coupled with a nonconference loss to Missouri, their credentials as a Rose Bowl team would be tarnished.

Still, with Ohio State barred and Michigan holding a victory over Purdue, the vote, the press speculated, would go in favor of the Wolverines. Should Michigan collapse, should Ohio State put it all together as it was so capable of doing, then those voices from the West Coast, and possibly in West Lafayette, would be heard in increasing numbers.

Ohio State had dazzled its opponents with the raw power of Jim Otis, the ball-handling artistry and passing of Rex Kern, and a defense that offered Jim Stillwagon. He was the key to an impressive five-man line, while in the secondary there was a roverback of intimidating proportions...Jack Tatum. Acclaimed national champions in 1968, the Buckeyes now had won twenty-two straight games.

The pre-game build-up was massive. Woody was a daily story out of Columbus, while the West Coast press added to the quickening pulse of the game. Every possible turn was explored. What the papers did not print, however, was a unique game plan outlined to the Michigan players by their coach, Glenn E. (Bo) Schembechler.

Schembechler, in his first year at Michigan, had groomed his team like a swimming coach pointing for a championship meet. Week-by-week the improvement came. It had started at midseason in Minneapolis where Michigan, trailing Minnesota

12

9-7, exploded in the second half and won convincingly, 35-9. Then in succession the Wolverines rolled: Wisconsin, 35-7, Illinois, 57-0, Iowa, 51-6.

When those sixty minutes of football in Iowa City were completed, Schembechler privately proclaimed, "This Michigan team can beat Ohio State." He carefully took another approach, much less emphatic, with the writers, but in the locker room, he laid it out for his team.

"I asked them if there was anyone who didn't believe we could win the next one. There wasn't one player who didn't have the confidence that we could. At least I knew of none.

"The next week in preparing for the game I put it straight to them. We would win if every man played his best game. It was as simple as that. Henry Hill, our middle guard, must outplay Stillwagon. Don Moorhead would outplay their quarterback, Kern. Jim Mandich would be better Saturday than Jan White at tight end. Every player knew what he had to do for us to win."

The preparations, the build-up, the speculation now were over. A midweek snowstorm gave way to a bright, crisp Saturday. Temperatures moved into the forties.

Ohio won the toss and immediately took the game to Michigan. Kern on the first play, as if to warn his opponents that no compromise would be made today, dropped back to pass, hesitated, and ran for twenty-five yards. Then it was Otis for seven, Otis for three, Otis for one, Otis for seven, down to the Michigan 11-yard line where the Buckeyes needed just a yard for a first down. The challenge was real.

Predictably, Kern sent his 235-pound fullback over the middle, right at Henry Hill. A walk-on playing without an athletic scholarship, Hill had been an undersized tight end at Martin Luther King High School in Detroit. He had not been recruited and decided to attend Michigan when Bo's assistant coach, George Mans, showed interest in him.

Hill and Otis met head on and when the officials measured the progress of Otis' charge at center, the stadium erupted. Inches short! "Henry Hill must outplay Stillwagon," Schembechler, looking from the sidelines, felt that his message was understood.

Still, this was the first thrust. The giant was alive, and

Michigan middle guard Henry Hill (39) stops Ohio State's Jim Otis in 1969 upset of Buckeyes in Michigan Stadium.

moments later Larry Zelina brought the Buckeyes across midfield with a brilliant punt return. Then a pass Michigan had not seen before, Kern to White on a slant across the middle, set up the touchdown, a short dive by Otis. The conversion attempt floated wide, but that seemed unimportant. Ohio State, as it had been all season, was in the lead.

Now Michigan had to come back. Moorhead started to throw. First to Mike Oldham for eight, then to Mandich for seven, and again to Mandich for nine. John Gabler, a seldom-used wingback, gained eleven yards on a counter play. Moorhead rolled to his left for six, then Garvie Craw, strong, determined, struck viciously at left guard for the touchdown. Frank Titas kicked the extra point, and Michigan had the lead.

There were nearly fifty minutes to play, and Ohio State, still strong, still talented, came back to score. Stan White booted the extra point perfectly. The officials, however, caught a Michigan player offsides, and now Hayes had a decision: take the point, or move the ball 1½ yards from the goal line and try for two. Hayes, perhaps thinking of Henry Hill denying them a mere yard, thinking that touchdowns may be hard to produce, went for the two points that just might force Michigan into a hard decision later. Kern immediately scrambled out to the left, looking to pass. He never had a chance. Mike Keller roared in from his right end position to hit the Buckeye quarterback, and from the opposite end, big Cecil Pryor, playing his finest game, swarmed over the staggering Kern. Michigan trailed by only five points.

Michigan promptly took the kickoff and drove 67 yards for a touchdown, never once facing a third-down situation. Craw scored his second touchdown from the 1, and when Titas kicked the extra point the Wolverines were up by two points, those two points Hayes figured he needed moments before. Schembechler had told the press earlier in the week, "They won't blow us out of there. This team is just too good for that."

Then it happened. The first, big, spectacular play that sent the momentum of the game to Michigan. Detroit Free Press sports editor Joe Falls had been among the consensus favoring Ohio State. Now watching from the front row of the press box he turned to another reporter. "You know, they just might be able to pull it off."

The play came on a punt to Barry Pierson on Michigan's 37. A senior from St. Ignace in Michigan's Upper Peninsula, Pierson started up the middle, broke through the first wave of white jerseys, and ran 60 yards to the Ohio State three. Two plays later Moorhead scored the touchdown and Titas' kick put Michigan ahead by nine points.

Again the Buckeyes came back, moving impressively to Michigan's 25-yard line. Then Pete Newell, a philosophy major, a member of the athletic board, powered through the Ohio State line from his defensive tackle position and caught the scrambling Kern for an 11-yard loss. The drive was stopped.

Michigan, however, would not let up. Quickly Moorhead had the Wolverines moving, and, unexpectedly, from the 3-yard line he fired a pass to Mandich in the end zone. The thunderous cheers that virtually shook Michigan Stadium faded imme-diately when a penalty nullified the touchdown. Tim Killian promptly kicked a short field goal with just 15 seconds left in the half, and Michigan ran into the dressing room with an unbe-lievable 24-12 lead.

There was no show of emotion in Michigan's locker room, except for Jim Young. He had come from Miami with Bo and was the architect of Michigan's proud defense. Young pounded his fist on the blackboard and shouted, "No more, damn it, they will not score anymore." Young then made some defensive adjustments, Bo talked quietly to the offense and they moved out into the long, dark tunnel and into the bright sunshine of the stadium. The greeting was deafening.

If there had been a tenseness before the game, it came in a new dimension now. There was an anticipation, a feeling that the Buckeyes surely would erupt. But then Pierson intercepted a Kern pass. He intercepted another pass, then another in what was one of the most inspired games Michigan fans had ever witnessed. When Pierson stole his third pass from reserve quarterback Ron Maciejowski, there was no doubt. Michigan had achieved one of the greatest upset victories in college football. Late in the fourth period the Buckeyes fans, their "We're No. 1" banners discarded, began their exit, and as they left, Tom Darden made it complete with Michigan's sixth interception of the day.

Fritz Crisler later called the 24-12 victory one of the finest

in Michigan history. *"I have never seen a team better prepared for a game than your Michigan team Saturday,"* was the note Schembechler received from the former Michigan coach and athletic director.

It was one of Michigan's finest hours. But we are getting ahead of our story. Michigan football goes back nearly a century...a century that had Saturdays like November 22, 1969, and Saturdays of heartbreak, too, like November 7, 1925, in the rain and mud in Chicago against a seemingly overmatched Northwestern team.

Bruce Dudley as sports editor of the Louisville Courier

18

Michigan bench erupts in joy after upsetting Ohio State in 1969. Frank Maloney (extreme right) later went on to become Syracuse's head football coach; George Mans (in center with clip board) was named head coach at Eastern Michigan; and defensive coordinator Jim Young (not shown) took over as head coach at Arizona.

Journal *caught some of the substance of Michigan football years ago. "Michigan's athletic achievements," he observed, "are not to be gauged by the mere number of events won. No indeed, for Michigan has been as magnificent in defeats as it has in victories."*

Bo Schembechler put it another way. Looking through a thick Michigan record book in his office the summer of 1974, he said, "This is an amazing record. I'll bet people don't understand how great Michigan football has been over the years."

That success, however, had humble beginnings.

The Man From Shanghai . . .
Or Anyone For Rugby?

Charles Gayley was not the typical student at the University of Michigan. Tall, slender, and with a clipped Oxford accent, he arrived from Shanghai where his father was serving as an American missionary and entered the junior class of 1876. His earlier education included schools in England and Ireland.

Gayley had deep interests in literature, writing, music, and sports, an unusual combination that would enrich his new university in each area. He made friends quickly, and in talking with his classmates he was delighted to learn they were engaging in games of "foot-ball," a game that strikingly resembled his favorite sport of rugby. He knew a loose football association had been organized three years earlier, but still the rules were unworkable. There were too many players. "Why not adopt the English rules?" Gayley suggested.

His knowledge of rugby impressed Michigan students, and when a report came from the east that Harvard and Yale had played a game under full rugby rules with one exception, that players should be limited to 11 on a side, Gayley convinced them to adopt the English game. Thus Michigan entered its "Modern Era" of football, though three years would pass before the sport moved to the intercollegiate level.

Gayley not only gave football at Michigan a vital direction, but went on to write *The Yellow and Blue* Alma Mater, then later wrote the *California Bear* while an instructor at the University of California.

When Michigan did travel to Chicago in 1879 to play

Racine College in the "first intercollegiate game west of the Alleghenies," it followed by a full decade the historic meeting of Princeton and Rutgers, a game which offered the embryonics of American football.

The earliest forms of football at Michigan resembled mass tug-of-wars. The student newspaper, the *Chronicle,* noted in 1862 that "42 sophomores were beaten by 82 freshmen," but it was not until eight years later on a Saturday in April when the class team of 1872 met the class of 1873 that football became more organized. A football association was formed in 1873, and with interest in the sport growing, an all-campus team was formed. Students then looked eastward for a game.

Cornell, much like Michigan, had been playing football games among classes, and through a series of letters by students from both schools they decided to play a game in 1873 on a neutral site. Cleveland, Ohio, was selected as a midpoint where both teams and some student supporters easily could travel. Only the permission of school officials was needed.

When Andrew White, who had watched the football fad take hold on his Cornell campus, learned of the proposed game, the Cornell president immediately wrote Michigan President James Angell a succinct and uncompromising refusal. "No, I will not permit thirty men to travel 400 miles to merely agitate a bag of wind," President White said in what provided his assessment of football and its value to his university. Fourteen years later Cornell played its first intercollegiate game.

Two years after the Cornell misadventure Michigan officials denied the baseball team permission to play any games outside Ann Arbor. Administration and faculty members began to exercise more control of Michigan's athletic teams.

Football organization remained loose, and another challenge, this one from the University of Chicago in January of 1877, had to be declined. James E. Duffy was later to recall that offer from Chicago:

"The challenge from Chicago...found us without an association to receive it, although foot-ball was supposed to be the great sport here. The formation of an athletic association had been urged but nothing came of it."

Then in 1878 the football and baseball associations joined forces to form Michigan's first Athletic Association. It immediately directed itself toward raising funds for a gymnasium, the most popular cause at that time among students. Football interests, now with the broadest student base ever, were ready to move their sport to the intercollegiate level. A challenge from the small Wisconsin college of Racine was accepted and a game scheduled for May 30, 1879, at the White Stocking Park in Chicago.

Football at Michigan had begun.

"Pond Forever"

Chicago—May 30, 1879

Even the brisk wind moving along the lakefront from the south failed to relieve the oppressive heat. Dust rose chokingly from the baseball grounds at White Stocking Park. Still, there was a picnic-like atmosphere surging through the Decoration Day crowd. They had come to watch what the *Chicago Tribune* had reported as the "first rugby-football game to be played west of the Alleghenies."

The Michigan team of 11 players and one substitute had left the Clifton House at 3:15 p.m. for the short trip to the park, located between Randolph and Washington. An hour later the Michigan players and a team from Racine College were on the field ready to play. Umpire A. J. Pettit, Michigan's only reserve player, as was the custom, served as one official, while a Racine substitute acted as the other official.

Racine's J. W. Johnson kicked the ball well downfield to Charles Campbell. He returned the ball "some distance by good runs and skilled throwing to others of our team," wrote a reporter from the student paper who had accompanied the team to Chicago. Strangely, he took little notice that Michigan was entering a new sports frontier—intercollegiate football. Still, students back at Michigan received seven telegraph reports, which were posted on a board near the medical building, detailing the progress of the game.

The game was, in today's descriptives, a defensive battle. "Scrummages"—where both teams had the opportunity of

23

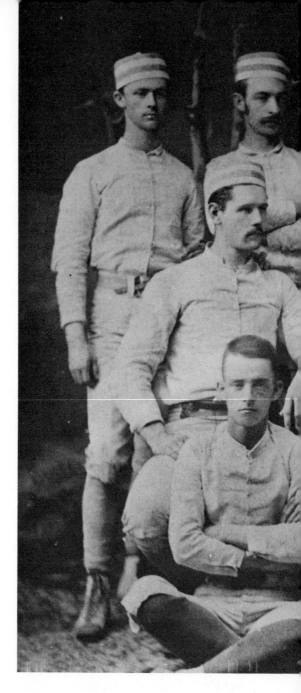

Michigan's first football team, in 1879. Players include (top row, left to right) Jack Green, Bill Hannan, Captain Dave DeTar, Charlie Mitchell, Frank Reed, and Albert Pettit, who served as an official. (Second row) Irving Pond, who scored the first Michigan touchdown, Tom Edwards, John Chase, Charlie Campbell. (Bottom row) Collins Johnston, Gay DePuy, and Ed Barmore. Michigan defeated Racine College in Chicago.

gaining possession of the ball—kept the ball moving in both directions.

Midway through the first "inning" Michigan worked slowly toward the Racine goal. Finally, a young civil engi-

neering student stamped himself forever in Michigan football lore. Irving K. "Ike" Pond, a rusher with considerable gymnastic ability, ran the ball for a touchdown—the first to be recorded by a Michigan player. Ironically the touchdown did not

Irving Pond scored Michigan's first touchdown in 1879 game against Racine.

represent points as tabulated in today's scoring. Games were decided on a majority of touchdowns. A goal kicked from the field counted as four touchdowns.

Pond, who was able to perform cartwheels and somersaults at the age of 82 and wrote many times of this historic game, recalled the game week vividly:

"...On Wednesday evening the eleven appeared on campus for the first time in their new suits. They presented quite a neat appearance. The uniform is of white canvas, close fitting, with blue stockings and belt. A large number of spectators came out to see the boys practice. They were opposed by a picked eleven.

26

The team left Thursday on the day express. A few of the students, among them our managing editor, accompanied them as spectators."

Pond left other marks on Michigan. He designed the Michigan Union Building and Michigan League and also designed similar student buildings at Purdue, Michigan State, and Kansas. His most remembered feat, however, remains that touchdown in Chicago. He was a superb rusher that day, and many times the crowd responded to his playing with cheers of, "Pond Forever."

Michigan captain Dave DeTarr, who had missed his try at a goal after Pond's touchdown, kicked a goal in the final two minutes to complete the victory. Michigan had one touchdown and one goal (officially recorded as a 1-0 victory). Racine "was not able to put the ball back of the university half-back."

While Pond and DeTarr attracted considerable notice with the ball, John Chase was equally as prominent with his tackling. Fans even then apparently appreciated defense, as the shout, "'Chase is there,' was heard at least 20 times," Michigan's student paper noted.

Later that evening at the Palmer House, university alumni gave the Michigan team a banquet. They celebrated a victory, a practice to become very familiar with Michigan alumni over the years.

Inspired by their success the Michigan players quickly searched for another game and made arrangements with the University of Toronto to play in Detroit that November. Again the defenses were strong, and the match ended in a scoreless tie. When the team arrived at the Ann Arbor train station that evening, a group of students and a brass band were waiting. Everyone proceeded to the court house where the festivities continued. Football was taking hold.

Michigan and Toronto played again in 1880 with Michigan winning, 13-6. Football interest now intensified on campus. The players and their supporters optimistically reasoned: "The best elevens of the west had been met and taken into camp, and all eyes were turned eastward." Michigan looked hopefully to a challenge from Eastern teams, and in 1881 that challenge was offered by Harvard, Yale, and Princeton. Michigan would play them all in one week.

27

From Freight Trains
To Dining Cars

There were few doubts on the Michigan campus: The football capitals of 1881 were in the East, and that was where the Wolverines went—a team of eleven regulars and two substitutes. They played three games within a week, the first intersectional schedule ever attempted in college football.

Such overly ambitious plans had little chance of success, but the results did establish Ann Arbor as the center of football power in the midlands and offered indications that these Wolverines would have to be seriously considered in the future.

Michigan met Harvard on October 31, losing one touchdown to none. On November 2 Michigan lost to a worried Yale team, two goals to none, and two days later lost to Princeton, one goal and two touchdowns to none.

The extremely creditable performance against three of the finest football elevens of the time prompted a quick invitation to join the Eastern College League. Michigan declined because of faculty objections, and in fact did not play an outside game in 1882, probably due to the unprecedented concentration of football that had been arranged in the East.

The following year, however, Michigan's largest schedule, listing five games, was approved, and again it included games with Yale and Harvard, this time on successive days.

Football rules were constantly changing, and the delay in these innovations reaching Western schools was natural. When Michigan's players arrived for the Yale game, they were told a new, oblong ball was to be used and a new scoring system employed. Yale promptly rolled over Michigan, 46-0.

Those numerical values assigned to scoring plays included: safety one point, touchdown two points, goal following a touchdown four points, and a goal from field five points. A year later the values would change again.

Following the Yale game Michigan met Harvard and lost, 3-0. They had agreed previously to play a second game the next day, but Harvard, taking notice of the closeness of the score, refused. Michigan claimed a forfeit, though it was never entered in its official records.

Still, Michigan was receiving its graduate degree in football and was quick to employ the modern arrangement of players—seven forwards, a quarterback, two halfbacks, and a fullback.

That 1883 trip eastward, however, would be the last one until 1890 as Michigan concentrated on Midwest opposition. The Wolverines won eight straight games from 1884 through 1887, holding every team scoreless, including Notre Dame.

These two universities, each destined for national prominence in football, met for the first time in South Bend, Indiana, in 1887 when Michigan unveiled a drop-kicker, James E. Duffy. Duffy, who was credited with a record fifty-five yard drop-kick field goal, gained prominence by serving thirty years on Michigan's Athletic Board, and near the end of his service cast the only dissenting vote on Michigan rejoining the Big Ten.

Michigan won that inaugural meeting with Notre Dame, 8-0, and the following year twice defeated the Irish at South Bend, 26-6, and 10-4.

Football by this time was the most popular sport on the nation's largest campus. Michigan in 1889 had 2,153 students. The graduating class of 1867 selected Maize and Blue as the school colors, and a proper nickname already was available. As early as 1861, students referred to themselves as "Wolverines."

Michigan won four games in 1890, losing only to Cornell, 20-5, but the Athletic Association decided to obtain the services of a regular, non-student coach. Mike Murphy, a popular and experienced trainer at the Detroit Athletic Club, was hired as a part-time coach for the 1891 season. Also on the Michigan campus at the time was a graduate student from Yale, Frank Crawford, who had learned his football in the East and was eager to help. Crawford immediately went to work contacting teams for the upcoming season. His efforts resulted in the first advance intercollegiate football schedule in Michigan history with nine teams listed. Crawford midway through the season was enlisted as coach along with Murphy, whose chief duties were as a trainer.

Michigan now was better equipped for football than ever before. The Athletic Association of the University of Michigan had been formed a year earlier in 1890, the first lasting attempt at athletic organization. Student members paid $3 annual dues which allowed them to participate in the management of athletics. Actually the association was controlled by five officers and nine directors, elected by students from various university departments.

The Crawford-Murphy coaching combination lasted just one season with Michigan winning four games and losing five. The following year another Yale man, Frank Barbour, was hired, and he sent the Wolverines on their first Western trip. Michigan defeated Wisconsin and Minnesota but lost to Chicago and Northwestern. That 1892 season was the most demanding yet attempted with twelve games scheduled, including one unusual contest in Ann Arbor with Purdue.

Several Michigan players, who were on the team earlier, missed the Purdue game, and when four Wolverines were injured and all available substitutes used, the game was forfeited, 24-0. One of those injured players was George H. Jewett, Sr., who had been the football co-captain and track captain at Ann Arbor High. Jewett became Michigan's first black letterwinner in 1890 as a freshman halfback with considerable ability.

After his injury in the Purdue game, Jewett returned five days later to play against Northwestern in Chicago. Author John Behee in his book, *Hail to the Victors*, wrote of that game, "As he was tackled, several Northwestern men piled on, leaving Jewett when it was all over with a badly bruised face. 'The crowd was indignant,' reported the student newspaper, *The Michigan Daily,* 'and requested Jewett to name the man who had maltreated him, but this he refused to do...' After sitting out for several minutes, the battered sophomore returned to the game and was heartily cheered."

Jewett, who did not enroll at Michigan in 1891, but was a varsity regular the following year, later transferred to North-

George Jewett, Michigan's first black letterwinner in football.
He was a starting halfback as a sophomore in 1890.

western and played two seasons.

Michigan extracted some revenge from Purdue the next season, winning 46-0, but this game in West Lafayette was not without its problems. Michigan's athletic funds in 1893 were exhausted by midseason, and after considerable difficulty, the team manager, Charles Baird, persuaded four professors to sign a note for $100. Roundtrip train tickets were purchased, leaving an operating balance of $2. A $10 loan from one player was secured, and the Wolverines left for Purdue.

The game attendance was small, and Michigan's share amounted to less than the $100 needed to repay its loan. Manager Baird, however, quickly secured a Monday game in nearby Greencastle with DePauw University. Michigan won that game and received enough money from the gate receipts to repay the loan, but had no funds left over to reach Lafayette where the team had tickets for its return to Ann Arbor.

Again, Baird's inventiveness took charge. After checking train schedules, he discovered a freight train would pass through Greencastle, headed for Lafayette. The Michigan players jumped the freight and rode in empty box cars, arriving in Lafayette at 1:30 a.m. Tuesday. The return to Ann Arbor was reported as uneventful.

Michigan's win over Purdue that season would have provoked strong protests today. Coach Barbour, mindful that Michigan had exhausted its supply of players the previous year and had to forfeit the game to Purdue, inserted himself into the lineup when injuries again depleted his reserves. The resourceful Baird, who became Michigan's first athletic director, served as the only available substitute, but he was not needed. Seven of the players who made the trip reportedly were not enrolled in the university.

These misadventures and other obvious abuses of academic policy moved Michigan to full faculty control in 1893. It was not unusual to use athletes who had not enrolled in school or had played football six or seven years. The legendary Walter Camp had a brilliant seven-year football career at Yale before a knee injury forced him to retire. Michigan could match this, however. Horace Prettyman started his varsity career in 1882 and finished in 1890, earning seven letters in football. Later he operated a famous training table for the football team.

These were not isolated cases. Suddenly President James Angell and the Regents decided that athletics must fit more properly into the overall university program. Accordingly the University Senate on December 9, 1893, created a Board in Control of Athletics which would hire all coaches and trainers and supervise athletics. The Board was comprised of five professors selected by the Senate and four students chosen by the Athletic Association. Later the undergraduate members were selected by a vote of the students. With this change the Athletic Association actually ceased to function as a policy group and in 1894 turned over $6,095.03 in cash and bonds to the new Board.

Charles Baird became Michigan's first athletic director in 1898 and guided Wolverine athletics for a decade.

The Senate in creating the Board directed that a position of Graduate Manager of Athletics be established, and in 1898 Charles A. Baird became Michigan's first athletic director.

Michigan now was geared to enter its "Golden Age of Football" with the opening of the 1894 season. A young Michigan medical student, who had played tackle on a championship Princeton team, William L. McCauley, was named to coach the team. Spectator stands for 400 were erected on Regents Field where ten acres of land had been purchased a few years before by President Angell. Interest was developing among faculty men to establish an intercollegiate athletic conference.

McCauley's 1894 team with an average team weight of just 170 pounds and a backfield that averaged 155½ pounds won nine games, lost one, and tied one. The Wolverines traveled to Ithaca, New York, on November 3 to play Cornell, losing 22-0,

William McCauley coached Michigan to a 26-3-1 record from 1894 through the 1896 season.

but had a return game in Detroit November 24, and the buildup for that second game was remarkable. A crowd of 14,000 was recorded, and Michigan justified all optimism by winning, 12-4, achieving its first victory over an eastern university and becoming the first western school ever to defeat an established football power from the East.

This was the start of an exciting seven-year period when Michigan teams would win fifty-seven games, lose just eight, and tie three. The Wolverines would play before growing crowds. They would join a new conference, capture their first championship, and begin to build a tradition of unusual proportions. Indeed, Michigan football would move from "freight trains to dining cars."

The Big Seven Arrives

By February, winter closes in tight on Chicago's lakefront, but inside the Palmer House the talk was warm and friendly as representatives of seven midwestern universities gathered in the large, paneled meeting room. They had been sent by their presidents, these faculty men, from Michigan, Illinois, Northwestern, Chicago, Purdue, Wisconsin, and Minnesota. Their assignment—to form an association that would establish common standards and control of intercollegiate athletics.

Chicago, which astounded faculty circles by giving its football coach academic standing, sent Amos Alonzo Stagg. Michigan was represented by Dr. C. B. deNancrede. Conway MacMillan of Minnesota was chairman of this impressive faculty group.

That meeting, February 8, 1896, gave birth to the Intercollegiate Conference of Faculty Representatives. To be called, in the years to come, the Western Conference, the Big Nine, and finally the Big Ten, it represented a revolutionary concept in the managing of intercollegiate athletics. Its formation led faculty men of that time to believe that many of the problems offered by a growing emphasis on football were solved.

Football had spread like a range fire, engulfing students, then alumni, and on into the sporting veins of millions. Newspapers, notably the Hearst papers, enlarged their sports sections to mirror the growing interest. But in the wake of this popularity, abuses flowed. Charges of rampant professional spirit, ranging through almost all universities, was made in a national magazine. The questionable status of athletes as students concerned faculty members. The rules, dictated by a few Eastern schools and fostering mass formations of players, were responsible for injuries and brutality in football.

It was natural that university officials, who had watched with only mild curiosity as their students "agitated a bag of wind," now became alarmed. Michigan President Angell was one of the first to respond, calling for a conference April 16, 1892, that included representatives of Northwestern, Minnesota, and Wisconsin. The Intercollegiate Association of the Northwest was formed and immediately adopted rules prohibiting any payments for athletic play and insisting that athletes be bona-fide students enrolled in their university at least two months before engaging in any scheduled game.

This loosely formed group survived only one year, but its efforts did not escape notice of Purdue's president, James H. Smart. He invited college presidents to convene January 11, 1895, to discuss faculty control of athletics. In a subsequent Chicago meeting, Purdue, Illinois, Northwestern, Chicago, Wisconsin, Minnesota, and Lake Forest Academy adopted a series of proposals aimed at regulating eligibility of athletes and establishing firm faculty control.

Michigan was specifically invited, but President Angell did not attend "due to a misunderstanding." He expressed his complete accord with the resolutions adopted by the seven schools. Those proposals were taken back to the faculties for study and one year later endorsed at the meeting in the Palmer House by the faculty representatives of the original group with one exception, Lake Forest, which had been replaced by Michigan. The Western Conference was a reality. On December 1, 1899, Indiana and Iowa made the conference the "Big Nine." Ohio State joined April 6, 1912.

That fall of 1896 saw the seven-team football conference open. Wisconsin won two games to claim the championship, while Michigan won two games but lost its final game with Chicago and finished second under a new coach, Gustave H. "Dutch" Ferbert. There had been a move by the student-alumni advisory board to have only former students as coaches, and Ferbert, who was on the advisory board along with James Duffy

Michigan's first two all-Americans, Neil Snow, kicking, and William Cunningham, holding. Cunningham was the first Wolverine honored in 1898.

and James Baird, was selected to replace McCauley.

Wisconsin swept by its three conference opponents in 1897 to repeat as champions. Michigan again posted a 2-1 record, defeating Purdue and Minnesota, but again losing to

Artist's drawing of Charlie Widman's touchdown run in 1898 against Chicago that inspired Louis Elbel to write the famed "The Victors" fight song for Michigan.

Stagg's Chicago team. That Thanksgiving Day game, staged indoors before nearly 10,000 fans in Chicago Coliseum, provided Michigan with $3,813 in revenue.

The next season, however, fortune played on Michigan's side in this growing rivalry with Chicago, the type which has filled college football with a special drama. The undefeated Wolverines in 1898 defeated Notre Dame, Northwestern, and Illinois on successive Saturdays. In Ann Arbor they were claiming that this was the best team yet to represent their university. In Chicago, Stagg's forces were not exactly hardship cases. They had lost just once and had the best fullback in football, Clarence Herschberger. Herschberger and Michigan's William Ralph Cunningham, a powerful junior center, were to become the Big Ten's first all-America selections.

Michigan won its only two conference games, and Chicago swept by all three of its league opponents. A crowd of 10,000 turned out in Chicago to see the championship of the Western Conference decided. Largely a Chicago following, they remained hopeful, cheering, until late in the game when a small, sturdy halfback, Charles Widman, ran nearly 65 yards for a touchdown that gave Michigan a 12-11 victory.

Louis Elbel wrote his famed "The Victors" as a tribute to that victory.

That championship was the first of many for Michigan, and they came in machine-like procession. Michigan closed out the century by hiring a new coach for the 1900 season, Langdon (Biff) Lea of Princeton, discarding the policy of hiring only former students as coaches.

Biff Lea coached Michigan's 1900 football team.

Keene Fitzpatrick was Michigan's trainer until leaving in 1909 to become a highly successful track coach at Princeton.

By now school spirit was reaching almost visible proportions. Baird was directing athletics full time at an annual salary of $2,000. Keene Fitzpatrick, who was later to become one of the nation's outstanding track coaches at Princeton, was hired as trainer. Michigan's stirring new fight song was being played at every home game by the Michigan Band of thirty men. It only remained for a new force, a catalyst, to move Michigan into the forefront of college football...it arrived in Ann Arbor in the summer of 1901. Astute, confident, showing an obvious penchant for showmanship, Fielding H. Yost would lead Michigan to the heights.

A Toast From Coast-To-Coast
Or . . . Here Comes Mr. Yost

The train moving slowly into the Ann Arbor depot was late, and this irritated Fielding Yost. He wanted, at least, to be on time. His car finally jerked to a stop, and Yost, with a heavy suitcase dangling easily from his hand, quickly stepped down to the platform. He glanced at the small group waiting under the pitched, wooden canopy of the station and saw a slender, impeccably dressed man start walking toward him.

"Are you Coach Yost?" the man asked.

"Yes, sir, I am," Yost replied.

"Well, I'm Charles Baird, and I'm very happy to meet you."

The two shook hands. Baird, greeting his second football coach since becoming Michigan's first director of athletics, looked appraisingly at this solidly-framed young man who resembled a football player. Finally, Baird said, "You look rather young to have had all this success in coaching. Just why are you so sure you can coach winning teams in this conference?"

"Mr. Baird," Yost said, "there are three things that make a winning football team. Spirit, manpower, and coaching. If your boys love Meeshegan, they've got the spirit, you see. If they'll turn out, that takes care of the manpower. I'll take care of the coaching."

Baird studied the 30-year-old Yost for a moment and said, "Well, you've got a real job ahead of you. You've got to beat Chicago."

There was no doubt about Yost's job. He was to produce a

winning football team, one that would defeat Chicago. That is exactly what Yost did in the years ahead, but in a style Baird could never have anticipated. His record as a coach, a builder, an image-maker made Michigan and Yost a standard of football excellence from coast to coast, and Yost did it with amazing quickness.

Yost sent Baird by railway express a box jammed with writings, newspaper clippings, recommendations, all dealing with his qualifications as a football player and coach. This shipment preceded him to Ann Arbor, and as the Yost legend would grow, that box became a suitcase. It could have been a trunk, such were his early successes.

Just past his 30th birthday Yost was restless, a football nomad of immense proportions. He came out of the West Virginia hill country completely engrossed in football. It was football that carried him westward, first to Ohio, then to the midlands of Kansas and Nebraska, and finally to the West Coast. Now football was returning him eastward to Michigan.

These travels, these associations, and his deep roots in West Virginia would have an important impact on Michigan football. Under Yost, Michigan became the most intersectionally—oriented football team in the nation. Close relationships with Eastern schools like Pennsylvania would make Michigan's decision to separate itself from the Western Conference much easier.

Fielding Harris Yost was raised in Marion County, West Virginia. During his teens he worked in the oil fields and served as a deputy sheriff in the rough coal mining area around Fairfield. He enrolled at Ohio Normal College in Ada, Ohio, in 1889 and played baseball and a game that only resembled football. After two years he dropped out of school to teach. Three years later he decided to obtain a law degree, and in 1895 entered the University of West Virginia and his football career began.

Yost was a 6-foot, 195-pounder with considerable strength, but his knowledge of football was limited. So he bought a football book and quickly became an authority on the rules, impressing his acumen on anyone who cared to listen.

It was a characteristic that would remain with Yost, who insisted that all his players know the rules. Once on a train trip

Fielding H. Yost as he appeared in Ann Arbor in 1902, carrying the only piece of equipment he ever needed—a football.

to Minnesota, Yost spotted a player reading a newspaper purchased in Chicago where the team had changed trains. Yost grabbed the newspaper with one hand, reached into his back pocket with the other, and shoved a rule book into the surprised player's hand. Yost often said, "In football, as in life, you've got to know the rules and your rights."

Yost took every advantage of the rules and liked to pull surprises, especially against Chicago and Stagg. These two coaches never were on the best of terms. There were reports that Stagg was unyielding on changing Big Ten policies that kept Michigan out of the conference for ten years. After Yost's 1902 team had defeated Chicago, 21-0, Stagg complained, "Michigan played a nice game, but it was their tricks that beat us...Their tricks were very clever."

Yost, in postgame comments, did not let the opportunity escape him of embellishing a victory over Chicago. "I only predicted a score of eighteen to zero. I guess we showed Chicago a few new ones, didn't we?" said Yost, referring to several new plays, including one double lateral that resulted in a touchdown.

Yost played guard and tackle for West Virginia for two seasons and was considered a strong, smart player who would not quit. During the 1896 season his West Virginia team played Lafayette three times, losing all three, but his talents were easily recognized by Lafayette's coach, Parke "Dink" Davis, who apparently talked Yost into transferring to Lafayette.

Years later Yost explained the transfer. "I had entered Law School at West Virginia and then thought I'd try engineering at Lafayette, so I transferred after having played three games in one week for West Virginia. But I found engineering not so pleasant and decided to return to West Virginia for my law studies."

During his short stay at Lafayette, Yost was able to play a key role in its startling upset in 1896 of mighty Pennsylvania. Penn had been using the famed "guards back" formation, a sensation in its day, and it remained for Yost's innovative mind to solve the attack.

Early in the game Yost noticed that when the guards were stationed behind the line, the five remaining linemen would move into a tighter formation. Yost, from his tackle position, was able to cut around the flank, move in behind the mass of interference, and stop the runner.

Yost transferred back to West Virginia and finished his law degree in 1897. He was 26 years old and ready to coach. "My main objective," Yost recalled, "was to see America first, and coaching offered me the best chance to do it."

No one ever worked his way westward in the manner of Fielding H. Yost. He did it with football championships, first at Ohio Wesleyan in 1897 when his team upset Ohio State, 6-0, and tied Michigan, 0-0.

He then moved on to Nebraska, and the Cornhuskers won the Trans-Missouri Association championship in 1898. The following year he shifted to Kansas and won another TMA crown.

Next came Stanford and another championship, but Yost did not stop there. He coached the Stanford freshmen to a title and in the morning helped coach the Lowell High team in Palo Alto, which won the Coast prep championship. After his season was completed, he coached the San Jose Normal team to a championship.

This totalled four championships in 1900 for Yost. He also remembered helping coach a Ukiah High School team, which claimed a title. Yost had a fondness for championships, and he never let one escape notice. Years later in a radio program Yost and Director Baird had an exchange that went like this:

Baird: "Mr. Yost, after reading that fifty-pound scrap book you sent me, tell me, is it true that you coached four teams simultaneously out there in California?"

Yost: "Five. I forgot to mention the high school team I coached in my spare time."

Baird: "According to the clippings, all four of your teams won championships."

Yost: "All *five* won championships. Yes, sir."

Yost brought this boundless energy to Michigan in 1901, and championships continued to flow. His first four teams won Western Conference titles, recording an amazing forty-two victories without a defeat and tying one game. That tie, in itself, was of historic importance. It was played in 1903 in Minneapolis and featured a piece of crockery that became the "Little Brown Jug."

45

Those were his famed "Point-a-Minute" years, though at times some criticism has been made of this literal fact. From 1901 through 1905 Michigan averaged forty-nine points per game, somewhat less than the required seventy. But Yost, typically, liked to explain that Michigan's 119-0 win over Michigan State in 1902 was achieved in just 36 minutes, the game being called at that point. The staggering 128-0 win over Buffalo was pulled off in 50 minutes, and a 130-0 blitz of West Virginia came in 36 minutes.

Few could deny that Yost's years at Michigan justified every glowing tribute contained in that hefty scrapbook which preceded him to Ann Arbor. He coached twenty-five Michigan football teams, and they won eighty-five percent of their games. He produced all-Americans when recognition of football talent was confined largely to players in the East. During the Yost years Michigan developed broad intramural programs as he established a policy that would endure—"Athletics for All." Yost directed the construction of an athletic plant that a half-century later remained as an example for others to imitate. He did it with a flair, a craftmanship, and with remarkable enthusiasm.

Yost, in a sense, was Michigan athletics. Or at least he symbolized a growing excellence in intercollegiate athletics that would remain with Michigan long after he had gone.

His two-story brick home on a hill off Stratford Lane became one of the social centers of Ann Arbor. Governors and senators were entertained there. Originally a Democrat, Yost became a strong, active Republican, giving radio speeches on behalf of candidates he favored.

A businessman with many investments, Yost's twenty years as athletic director saw Michigan produce $8,742,145 in revenue. When he retired in 1941 the cash surplus was $99,405.96, but more importantly he left an athletic complex that would be impossible to construct today. An 18-hole championship golf course, the nation's first field house, an ice rink, a women's physical education building, and a giant intramural building all rose during Yost's years as director. Then in 1927 came the dedication of a giant bowl that would eventually seat more than 100,000 persons and rank as the showcase for intercollegiate football—Michigan Stadium.

Perhaps Yost's endowment to Michigan could be measured by another yardstick. He brought with him a rare spirit of almost instinctive confidence that was shared by his players. There was something pleasingly arrogant about his contention, "Who are they that they should beat a Meeshegan team?" Or his comment on Louis Elbel's famed "The Victors," which the Michigan Band has made as much a part of a touchdown as the extra point: "I reckon it's a good thing Louis Elbel was a Meeshegan student when he wrote that song. If he'd been at any other Big Ten school, they wouldn't have had much chance to use it, y'know."

A friend once asked writer Ring Lardner, "Did you ever talk to Fielding Yost?"

"No," replied Lardner, "my father taught me never to interrupt."

"We Want Heston"

Yost began his coaching career at Michigan in September, 1901. He was employed just for the football season at $2,300 per year plus living expenses, a quite lucrative package for a young man who was forced to leave his coaching position at Stanford when the school adopted a policy limiting coaching jobs to alumni only. An excellent group of players was returning from the 1900 season in which Michigan won seven games, lost to Iowa and Chicago, and tied Ohio State. Not winning the "big game" caused some criticism of the football team. The athletic fund was exhausted and the equipment barely adequate.

The training camp at Whitmore Lake was lively as Yost appeared everywhere. It was clear that this new coach would insist on speed, a clear departure from the usual dependence on massive line assaults, so popular at the time. He immediately moved 165-pound Harrison "Boss" Weeks into the quarterback position. Weeks was an obvious leader. Yost once said, "If Weeks lined his team up on a cliff and said, 'Charge,' they would all charge."

During the training exercises Weeks, while still on the ground from the previous scrimmage play, would call signals for the next play. If a player did not move into the next formation fast enough, Yost would shout, "Are you just a spectator? Hurry up, hurry up!" A Detroit sportswriter immediately began referring to the new Michigan coach as "Hurry Up" Yost.

Yost was convinced Michigan had material that could

win. Neil Snow, who played brilliantly in Michigan's 1898 win over Chicago, was the fullback and defensive end and would be selected as an all-American. George "Dad" Gregory along with Bruce Shorts, a place kicker, and Dan McGugin, later to become Yost's brother-in-law and coach against Yost, and Everett Sweeley, the punter, all were experienced linemen. Al Herrnstein was an exceptional halfback.

Joining these veterans was a freshman from California. Yost, who had known him briefly when he coached San Jose Normal, wrote him encouragingly about Michigan and football. With a pasteboard suitcase and a one-way ticket from San Francisco, William Martin (Willie) Heston arrived in Ann Arbor in 1901, destined to become one of the greatest halfbacks in college football history.

Heston was a guard and captain of the San Jose Normal football team which tied with Chico State for the conference championship. When the two schools agreed to a playoff game, Heston and quarterback Billy Messe traveled 18 miles to Palo Alto and asked Yost to coach the championship game. Yost agreed. Heston, running at halfback, led San Jose to a 46-0 victory.

The following summer Yost wrote Heston, informing him that he had signed a three-year contract to coach the Michigan football team and offering Willie a chance to play football. Yost extolled the opportunity available to receive an "excellent education." Heston, however, decided to return home to Grant's Pass, Oregon, with the $315 he had saved from a teaching position and summer work as a teamster and stevedore. On the way to the San Francisco ferry to purchase his ticket Heston made a chance acquaintance with a young man from Toledo, Ohio, who had bought a roundtrip ticket to the coast to attend a Christian Endeavor Convention. The man had decided to remain in California and offered Heston the unused part of his ticket for $25. Heston checked the validity of the ticket and immediately made up his mind to travel east and enroll in the Michigan Law School. With the ticket and a new suit he took the next train to Toledo and then the interurban to Ann Arbor.

Upon his arrival Heston learned that Yost was not expected for several days. On the third day after arriving in Ann

49

Harrison "Boss" Weeks was Yost's fiery captain and directed his first two "Point-a-minute" teams, 1901-02.

Arbor he was standing on the corner of Main and Huron Streets when he was nudged in the knee from behind, and a pair of strong arms lifted him off his feet. A surprised Heston turned his head and saw his old coach.

"Why you little son-of-a-gun!" yelled Yost while bystanders stared. "You made it, didn't you? I always figured you'd come with me."

Then the always exuberant Yost added: "Where's your luggage? Let's get going. I've got a lot of groceries to pick up for our training camp. You're lucky, ya know, you came along when you did."

It was a start of a friendship that only death would end. "He was like a father to me," Willie would say years later. Yost maintained that Heston, "was the finest halfback I've ever seen play football."

Heston led Michigan to an undefeated season in 1901 and a remarkable 49-0 victory over Stanford in the first Rose Bowl game ever played. His speed and strength became legendary. In a game against Ohio State, Heston broke loose on one of his sweeping runs. Only Ohio's safety man, Clarence Foss, blocked his path to the goal. Foss, despite his 145 pounds, was a courageous athlete and slammed into Heston around the waist. Heston merely picked him up with his free hand and carried him 15 yards to the goal line for a touchdown.

One of Heston's most remarkable runs occurred in 1903 against Chicago. It came on the first scrimmage play of the game after Michigan had returned the Chicago kickoff to the

Willie Heston, Michigan's first all-American halfback, scored 71 touchdowns in his career and never played in a losing game for the Wolverines.

35-yard line. Yost had directed his quarterback, Shorty Norcross, to call the famed "tackles back" formation. They moved back behind their regular line positions, and the ends crowded in toward the center. Norcross handed off to Heston sweeping around his right end behind a wave of blockers. Heston broke through the mass of interference and headed downfield with only one defensive player to beat, the swift Chicago all-American quarterback, Walter Eckersall.

Eckersall moved in on Heston and made a dive for Willie's legs. Heston, showing the lightning reflexes that helped him score seventy-one touchdowns for Michigan, timed Eckersall's dive perfectly and leaped into the air. As Eckersall slid on the snow covered field, Heston continued unchallenged for the touchdown.

Plays like this led Heston to offer advice to other runners: "Use your eyes for searchlights and jump the dead ones." In modern times Vince Lombardi simply advised, "Run to daylight."

Heston was 5-feet, 8-inches, weighed 184 pounds, and was one of the fastest football players in Michigan history. Several

Willie Heston (top center of picture) gains fifteen yards against Minnesota in the historic 1903 Little Brown Jug game. The checkerboard markings were extended over the entire field in 1904 and permitted the first player receiving the ball from the

times he ran against Michigan's Olympic sprint champion, Archie Hahn, and beat him every time at 40 yards. Beyond 40 yards, however, it was Hahn's race. Keene Fitzpatrick claimed that Heston "was one of the fastest runners I ever saw at 40 yards."

However, Heston had to wait for his chance to play for Michigan. Yost used him only briefly in Michigan's 50-0 win over Albion in the 1901 opener, but still Heston scored. "I got in the opener for a few minutes," Heston recalled, "and I spotted a big gap between their center and right guard. I also noticed their quarterback tossed a rather long, awkward pass to the ball carrier, so I edged up, darted through the gap, and intercepted a lateral for a touchdown." He did not start against Case the next week but still scored four touchdowns.

It was not until the third game against Indiana that Michigan students began shouting, "We Want Heston." For the first ten minutes of the game the heavier Hoosiers were stopping every offensive play Michigan could run, and finally Yost turned to Heston and said, "Well, let's see if you can do any better." On his first play Heston circled end for 25 yards and a

center (quarterback) to carry the ball any place on the field beyond the line of scrimmage, providing he ran five yards outside of the spot where the ball was put in play.

touchdown, and Michigan rolled to a 33-0 win.

Michigan made it four straight shutouts with a 29-0 win over Northwestern, then astounded the football world with a performance on Regents Field that was not, at first, believed back East. The University of Buffalo travelled to Ann Arbor with hopes of giving Michigan a tough battle. The Buffalo team had surprised many by defeating Columbia 5-0 in its opener and came to Ann Arbor convinced that it could give Yost's team a strong afternoon. They left completely bewildered.

Michigan scored twenty-two touchdowns and eighteen goals in just 50 minutes of football to record one of the highest scoring victories (128-0) at that time in college football. The Wolverines gained 1,261 yards rushing the ball as the rule that allowed the scoring team to receive the kickoff worked admirably to Michigan's advantage.

At one point in the game an apparently dazed Buffalo player staggered over to the Michigan bench. Yost grabbed him by the arm and said, "Son, your bench is on the other side of the field. You're confused."

"No, coach, I'm not," the player replied. "I know exactly where I am."

The Buffalo paper carried this note on the game:

"One-hundred and twenty-eight to 0. It is unique and astonishing, even if every Buffalo man were a cripple before he got on the train to leave for Ann Arbor."

Michigan proceeded to roll through the remainder of its schedule, defeating the Carlisle Indians, 22-0; Ohio State, 21-0; Chicago, 22-0; Beloit, 89-0; and Iowa, 50-0. The win over Iowa gave Michigan a perfect 4-0 record in the Western Conference and the championship.

It was not the final game of the season, however, as a group of entrepreneurs on the West Coast was searching for an attraction to augment the popular "Tournament of Roses Parade" in Pasadena, California. What better attraction than this Michigan team with Heston and Yost. Leland Stanford College also thought that Michigan would make a proper opponent, one with which it could deal.

The Rose Bowl

A polo match as the sporting highlight of the Tournament of Roses Parade in Pasadena had been satisfactory, but something more dramatic was needed in 1902. "Why not a football game?" offered one member of the committee, and immediately Tournament President James Wagner started a series of correspondence with the "best team in the West"— Fielding H. Yost's Michigan team.

There were reports that Michigan was planning to play a football game on the West Coast during the Christmas Holidays, and Wagner's letter to Director Baird invited the Wolverines to play on January 1, 1902, against one of the "Pacific Coast Universities." Details were hammered out in an exchange of letters with Baird extracting one concession from the tournament committee. Michigan would receive $3 per day meal money instead of the proposed $2, this in addition to a $3,600 guarantee for expenses. That modest expense budget would increase to $45,889.05 when Michigan played in the 1951 Rose Bowl, and in 1970 Michigan would submit a budget calling for $79,128.50.

When Stanford defeated California 12-0 for the 1901 championships of the Pacific Coast, the opponents for the first Rose Bowl game were set.

Michigan started preparation in December, using Waterman Gymnasium for indoor work and going outdoors to run plays. This setup was not to Yost's liking, and it was during this period that he wondered, "Why not construct a large building with high ceilings and a dirt floor which could be used for indoor practices?" Twenty-four years later such a building was built at Michigan, and Yost tabbed it a Field House, the first such structure of its kind.

Despite the weather the Wolverines were able to regain most of their regular season sharpness under the conditioning

Before the Rose Bowl game, Michigan's team rode in the parade. Fielding H. Yost holds a Michigan banner in upper right, and standing next to him is Willie Heston.

program of Keene Fitzpatrick. They left Ann Arbor on December 17 with temperatures below freezing and six inches of snow on the ground. By this time the Wolverines had national recognition with their unprecedented trip westward. During a change of trains in Chicago the president of the Pullman Car Company told his manager, "Give the Michigan boys the best there is: the best is none too good for them."

Eight days later Michigan's party of fifteen players, Yost, Baird, and trainer Fitzpatrick arrived in Los Angeles and was greeted by newspaper reports listing three reasons why Stanford should win. First, the Michigan team would not be expected to adjust to the vast change in temperatures and would probably wilt in the second half. Also, the game would be played on dirt and not grass, to which Michigan had been accustomed. The third reason was particularly insulting to Michigan's freshman halfback, Willie Heston, who recalled the story:

"The papers stated they had seen me play on the San Jose Normal team, and if I could win a regular position in the Michigan backfield, Michigan could not be very strong."

On the Saturday preceding the game Stanford's captain,

The start of the Rose Bowl. This was the scene on New Year's Day of 1902 when Michigan played Stanford in the first Rose Bowl game.

Ralph Fisher, called on Yost and offered to take him for a ride. He had a two-seated buggy, drawn by two horses. Heston and two of his teammates climbed into the back, and the five started off. They had not gone far when Yost asked Fisher if it would not be a good idea to cut the halves to twenty-five minutes because of the heat.

"We can't do that, Mr. Yost," Fisher replied. "We have sold a great many tickets for the game, and they are entitled to see two full thirty-five minute halves." The subject was dropped.

New Year's morning found the Michigan team, outfitted in its new uniforms, waving colorful Michigan banners, and riding a large carriage in the Tournament of Roses Parade. Thousands jammed the parade route, and following the parade Pasadena experienced its largest traffic snarl ever as fans headed for the football grounds.

Stands had been erected for 2,500, but more than 8,000 spectators managed to surround the field. Hundreds more parked in carriages behind a wire fence while still others sat atop a wooden fence surrounding the field.

Quarterback Boss Weeks looks like a T-formation quarterback as he runs the Michigan offense against Stanford in the 1902

The game opened with a blistering sun moving the temperature into the mid-80s, and Stanford appeared every bit as capable as the papers reported. Two gallant goal line stands held off the Wolverines until deep into the first half when Stanford's field goal attempt from 40 yards out missed and

Rose Bowl game.

Michigan took over on its 20. Fullback Neil Snow started to ram the tiring Stanford line, and Michigan drove past midfield. Then Yost's artistry appeared. A fake kick sent most of Stanford's defense scurrying in one direction, and Heston like a thunderbolt ran down the sidelines for 35 yards. A few plays later Snow scored the first of his five touchdowns, charging in from the five.

Everett Sweeley, who averaged 43 yards with his punting, continued to keep Stanford deep in its territory with his kicks. Then, with a couple minutes left in the first half, he kicked a 23-yard field goal. Almost immediately Curtis Redden returned a weak Stanford punt 25 yards for a touchdown, and Bruce Shorts kicked the extra point for a 17-0 Michigan lead at half time.

Snow scored his second touchdown early in the second half, and after Redden picked up a fumble and ran 25 to score, the rout was on. Snow, who later was named the player of the game by the Helms Foundation, scored three more times, and finally Al Herrnstein recorded the final touchdown.

A few minutes later Stanford captain Fisher walked over to the Michigan bench and conferred with Michigan's captain, Hugh White.

"If you are willing, sir, we are ready to quit," Fisher said.

Stanford had suffered six injuries and had no reserves left. One lineman, William Roosevelt, the cousin of President Theodore Roosevelt, had suffered a broken leg but played until he sustained three fractured ribs.

Michigan consented to calling the game with eight minutes left.

The 49-0 victory capped one of the most unbelievable seasons in college football history. Michigan had outscored its opponents, 550-0, winning eleven straight games. Willie Heston, too, made believers out of his West Coast critics. He gained 170 yards in 18 carries for a 9.4 average as Michigan recorded 527 yards on the ground and advanced the ball a whopping 881 yards by kicking. Kicking would become a trademark of Yost's teams.

Michigan used only eleven players in the game. As the Wolverines were preparing to leave their hotel Monday night after the game, the four substitutes were missing. Yost dispatched Heston to find them, and after searching the hotel he found the four in the rear of the building.

"There they were," recalled Heston. "They had gone up to their rooms after dinner, put on their brand new football togs, came down, and went out the back entrance. They found a garden hose, wetted themselves down, and were rolling on the bare ground so they would not have to go back to Ann Arbor with clean, new suits."

The four Michigan substitutes were not the only ones concerned over the results of the game. The tournament association, though realizing a profit of $3,161.86, thought the wide difference in the score would make an annual game unappealing to spectators. The following year they replaced the football game with a chariot race, and it would be sixteen years before the Rose Bowl would again feature a post-parade football game.

A Water Jug Becomes Famous

Michigan claimed the championship of the West in 1901, but in Madison, Wisconsin, there were dissenters. The two teams had not met, both finishing their seasons undefeated, but this dispute would be resolved the following year when they played in Chicago. The November 1 game immediately was labeled as the one to decide the conference title.

Yost opened the 1902 training camp at Whitmore Lake with most of the players returning from his Rose Bowl team. Missing, however, was Neil Snow, the outstanding fullback and strong defensive end. Caspar Whitney, editor of *Outing Magazine* and considered one of the leading authorities on football, along with Walter Camp, named Snow to the end position on his all-America team. Snow was the only player outside the East to be honored in Whitney's 1901 selections. Snow, a ten-letter winner at Michigan, later died unexpectedly of a heart attack at thirty-four.

Michigan started the season impressively with an 88-0 win over Albion, defeated Case 48-6, then overwhelmed Michigan Agricultural College (now Michigan State University), 119-0. Notre Dame, which had lost its five previous games with Michigan, fell 23-0. Next came Ohio State. The week before the game, Ohio's first-year coach, Perry Hale, fresh from success as a player at Yale, announced that, "Michigan had never played a hard team." The Wolverines responded with an 86-0 victory.

With six straight victories behind them, the Wolverines were now ready for Wisconsin. Temporary stands were erected at Marshall Field in Chicago to accommodate 25,000 fans. It was one of the largest crowds to see a game in the Midwest. Both teams offered powerful defenses, and Wisconsin's plan centered around stopping the end sweeps of Heston and Herrnstein. Yost, anticipating this, instructed quarterback Boss Weeks to use the fullback, Paul Jones, up the middle. Jones, who later became a U. S. District Court judge in Ohio, opened the game with a series of rushes to either side of center and managed to work the ball to the Wisconsin 10-yard line, but his final effort did not please the critical Weeks, who yelled at his fullback, "Jonesie, you're not doing a G-D- thing." Weeks on the next play handed off to Heston for a touchdown.

Minutes later a section of the bleachers collapsed, injuring several spectators and delaying the game. The 6-0 score for Michigan held up the rest of the game, and the Wolverines remained undefeated. The following week Michigan ran up a 107-0 score on Iowa, and newspapers began referring to Yost's "Point-a-Minute" team. Michigan scored 644 points to 12 for the opposition and won eleven straight games, including a season-ending victory over Chicago.

In two seasons Yost accomplished what Baird said he must do: win and beat Chicago. There were indications that this success would continue in 1903. Yost, however, faced the problem of replacing his master quarterback, Weeks, and halfback Herrnstein, who scored thirty-seven touchdowns in two years.

Fred (Shorty) Norcross, a 5-foot, 8-inch, 139-pound track sprinter, was tried at halfback and eventually took over at quarterback. Tom Hammond was inserted into the fullback position and four other new players added to the lineup. Michigan never missed a step! Seven straight wins ran Yost's streak to twenty-eight, but looming ahead were the powerful Gophers of Minnesota, and their meeting on a cold October Saturday in Minneapolis would add another layer to Michigan's football tradition.

Never had a football game so excited the Minneapolis area. All seats and standing room areas were filled as the largest crowd ever assembled in the West for a football game—estimated between 25,000 and 30,000—jammed Northrop Field to watch these two unbeaten teams, clearly the powers of the

West.

The hostility present was evident to the Wolverines. Trainer Fitzpatrick had sent the student manager, Tom Roberts, to purchase a drinking container for the team, expressing suspicion at having the water supplied by Minnesota. Roberts was able to obtain a five-gallon, putty-colored jug for 30 cents at a nearby variety store.

The game quickly settled into a nose-to-nose battle of defenses. The field was 110 yards in length, and three downs were allotted to gain the necessary five yards for a first down. Nine-man lines were employed. Forward passing was illegal.

The tone of the game was established early when a booming Minnesota punt sailed to Michigan's two returners, Norcross and Herb Graver. Graver was hit almost immediately; and, as he fell forward, Minnesota's huge tackle, Webster, hit him head on, straightened him up, and then slammed him backwards. Graver got up, wiped the blood off his face, and turned to Norcross. "Norky," Graver said, "This is going to be a rough afternoon."

Later Heston was knocked out. Joe Maddock, a tackle who also carried the ball, was laid out. Seldom had a college game been waged with such intensity.

With 12 minutes left in the game, Michigan worked the ball to the Minnesota 5-yard line. Maddock, fully recovered, hit the Gopher wall twice and on his third attempt scored. Hammond kicked the extra point, and it appeared Michigan would win.

With Minnesota's cheering thousands responding to each play the Gophers continued to press on offense, and finally after Michigan punted out to its 45 they started to move. With two minutes left, Boeckmann, a reserve fullback, scored for Minnesota. When the fans realized that the touchdown was good, they swarmed over the field, 5,000 strong. When the field was cleared, Captain Ed Rogers, from a difficult angle to the right of the goalposts, kicked the extra point to tie the game at 6-6. There was no holding them back now; fans engulfed the field with 2 minutes left to play, and the game had to be called.

One sportswriter wrote, "Everything that wasn't nailed down went high in the air, hats, canes, umbrellas, and cushions. Dignity was cast to the winds."

The Little Brown Jug

Both teams finished their season undefeated, but what was more remembered from this game developed in later weeks. A janitor, Oscar Munson, found the Michigan water jug Monday morning while cleaning up and took it to the athletic director. It was labeled "Michigan Jug 'Captured' by Oscar." When Michigan inquired about the jug, Minnesota promptly replied, "If you want it, come up and win it." The Little Brown Jug rivalry began.

Because of the violent nature of the game, athletic

relations between the two schools became strained, and it would be six years before Michigan would return to play Minnesota again. Michigan won that 1909 game, and Minnesota did not see the Little Brown Jug for ten years.

Michigan completed the 1903 season with an easy 28-0 victory over Chicago, Yost's third straight over Stagg and third straight undefeated season. Financially the improvement was equally as impressive. Football profits rose from $131.57 in 1898 to an astounding $15,792.25 in 1903.

Michigan was now riding a success road never before traveled in college football. The Wolverines simply could not be beaten and in 1904 swept by ten straight opponents for their fourth straight championship. They pounded Kalamazoo 95-0 and steamrolled West Virginia, a team that had lost only to powerful Penn State in six previous games, 130-0. Michigan played only two conference games, defeating Wisconsin and Chicago, but under the rules of the time shared the Western Conference title with Minnesota, winner of three games without a loss.

The victory over Chicago was Heston's final game for Michigan. He played brilliantly, as did a young sophomore for the Maroons, Walter Eckersall. But the end of an era was in sight, and Eckersall would have a hand in the foreclosure.

An Era Ends . . . Barely

Adolph "Germany" Schulz had the strength of a black-smith. He came to Michigan from Fort Wayne, Indiana, 4 inches over 6 feet and weighing 245 pounds. He played center where his enormous hands allowed him to snap the ball with one hand and use the other for blocking. But it was on defense where he provided football with a new dimension.

Schulz, though gentle and able to absorb great punishment on the field and remain smiling, stood in awe of no man. He played football his way, and one of his innovations was dropping a yard or two behind his regular defensive line position. The first time Coach Yost saw that move he was horrified and quickly yelled at Schulz:

"Dutchman, what are you trying to do? You're supposed to play in the line."

"I think it's better to play behind the line," replied Schulz.

"They'll run over us," screamed Yost.

"Listen, Yost, I can see things better back there. If anybody gets by me, I'll move back into the line and stay there."

Yost, who was never able to fault Schulz' judgment or performance, went along with him. In a few years the position of linebacker became a permanent part of defense. Michigan was able to use a six-man line, and with the advent of the forward pass in 1906 this was a decided edge. Schulz went on to earn all-American honors in 1907 and was selected on all-Time all-America teams, first by Grantland Rice and a half century

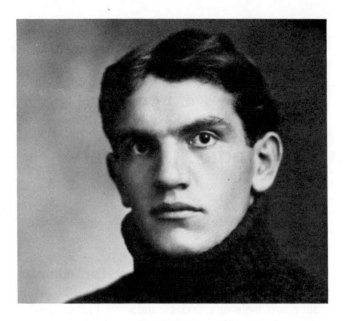

Germany Schulz, 1907

Ernie Vick, 1921   Jack Blott, 1923

All-American Centers
Michigan's short punt formation relied on great centers, and the Wolverines usually had one. These six centers all gained all-American honors. Germany Schulz was named to the all-time college football team of the first half century. Maynard Morrison earned all-American honors in 1931, the first of three

Bob Brown, 1925   Maynard Morrison, 1931
Charles Bernard, 1932-33

successive years a Michigan center was accorded the honor.
Chuck Bernard twice was named all-American, in 1932 and
1933. Bob Brown, later to serve Michigan as a regent, was
called by Yost "the finest captain I ever had." Jack Blott later
served Michigan as an assistant coach, while Ernie Vick went on
to play major league baseball.

later by the Associated Press.

Michigan continued to blitz its opponents during 1905. With Schulz leading the defense, the Wolverine goal line went unpenetrated through twelve games. Early in the season, however, a tough 18-0 win over Dan McGugin's Vanderbilt team indicated that the Michigan offense was not the explosive unit of Heston's years. Heston had a chance to see the Michigan team a few weeks later when he brought his Drake team to Ann Arbor and lost, 48-0. A 12-0 victory over Wisconsin then put the Wolverines in line for another championship, and that was decided in the final game against Chicago.

A crowd of 27,000 was on hand in Chicago, lured by the prospect that Stagg's finest Maroon team would finally stop the Michigan streak of playing fifty-six games without losing. Midway through the first half Walter Eckersall sent a low, driving punt between Michigan's Al Barlow and Denny Clark near the goal line. Clark picked up the ball in the end zone and tried to run it out. He shook off two tacklers and moved a couple yards out into the field when Chicago's Maurice Catline drove hard into the Michigan halfback, forcing him back into the end zone. It was a safety, and Chicago's great defense made that stand up for a 2-0 victory.

Clark was visibly upset over the play. Later he explained the play: "When I ran out of the end zone, I saw I was going to be tackled. I called 'Down!' but the referee was too far upfield and never heard me."

The loss was Michigan's first in fifty-seven games. The Wolverines scored more points (495) and allowed fewer (2) than any team in the nation and still lost one of their games. But their five year record stood as the finest ever achieved in football. They won fifty-five games, lost one, and tied one, scoring 2,821 points against 42 for the opposition.

An era had ended, but a new era for Michigan and college football was beginning. Critics of the sport were being heard in growing numbers. They attacked the brutality of the game and, dramatically, Northwestern University announced that it was withdrawing from intercollegiate football. President Theodore Roosevelt ordered the colleges "to clean up the game," and a series of wide-ranging rules came forth, including the legalization of the forward pass.

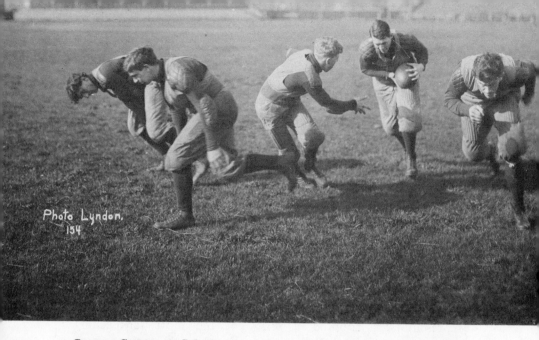

Center Germany Schulz, far left, leads the Michigan backfield through a drill as quarterback Fred Norcross hands off to Tom Hammond in 1905.

In Ann Arbor, Michigan President James B. Angell thought more should be done. He proposed a conference meeting in Chicago to deal with the serious problems of football. His concerns would trigger wide-reaching reforms and at home result in a storm of protest, forcing Michigan onto an island.

"Then There Were Seven"

The "Angell Conference" convened January 19, 1906, at the Chicago Beach Hotel. After two days the group of faculty representatives adopted a series of the most far-reaching regulations of football in history, and with their passage Michigan would stand alone.

The Western Conference approved the following regulations:

1. Students must have a year of residence before competing in athletics,
2. They must maintain proper grades,
3. Participation is limited to three years,
4. Training tables are abolished,
5. Universities may play a maximum of five games,
6. Coaches must be regular members of the instructional staff at their universities,
7. There must be absolute faculty control.

Battle lines immediately were drawn at Michigan. Faculty men generally approved the regulations, while alumni and students clamored for Michigan's withdrawal from the conference. Three of the regulations were particularly opposed by athletic interests at Michigan. The retroactive provision of the three-year rule would deprive several outstanding Michigan athletes of their senior year of competition, including Tom Hammond, John Garrels, who was a football player and outstanding track performer, and members of several other athletic teams. Secondly, a training table was thought essential for athletes. And finally, a limitation of five games would sever

74

Michigan's strong ties with Eastern teams.

Michigan's Board in Control, in an April 12, 1906, meeting, adopted the regulations but requested the conference to modify its three-year rule by removing the retroactive feature. A month later, however, Director Baird was authorized to surrender Michigan's "membership in the conference," if he thought it best.

In November the Board again asked the conference to modify the objectional features of its regulations. On January 25, 1907, the Board asked the Regents for advice. A series of meetings was held on the question until the Regents, on November 15, 1907, passed a resolution changing the organization of the Board.

The new Board of five faculty members, one alumnus, and two undergraduates voted that the Michigan delegate to the next conference meeting work for the passage of rules that would secure a seven-game schedule, a training table, and repeal of the retroactive three-year rule.

These proposals all were rejected at the Western Conference meeting of January 4, 1908. The Board on January 14 voted 5-3 to withdraw, and on February 1 Michigan officially left the conference.

Despite this concern over Michigan's place in the conference, Yost managed to have a new football field ready for the 1906 season. The Wolverines had played on Regents Field, but seating was limited to about 15,000. Dexter M. Ferry of Detroit, a generous benefactor of the university, had purchased and donated to the athletic department twenty acres to the north of Regents Field. A new field was constructed with seating for 18,000. Concrete stands were erected in 1914, expanding the capacity to nearly 25,000, and this capacity was increased to 46,000 with further additions. The entire athletic complex was named Ferry Field.

Michigan played only one conference team in 1906, dedicating new Ferry Field with a 28-9 win over Illinois. No league games were played in 1907. The Wolverines suffered only two defeats in those two seasons, both to powerful Pennsylvania.

The meeting with Penn in 1907 again demonstrated Yost's ability to immediately take advantage of the rules. The forward pass had been approved the year before, and Yost already had

his players throwing spirals rather than the end-over-end style of the day. One restriction, however, stipulated that the pass must cross the line of scrimmage at least five yards to the left or right from where the center snapped the ball.

Trailing 6-0 Michigan worked the ball to Penn's 30-yard line where Yost unveiled his play. Schulz stood 15 yards in from the sidelines with five linemen to his left toward the center of the field. He snapped the ball diagonally back to Bill Wasmund who lateraled to Dave Allerdice moving to his left. Allerdice then fired a pass to Paul Magoffin, the captain, who had sprinted down the right sidelines, then cut directly over in front of the goal posts. The pass went for a touchdown, but when Pennsylvania complained, the officials ruled that the pass had not crossed the scrimmage line more than five yards from

Michigan captain David W. Allerdice punts from his own goal line in 1909 action versus Pennsylvania in Philadelphia's Franklin Field. Michigan won, 12-6.

where Schulz had snapped the ball. It was a hotly disputed play, and Yost in future years made a practice of informing officials of his trick plays.

Michigan continued to play successful, though not spectacular, football with Notre Dame, Ohio State, and Pennsylvania supplying the main opposition. In 1909, after barely edging Marquette, 6-5, and losing to Notre Dame, 11-3, the Wolverines upset "Pennsy" to become the first Western school to record a victory over one of the Big Four—Yale, Harvard, Princeton, or Pennsylvania.

The following week Michigan upended mighty Minnesota and took possession of the Little Brown Jug. This game also created the setting for one of the classic football encounters of all-time, the 1910 Michigan-Minnesota game in Ann Arbor.

The Forward Pass
Comes Of Age

Minnesota had lost one game in 1909, and now, a year later the Gophers were undefeated, unscored upon, and ready for Michigan. Coach Henry "Doc" Williams had perfected his "Minnesota Shift" which had demoralized six straight opponents.

Michigan was not an imposing team in 1910. The Wolverines managed only two victories and three ties before meeting Minnesota. Their schedule had been abbreviated when a game with Notre Dame was cancelled. Michigan claimed that Notre Dame had two players who had played at least four years at two other western colleges. Notre Dame denied the charge, refused to withhold the pair, so the game was called off.

Minnesota was huge. Tackles Jim Walker, 235, and Paul Young, 225, flanked center Babe Morrell, who weighed 240. Michigan had speed and Albert Benbrook, a cat-like giant at 6-5, 265 pounds. Ferry Field was jammed to capacity, and thousands more were perched in surrounding windows, rooftops, trees, and on telegraph poles. It was billed as the battle of giants, and no one was disappointed.

Yost had devised a counter plan for the Minnesota Shift. The Gophers had confused their opponents by lining up in one formation, suddenly shifting to another formation, and immediately snapping the ball. Yost had his tackles shifting with Minnesota, matching power with power. Minnesota's defense was equally effective, and the teams waged a bruising battle of punts and defense. Clark Shaughnessy, the famed football

Al Benbrook cleared the way for Stanfield Wells in defeat of Minnesota in 1910.

Stanfield Wells broke a new frontier with the forward pass in 1910.

coach, was on the Minnesota bench that day, a third string substitute. He later wrote, "The play was as fierce in physical contact as I have ever seen. I doubt that it has ever been equalled on a football field. That was the heyday of grubbing, manpower football."

There were six minutes left when Michigan took possession of the ball on Minnesota's 48, and Yost's genius once more began to unfold. Michigan unexpectedly went into a shift with all-American Stan Wells moving into the backfield from his right end position. Wells took the ball from quarterback "Shorty" McMillan and started to his left behind massive interference. Johnny McGovern, the Gophers' brilliant all-American quarterback, watched the play unfold from his safety position and suddenly shouted, "Look out, a pass!" Too late! Stan Borleske, who had shifted from left end to the right side, broke quickly down field, and Wells had the ball in the air. Borleske made a leaping catch on the 30, and McGovern immediately shoved him out of bounds.

Michigan lined up immediately. No signal was called. Again Wells shifted into the backfield and, using the identical play, passed to Borleske on the Minnesota 3-yard line.

Two minutes were left. Michigan sent Wells into the massive Gopher line...once, twice...but they held. Benbrook, who had blocked a field goal kick and played magnificently the entire game, walked over to quarterback Neil "Shorty" McMillan. "Run it over me this time," ordered the giant, "and make it Wells." Wells once more took the snap and drove straight for Benbrook, over the weak side. Benbrook bent the Gopher line with his massive body, and Wells lunged over his shoulder and across the goal line. Fred Conklin's extra point gave Michigan a 6-0 victory.

The game was a classic in its day but, more importantly, established the forward pass as a means of victory. This was the first game of major significance to be decided by the pass. Yost called this game "the finest I've ever seen," and always maintained that the forward pass came into its own on November 20, 1910. Three years later Notre Dame's Gus Dorais and Knute Rockne used the pass to bewilder Army.

That Minnesota game also marked the last association Michigan would have with a Western Conference team until 1917. The league passed a "non-intercourse" rule prohibiting its members from having athletic relations with any institution that had been a member of the conference and ceased to be such a member. Many thought the rule was a means of boycotting Michigan, but there were reports that at least one school was ready to leave the conference and that this action was aimed at discouraging further defections.

Michigan, however, was on top of the football world, and her horizons would expand with intersectional games.

Of Men And Spirit

The brilliant pageantry that would surround college football was beginning to form a vibrant, intoxicating air around the Wolverines. There were heroes to cheer, songs to be written. The bands became bigger, the crowds larger. America had adopted football.

Alumni identification with Michigan intensified, and in 1913 they even had a song to recall their undergraduate years. Joe Parker ran the most popular student saloon in Ann Arbor. Located on South Main Street, its oak tables were covered with initials, and the beer was always cold. The place was usually packed, and a few blocks away the Oriental Bar took care of the overflow. It was with some nostalgia that alumni and students would sing:

> *I want to go back to Michigan,*
> *To dear Ann Arbor town.*
> *Back to Joe's and the Orient,*
> *Back to some of the money I spent.*
> *I wanta go back, I gotta go back*
> *...to Mich-i-gan.*

And back they came by the thousands to watch the Wolverines. To watch their heroes, like Johnny Maulbetsch, the German Bullet from Ann Arbor, like Stan Wells, Jimmy Craig, Ernest Allmendinger, Miller "Brute" Pontius, Frank Culver, Cedric "Pat" Smith, and Frank Steketee. They were college all-Americans.

Charles Baird resigned as athletic director to join a bank in

Kansas City in 1909, and his assistant, Philip B. Bartelme, took over. A year later trainer Keene Fitzpatrick left to become Princeton's track coach, and Dr. Alvin Kraenzlein replaced him.

Fred Lawton, whose prose and verse would forever record his special feeling of Michigan's tradition, decided that the Wolverines needed a new song. He met Earl Moore on a street corner in Detroit one October afternoon in 1911, and they agreed to collaborate. While riding the trolley to Lawton's home, where the closest piano was available, the words came to Lawton.

Varsity, we're for you,
here for you,
to cheer for you
We have no fear for you—Varsity.

Philip Bartelme was Michigan's athletic director from 1909 until 1921.

Lawton later completed the other stanzas, Moore put them to music, and this robust song soon rivaled "The Victors" in popularity.

With the Western Conference "boycott" in full force against Michigan, such schools as Marietta, Mount Union, and Lawrence began to appear on the Wolverine schedule. Still, Yost was able to meet Harvard, Cornell, and Pennsylvania with some success. These games maintained Michigan's national prestige and provided a showcase for Eastern writers, who selected several Michigan players on their all-America teams. Jimmy Craig was one halfback who benefited from Michigan's long series with Penn, a series that ran uninterrupted from 1906 through 1917. Craig's moment came in 1911.

A capacity crowd, ignoring a snowstorm whipped by 30 mile per hour winds, turned out at Ferry Field to watch Michigan battle Penn, and it appeared that the Wolverines were headed for another defeat. They had achieved only a victory and tie in six previous meetings with the Quakers. Late in the fourth quarter, trailing 9-5, Yost decided to unveil one of his special plays. The ball was snapped, and nine Wolverines charged to their left. Craig, with only Otto Carpell for protection, faded to his right for an apparent forward pass. The entire Penn team moved right with the formation. Craig, a sprinter, whose brother, Ralph, won two Olympic gold medals at 100 and 200 meters, charged 25 yards down the sidelines unchallenged for the winning touchdown.

Three years later another swift Michigan runner made his mark on Eastern football critics. Johnny Maulbetsch, just 5-feet 7-inches and 153 pounds, bulldozed his way through Harvard's great defense for 133 yards in thirty rushes, most of them off the vaunted Harvard tackles. He gained more yardage than the entire Harvard backfield, and though Michigan lost, 7-0, Ring Lardner in 1914 wrote:

"After this, if any Easterner tells you that the game played back East is superior to that played in the Midwest, try not to laugh yourself to death. Johnny Maulbetsch of Michigan shot that theory full of holes."

A week later Maulbetsch scored two touchdowns and accounted for 120 of the 127 yards Michigan gained against Pennsylvania to spark a 34-3 win before an overflow crowd of

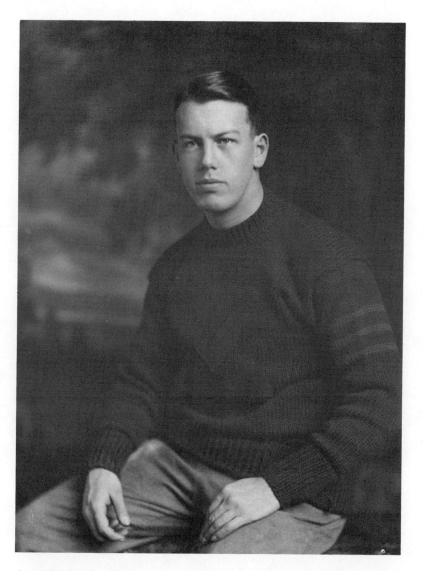

Jimmy Craig was one of Michigan's greatest halfbacks, and followed Willie Heston as the second runner to become an all-American in 1913.

25,000 at Ferry Field. That 1914 Michigan team scored 233 points, the largest total since Yost's last Point-a-Minute squad of 1905.

Desire was a Maulbetsch trademark, and his unique

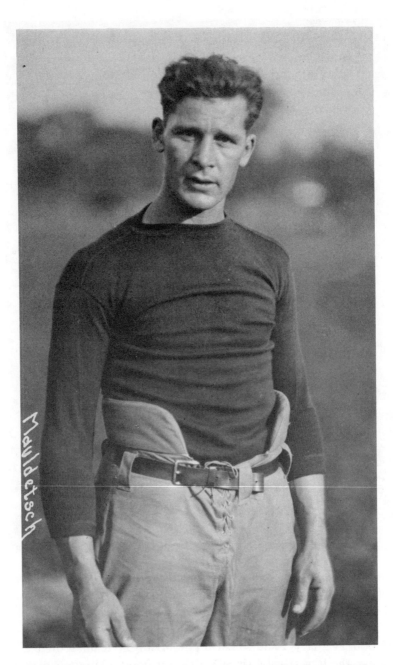

Johnny Maulbetsch was an all-American halfback for Michigan in 1914 as a sophomore. One of three Michigan football awards is made in his honor.

running style was an extension of it. Crouched low, using one arm as an extra leg, he had to be tackled from the top to be stopped. He played three seasons, 1914-15-16, for Michigan. There is a football trophy awarded annually in his honor to the Michigan freshman who exhibits character, capacity for leadership, and desire. There is another tribute to him, written by Fred Lawton. The last stanza reminded Michigan men of that Harvard game:

> *He didn't make the touchdown,*
> *and we didn't win the game,*
> *But little Johnny Maulbetsch*
> *led the Wolverines to fame,*
> *For, in those glorious minutes,*
> *when young 'Mauly' gave his all,*
> *We learned of Michigan 'spirit'*
> *from his words, 'GIMME DA BALL!'*
> *His spirit burst into a flame*
> *when victory hopes were slim,*
> *The 'Victors' and the 'Varsity'*
> *became a part of him!*
> *You ask the meaning of this*
> *Michigan 'spirit'—yours and mine?*
> *Just think of Johnny Maulbetsch*
> *when he hit that Harvard line!*

Michigan won six of nine games in 1914 with Maulbetsch scoring twelve touchdowns and Tommy Hughitt providing the leadership at quarterback. But it was the final game, a 28-13 loss to Cornell, that caused a near-riot on the Michigan campus.

A letter was uncovered from a local pool hall operator, Joe Reinger, offering to fix the Cornell game. The letter to H. P. Bailey of Massachusetts insisted that Hughitt and Maulbetsch were "enemies," and Reinger promised that Michigan would lose. The letter was published and 2,000 angry students stormed Reinger's pool hall, but Germany Schulz, Michigan's assistant coach, pleaded with the crowd to "stand by Michigan." He turned what could have been a riot into a victory rally. Reinger passed the letter off as a joke but later sold his pool hall and left town.

Michigan suffered through a disappointing 1915 season, losing three of seven games, but with Maulbetsch as captain in

1916 the Wolverines won seven straight before losing to Cornell and Penn. One of those victories, 9-0 over MAC (now Michigan State University), involved one of the weirdest plays in Michigan history. Quarterback Clifford Sparks, playing in his first "big" game, knelt to hold a field goal attempt for Maulbetsch from the 32. The center snap went high over Sparks' head, but he leaped up, grabbed the ball, and promptly drop kicked a field goal.

Victories, however, appeared shallow. The old rivalries with Wisconsin, Chicago, and Minnesota could not be replaced. Michigan was ready to leave its island exile.

A "Loser" Wins

Ralph Aigler picked up the morning edition of the *Michigan Daily* in 1913 and was startled by the front page story. He had been appointed to the Board in Control of Athletics by Dean Henry Bates of the Law School. Aigler, a law professor, decided he should accept the post. That decision started Michigan on a return course to the Western Conference.

Aigler discovered later that a debate he lost, actually, was responsible for Dean Bates' appointment. He spoke in favor of Michigan resuming membership in the conference, and Frank Murphy, a law student, took the opposite side. No official vote on the debate was taken, but the Detroit papers, which at the time saw nothing good in the conference for Michigan, reported more points were scored by Murphy, who would later serve on the U. S. Supreme Court.

Aigler immediately set about changing Michigan's athletic course. He received support from all three of the student members of the Board, and the *Michigan Daily* reversed its conference stand to favor resumption of membership. The Regents in 1915 also took a decisive move by ordering that the four faculty members of the Board should be named, not by the deans, but by the University Senate. At the next Senate meeting only Aigler was returned to the Board. Three new members, all known to be pro-conference, were elected. Aigler was elected chairman.

Aigler began canvassing the attitude of faculty representatives in the conference to learn what steps Michigan must take

89

Ralph Aigler was chairman of Michigan's Board in Control of Athletics and served as the faculty representative to the Western Conference from 1917 until 1955.

to rejoin the "family." Aigler visited seven of the nine schools and reported, "It was obvious that the Conference would welcome Michigan's return." The main stipulation, he found, was that President Harry Hutchins must assure the conference that Michigan had "faculty control of athletics."

Anti-conference feelings were particularly strong among alumni in Detroit, and Bartelme, as athletic director, also was opposed. There were many avenues of resentment running against the conference, especially the "boycott" action it had evoked. Aigler discovered, however, that Professor Paige, the Minnesota faculty representative, had proposed the boycott rule not as a slap at Michigan but as a means of quieting a movement at his own school to withdraw from the conference.

Finally in the fall of 1916, while Aigler was accompanying the football team to Cornell, director Bartelme turned to him and said, "I am getting tired of begging for games to fill out our schedule. Michigan ought not to have to do that. I believe the thing to do is to get back to our own group, and that means joining the conference."

The alumni began to clamor to rejoin the conference, and in 1916 the Detroit Alumni Club voted 358-58 to return to the league.

Aigler, buoyed by a change in attitude of a man he respected and the obvious support of Michigan's alumni, intensified his efforts. On April 27, 1917, he presented to the Regents a resolution of the Board that requested that the University Senate be given veto power over all actions of the Board. The next day the Regents approved the resolution, and faculty control was firmly established. Michigan, which also eliminated its training table, applied for membership in the Western Conference effective November 20, 1917, the day a tentative game was scheduled with Northwestern in Evanston. Michigan's request was approved by the conference.

The Wolverines rolled by eight straight opponents in 1917 before old rival Penn prevailed, 16-0. Then Northwestern shattered their re-entry into the conference with a 21-12 victory. Michigan, however, played without its superb quarterback "Beak" Weston, named to Walter Eckersall's first team all-American, and center "Paddy" Lambert, on Eckersall's second team of all-Americans. Captain-elect Pat Smith, a fullback, was playing for Great Lakes Naval Training School, and Ernest Allmendinger, a guard, was starring for Fort Sheridan. Both were named on Camp's Service all-America team that season.

But Michigan was back. In a decade of playing outside the conference Yost's teams compiled a 52-16-7 record, a record devoid of championships.

A Call For Help Answered

World War I was raging in Europe, and a flu epidemic was spreading through the United States. The 1918 college football season nearly collapsed. These events made a medical career all the more important for Angus Goetz, a regular tackle on Michigan's football team.

Discouraged by the cancellation of the first three football games, Goetz walked into Yost's office and said: "Coach, I've decided to quit football."

A startled Yost looked at his big lineman for a moment, smiled, and asked, "What's the matter? Is there something I can do?"

Goetz, consumed with his medical studies, explained that late classes and laboratory courses prevented him from attending practices on time, and with the war and epidemic he felt it necessary to sacrifice football.

Yost listened until Goetz finished, then said, "Y'know, we have our most important games coming up, and that means a lot to Meeshegan." The Yost charm and persuasion took hold. He was not about to go into the Chicago game without his best tackle. Goetz reconsidered and remained on the team. It was a fortunate decision for Michigan.

The Wolverines, meeting Chicago for the first time in thirteen years, blanked the Maroons, 13-0, and one of those touchdowns came on a blocked field goal and a 50-yard run by Goetz. Michigan then defeated MAC, 21-6, and Goetz scored again, this time by picking up a fumble. He scored his third

Angus Goetz nearly quit football during World War I, but remained to become the first player under Yost to be elected twice to captain the Wolverines, 1919 and 1920.

touchdown of the season on a blocked punt in a 14-0 win over Ohio State.

Michigan won all five games on its abbreviated 1918 schedule as two freshmen, Frank Steketee from Grand Rapids and Ernie Vick from Toledo, started their outstanding careers. Steketee, a fullback with a talented foot, earned all-American honors in his first season. Vick became an all-American center his senior year, and Goetz was elected captain for the 1919 season.

Victories over Chicago and Ohio State gave Michigan a 2-0 conference record. Illinois was undefeated in four league games, and Michigan pressed for a post-season game with the Illini that would decide a champion in 1918, but they refused. Reports out of Ann Arbor strongly hinted that Illinois might have "cold feet." When Coach Bob Zuppke heard this, he quickly fired back, "Michigan's record the last ten years is not awe inspiring enough to give anyone cold feet," and a burning rivalry was beginning to be stroked, one soon to erupt on the football field.

But troubled times were ahead for Michigan.

Yost opened his 1919 training camp missing several players who had joined the armed service. All-American Steketee was ineligible. Michigan proceeded to win only three of seven games, the worst record of any Yost team. Students and alumni were visibly upset, and criticism of Yost began to form. He immediately went on the offensive, calling for support, for more players, more spirit. Students and alumni responded as never before, to such an extent that Yost had to caution some alumni for being too "overindulging in their recruiting efforts." Fraternities threw their support behind Yost, and one campus message urged, "Your duty is to talk Michigan and search out all available prospects in your local area during Christmas vacation." Alumni, as far away as New York, pledged support.

For 1920, however, Yost would have to go with the material on hand. A brilliant engineering student from Grand Rapids, Paul Goebel, and Frank "Cappie" Cappon from nearby Holland joined the varsity. Steketee returned. With Goetz as captain, the first player under Yost to be selected for this honor in successive years, the Wolverines turned in a creditable season. They won five games, losing only to Illinois, for the second straight year, and eventual champion, Ohio State. They posted a

Paul Goebel, an all-American end at Michigan who could pass.
He captained the 1922 Wolverines.

satisfying 14-0 win over Chicago, a team containing a player destined to command an important role in Michigan athletics, Herbert O. "Fritz" Crisler. Michigan capped the season by edging Minnesota, 3-0, on Steketee's field goal.

The discouragement of 1919 turned into heady optimism for 1921. Ohio State and Illinois had dominated the Western Conference championship every year since 1916, but students and alumni now were talking of Michigan's first title in sixteen years. Those heavy recruiting efforts were ready for harvest with the most promising product coming in the smallest package. Harry Kipke, a high school sensation at Lansing, was just 5-foot-9 and weighed 158 pounds, but he could do it all—run, pass, punt, catch the football. He was joined by Doug

This 1920 action shows Michigan's Frank Steketee gaining 15 yards on an end run against Michigan State. Steketee was an all-American fullback in 1918 and an excellent place kicker.

Roby of Holland and Bernie Kirk, a brilliant athlete who had transferred from Notre Dame.

Phil Bartelme, who had guided Michigan athletics since 1909, suddenly resigned as athletic director, and Yost was named to replace him. With a salary as athletic director, Yost volunteered to coach without pay in 1921. He continued this practice in 1922-23-25-26.

Michigan, with Kipke running and kicking superbly, opened the season with three straight shutout victories to set up an important meeting with Ohio State. A record Ferry Field crowd of 45,000 turned out for this growing rivalry, but Kipke was injured early in the game, and the Buckeyes won, 14-0. It was a disappointing loss, and critics of Yost quickly returned. One headline appeared in the *Michigan Daily* over a "Letter to the Editor" suggesting that "Yost Has Seen His Day." The following week Steketee's field goal defeated Illinois, 3-0, and most of the criticism subsided. The Wolverines then turned their attention to the powerful Badgers of Wisconsin.

Michigan brought a young group of Wolverines to Madison on Friday, and Irwin Uteritz, a 143-pound quarterback, was trying to keep the pressure off his teammates. While dressing for practice he kept looking at Cappie Cappon. Cappon was nearly bald, but had a massive chest of hair. Uteritz had seen something comical in Cappon all season and walked up to the big halfback. Suddenly the young sophomore applied a lighted match to Cappon's chest. The stunt broke up the dressing room with laughter and eased much of the tension that had been building.

Wisconsin was a two or three touchdown favorite, but this was one Yost wanted badly. He was so emotional before the game he could not finish his pre-game talk. Captain Bob "Duke" Dunne took over, and there was hardly a dry eye among the Wolverines when they charged onto Randall Stadium. Wisconsin, however, scored first as a Michigan punt was short and bounced crazily back into the end zone when a Badger fell on it for a touchdown.

Michigan took the ensuing kickoff and worked the ball past midfield to Wisconsin's 32. Now it was time for Yost to dust off a play that went back to 1910—the Minnesota end back play. End Paul Goebel dropped off the line into the backfield, took a quick lateral, and immediately passed downfield to Doug Roby, who caught the ball for a touchdown. The game ended in a 7-7 tie, but for Yost, it represented a victory of sorts.

The following week Michigan routed Minnesota, 38-0, and finished the season with a 5-1-1 record. Iowa won the championship, but Michigan was ready to offer a serious challenge in 1922.

"Kipke's Dedication"

Ohio State's imposing new football stadium in 1922 was the largest in existence west of the Yale Bowl, and the Buckeyes wanted to dedicate it properly. The crowd of 72,500 had come to watch their Bucks defeat the Wolverines for the fourth straight season.

Michigan, however, took a 3-0 lead when Paul Goebel blocked a punt and kicked a 28-yard field goal in the first quarter. The Wolverines continued moving in the second period and had the ball on Ohio State's 34. Quarterback Irwin Uteritz took the snap from center, started to his right, and faked a handoff to the end coming around. Harry Kipke also was moving right from his tailback position, but suddenly he whirled to the left and took a short shovel pass. Two Ohio State defenders reversed their charge, but too late. Kipke had them both by a couple of steps. As he slid across the goal line, Kipke turned to the official, tossed him the ball, and said, "Well, the place is really dedicated now."

He had scored on Yost's famous "Old 83," a play that scored dozens of touchdowns for Michigan over the years. But Kipke was not through with his dedication. In the third period he intercepted a pass and ran 45 yards to score, and after intercepting another pass Kipke drop-kicked a field goal from the 37 as Michigan rolled to a 19-0 victory.

After the game Walter Camp told the Michigan halfback, "Kipke, you're the greatest punter in football history." Camp had just seen one of the greatest exhibitions of kicking in the

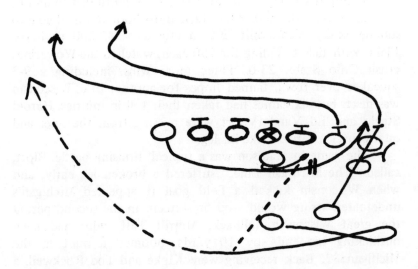

Michigan's famed "Old 83" scored dozens of touchdowns. The play starts to the right with the quarterback riding the line of scrimmage, faking to the end coming around, and pitching back to the tailback, who had started to the right, circled back, and headed for the wide side of the field.

history of football. Kipke punted eleven times. The first two sailed into the end zone, and the next nine went out of bounds inside Ohio State's eight-yard line. The punts averaged 47 yards.

The Wolverines never let up. They blanked Illinois, 24-0, as Bernie Kirk ran 80 yards for a touchdown. They smashed Michigan State, 63-0, edged stubborn Wisconsin 13-6, and finished with a 16-7 win over Minnesota. Only a scoreless tie in a dedication game with Vanderbilt tarnished an otherwise perfect record. Michigan claimed its first championship since 1906, sharing the crown with Iowa. Kipke and Goebel joined the growing list of Michigan all-Americans. Kirk was selected on Camp's second all-America team, an honor that was read to him in his hospital bed. Kirk was injured in an automobile accident shortly after the season, and meningitis set it. Five days later he died.

Michigan's string of undefeated games continued to mount in 1923. Case fell, 36-0. After Jack Blott booted a field goal to subdue pesky Vanderbilt, 3-0, a crowd of 45,000 at Ferry Field, with tickets selling for $50 each, watched the Wolverines crush Ohio State, 23-0. Three more wins, including a 9-3 squeaker over Iowa, fanned hopes for another title. Wisconsin was next, but six games had taken their toll in injuries. Harold Steele and Ed VanderVoort were missing from the line, and quarterback Uteritz broke his leg.

The game in Madison was a typical, bruising battle. Blott, called "The Michigan Line," suffered a broken leg early, and when Wisconsin kicked a field goal it appeared Michigan's undefeated string would stop at sixteen. In the second period the great Wisconsin fullback, Merrill Taft, who had been outkicking his ends by 10 yards, boomed a punt to the Michigan 32. Back receiving were Kipke and Tod Rockwell, a replacement for Uteritz. The ball struck Rockwell on the chest and bounded to his right. Kipke's block took out the first Badger end downfield. Rockwell picked up the ball and started to run. A second Badger came in and tackled him, but Rockwell, only partially down, shook loose. He was hit again but did not stop. Rolling to the sidelines he evaded a diving tackle by Marty Below. The Michigan runner picked himself up, reversed his field, and shot into the open. Several Badgers paused, thinking the play was over. Two defenders resumed their chase, but it was too late. Rockwell continued to the goal as Wisconsin rooters jeered his efforts.

Referee Walter Eckersall, wondering whether Rockwell had stepped out of bounds, consulted with the other officials. He was assured Rockwell was at least ten feet from the sideline. Suddenly the signal was given. Touchdown! The stands erupted, threats were hurled at Eckersall. But it was only the second quarter, and the Badger fans knew there was plenty of time for victory.

Michigan's defense held the Badgers through the second half, and with just seconds to go Wisconsin's only hope was a long pass. Taft unleashed the longest throw of the day, deep into Michigan territory. Players on both teams leaped, the ball was tipped and came down in the hands of a Badger end. He

Harry Kipke, captain, all-American, coach at Michigan. The nine-letterman is regarded as one of college football's greatest punters.

started to run, was hit, fumbled. Wisconsin's halfback Harris raced in, picked up the ball, and headed for Michigan's goal. Butch Slaughter, charging downfield nearly 50 yards, dived for Harris, his fingers just barely hooking his waist. Slaughter hung on, and Harris finally stumbled to the ground, 15 yards short of the Michigan goal. The all-American guard saved the day.

The game ended with that 6-3 score still on the board, and Wisconsin fans by the thousands immediately stormed the field. The first to reach Eckersall landed a blow on his head. Tom Jones, Wisconsin's athletic director, ran to Eckersall, pulled an automatic pistol from his coat, and waved it at the crowd. Realizing the danger, Below, the Wisconsin captain, recruited some of his teammates, and they moved in to form a circle

Butch Slaughter, an all-American guard, saved the day for Michigan in 1923 with a last-second tackle of a Wisconsin receiver headed for a touchdown.

around Eckersall who was escorted to the dressing room. Both teams formed a line outside the dressing room as Below told Eckersall, "You're coming with me, let's go." They walked out between the cordon of players to a waiting car, and Eckersall was driven to Milwaukee.

The rule of 1923 stated that a runner's forward progress must be stopped while in the grasp of a tackler before the play is over. Events had evened out for Michigan. In 1912 Michigan had a 20-14 lead late in the game when George Thompson punted to Cornell. Otto Carpell raced downfield and made a jarring tackle on Cornell's halfback. He went down, got up immediately, and ran for a touchdown that won the game, 21-20. After the Wisconsin turmoil, the rule was changed, terminating a play when the ball carrier hit the ground.

Michigan completed a perfect season in 1923 with a 10-0 win over Minnesota, again creating a tie for the Western Conference title, this time with Illinois.

It was the final season for two Michigan all-Americans. Kipke would return to become an assistant coach, and Goebel, in a sense, would never leave. The tall, slender end, who always retained the humility of a champion, became mayor of Grand Rapids, a regent, and devoted a near life-time of service to the university.

Reports had persisted that Yost would retire as coach. Just before the 1924 season opened, the Wolverines had a new coach for the first time since 1901—George Little from Miami of Ohio.

Michigan's Tod Rockwell on his way to a disputed touchdown against Wisconsin in 1923. The run won the game for Michigan, 6-3. Rockwell was tackled several times, hit the ground, but never stopped. This play triggered a rule change that terminated a play when any ball carrier hit the ground.

A Ghost Gallops

Mammoth concrete football stadiums began appearing on college campuses in the early 1920s, and Michigan was a popular and willing participant in their dedications. Emotion was always on the part of the home teams on these afternoons, but Yost never backed down from accepting a dedication game. "It's an honor, y'know," Yost would explain.

Michigan had traveled to Nashville for Vanderbilt's dedication in 1922 and escaped with a 0-0 tie. That year Harry Kipke made sure Michigan properly dedicated Ohio State's vast horseshoe, leading the Wolverines to a 19-0 victory.

Michigan helped Michigan State dedicate its stadium in 1924, and the fired-up Spartans nearly pulled off an upset before losing, 7-0. Michigan's second dedication game of 1924 was scheduled in Champaign, Illinois, October 18.

The papers immediately called it the "biggest game on Michigan's schedule." Headlines asked, "How Will Michigan Stop Grange?" By the end of the week Coach George Little, finally irritated by the question, shot back: "With everyone talking about whether Michigan is going to stop Grange, they are overlooking that Illinois is going to have to do a lot of work stopping what we have."

Michigan's defensive plans were aimed directly at Grange, an all-American his sophomore year and showing the same skills as a 22-year-old junior. His threat took on additional substance with reports the Wolverine ends were not as capable as they had been in previous years. Kipke and Blott also were gone.

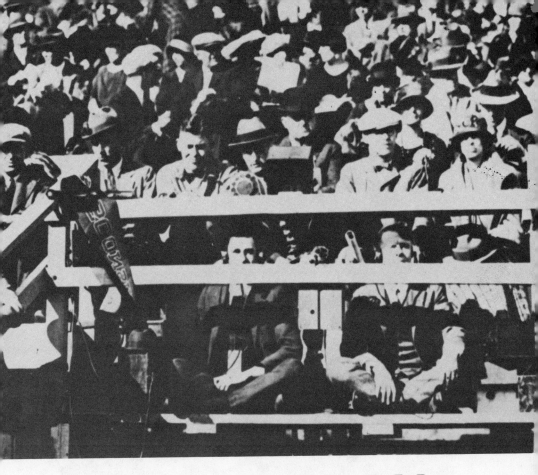

The first play-by-play of a college football game by Ty Tyson and Doc Holland was in 1924, but the two announcers from WWJ in Detroit had to buy tickets to attend the game.

On Saturday all 70,000 seats in the stadium were filled for the opening kickoff. Herb Steger's kick sailed long and straight to Grange. He took a few steps to his right, cut back up center, and broke through the first wave of charging Wolverines. The "Redhead" with number 77 across his back was just a blur from then on, racing 95 yards for a touchdown. Grange was just starting. He scored the next three times he handled the ball, on runs of 67, 56, and 44 yards, as Illinois took a 27-0 lead in the first 12 minutes. Grange returned in the second half to score his fifth touchdown on a 15-yard end run.

Those five touchdowns and Grantland Rice insured the "Galloping Ghost" his place in football history. But Michigan,

"Fight like Steger"—That was the motto that emerged from Michigan's 1924 game with Illinois. Despite Red Grange's five touchdowns and the impossibility of victory, Herb Steger, at far right, without a helmet, powers through the Illini line, leading Michigan to a final touchdown.

even in the 39-14 defeat, showed something of which tradition is made. Late in the fourth quarter, with no chance for victory, the thousands of Michigan fans who made the trip to Champaign watched in amazement as Steger, eyes blazing, without a headgear, continued his bull-like charges into the Illinois line. The Michigan captain did not quit until he scored that final touchdown.

Steger had never played on a losing football team. Not during his four years at Oak Park High near Chicago, nor in his first two seasons at Michigan. He did not know how to lose, and at Michigan there came a motto, "Fight Like Steger."

The game offered another twist. Late in the fourth quarter an unknown substitute appeared and threw two passes. A week later Wisconsin played Michigan and discovered his name, and before long the entire nation was reading about this sophomore. Michigan would revisit Mr. Grange and his Illini a year later, and they too would come to know Benny Friedman.

Yost watched the dismantling of his team by Grange from the stands. He was noticeably upset. So, too, was his wife,

George Little coached Michigan's 1924 football team.

Eunice, who was by no means an expert on football. Finally, after Grange had scored his fourth touchdown, she tugged at Yost's sleeve and said, "Fielding, can't you do something about that."

Yost, not on friendly terms with retirement anyway, decided to take personal charge of the preparations for the Wisconsin game. Two changes were made. Steger took over the signal calling from Tod Rockwell, and Friedman started the game at right halfback. The results were dramatic. Friedman threw a long, arching spiral to Steger for Michigan's first touchdown, a play that covered 62 yards. Later he sprinted 26 yards to score as Michigan won, 21-0.

The next week against Minnesota, Friedman rifled a 35-yard scoring pass to Bill Herrnstein as Michigan won, 13-0. Victories over Northwestern and Ohio State followed before Iowa upset the Wolverines in their final game, 9-2. They won six of eight games and finished with a comfortable 4-2 record in the conference. Chicago claimed the championship on three wins and three ties.

The shocking loss at Illinois and the defeat to Iowa, however, remained with Yost. After the season, Little went to Wisconsin as athletic director and football coach, and Yost officially restored his title as Michigan's football coach for 1925. The talent returning was remarkable. Bob Brown, considered by Yost as one of the finest leaders to play for him, was elected captain. Tad Wieman remained on the staff, and Yost added Cappie Cappon, Jack Blott, and Harry Kipke, fresh from Missouri. Joining the varsity was a brilliant group of sophomores. To win, Yost had said, you need "manpower, spirit, and coaching." He was convinced all three were available for 1925.

The Benny-To-Bennie Show

Line coach Tad Wieman walked over to the big, blond sophomore end and said, "Son, you don't even know how to line up properly. Why don't you report over there to Coach Mather."

Bennie Oosterbaan looked at Wieman, unable to speak. Finally he stammered out an "Okay" and trotted to the far south end of Ferry Field where Ed Mather was working with players that Bennie knew were never going to play football at Michigan. They were the lowest scrubs.

Mather, a basketball coach in the winter, listened to Oosterbaan's story, then said, "Why don't you quit football and come out for basketball. We know you can play basketball."

"Coach," Oosterbaan replied, "if you don't mind, I'll wait for the scrimmages and see how I do." There was a confidence in his voice that Mather respected. "All right, we'll wait until Saturday."

That Saturday, Oosterbaan received his chance in a scrimmage, and immediately Yost knew he had a brilliant prospect moving up to the varsity. After just three games Yost would call him the greatest pass receiver he had ever seen.

Michigan's promising 1925 season opened at Ferry Field against Michigan State with Benny Friedman at quarterback and Bennie Oosterbaan on the bench. Friedman quickly put Michigan ahead by running 65 yards from scrimmage. A few moments later he passed 40 yards to Bruce Gregory for another touchdown.

The Wolverines had a 14-0 lead in the third quarter when Yost decided to see what his sophomores could do, and in came Oosterbaan and halfback Louis Gilbert. They did not waste time. A pass was called, and Gilbert took the ball at State's 35. Oosterbaan broke easily from left end and cut across the middle near the 10-yard line. He took Gilbert's perfect pass in full stride, shook off an Aggie tackle, and ran into the end zone.

Later in the period Friedman dropped back to pass from the Aggie 22. Again Oosterbaan's long, smooth strides had him clear near the goal line. The ball came in high, but he stabbed it with one hand and fell into the end zone. The Benny-to-Bennie passing combination had arrived.

Friedman and Oosterbaan were the most devastating aerial act ever to confront Western Conference teams. Friedman, powerfully built and under six feet, outspoken, confident, was a junior from Cleveland. Oosterbaan, 6-feet, 192 pounds, quiet, possessed enormous athletic abilities. They shared a common bond. Both had to wait for acceptance of their talents, Friedman a little longer than Oosterbaan. Friedman, as a sophomore, was relegated to the "scrubs." Discouraged, he

Benny Friedman was twice an all-American, the finest passer of his time, a great kicker and defensive player.

The most feared passing combination of the 1920s was "Benny to Bennie"—Benny Friedman, left, the passer, to Bennie Oosterbaan, the end. They were named all-Americans in 1925 and 1926 and rank as one of the finest passing combinations in college football history.

wanted to quit football, but a talk with assistant coach Wieman convinced him to stay. After showing Friedman how Michigan's lineup changed from game to game, Wieman told him, "When your time is called, you have to be prepared." Head coach George Little, however, did not consider Friedman a quarterback prospect, and in 1924 Benny rode the bench in the first two games. Finally, after the Illinois game, Yost directed that the sophomore be played.

The 39-0 victory over Michigan State that opened the 1925 season for Michigan was just a warmup for the two "Bennies." Friedman shocked Indiana with five touchdown passes, two of them to Oosterbaan, in a 63-0 rout. But it was the following week against Wisconsin that Friedman looked forward to with some emotion.

The Badgers were strong again and coached by George Little. Friedman, who had something to prove, recalled, "It was Yost who prevailed on Little to start me after that Red Grange holocaust. I could not play quarterback for Coach Little, because I did not personify what he wanted. Now, under Yost, I was the quarterback, and this game meant much to me."

Yost had devised a special play to take advantage of the coverage he expected Wisconsin to give Oosterbaan. Friedman liked the play and asked Yost if he could use it on the first play of the game. Yost agreed.

Wisconsin elected to kick off, and Bruce Gregory brought the ball out to the 30. Friedman called the play. Oosterbaan, who was to be used as a decoy, shifted from left to right end. Before the Badger defense could respond, Friedman took the quick snap, faded back, faking a pass to Oosterbaan sprinting downfield. He then turned and threw to Gregory, in the area vacated by the Wisconsin safetyman, who was chasing the decoy. Gregory scored easily.

Wisconsin elected again to kick off. The ball sailed to Friedman on the 20. He broke through the first wave of Badgers, cut to the sidelines, and ran 80 yards to score. Friedman kicked the extra point, and in just 36 seconds Michigan had a 14-0 lead over a stunned Wisconsin team. Later Friedman passed 10 yards to Oosterbaan for the final touchdown in the 21-0 win at Madison.

The victory over Wisconsin was satisfying, but the next game was one Yost had looked forward to for a year. Michigan was to revisit Champaign where Red Grange was in his third year of all-American status. And Yost was ready.

Mr. Brown "Meets"
Mr. Grange

Bob Brown had replayed the game for a year, but a comment by Coach Yost remained with him. They had been in the dining car on their trip home from Champaign where Red Grange had just run wild against the Michigan defense, and Yost asked, "Bob, where were you? Why didn't you meet him at the crossroads?"

The plan had been for Michigan's six-man line to take away all the inside running of Grange and for the linebackers and halfbacks to stop him outside. From his linebacking spot that day, Brown had seen Grange run for four touchdowns in 12 minutes. That had never happened before to a Michigan team.

Yost watched the game in 1924 from the stands, but now, a year later, he was returning as head coach and with a team undefeated and unscored upon. The six-man line of 1924 had been replaced by a seven-man front with a diamond shaped secondary. The target was Grange.

Rain had turned Memorial Stadium into a field of mud, but still 67,000 fans were in the stands for the rematch. Michigan received the kickoff, and the battle was on!

Illinois held and took Michigan's punt at its 39. On the first play Grange slammed hard at tackle. One yard. Two plays later the "Redhead" darted around right end. Fifteen yards. A few plays later Grange fired a pass, but Bo Molenda was there for the interception. Still, Michigan could not move and again turned the ball over to Illinois. Grange tried the end. Two yards.

Bob Brown had his eyes on Red Grange in their 1925 meeting.

He tried Michigan's tackle, but Brown moved in swiftly from his linebacking position to grab him for a yard loss. Then it was Harry Hawkins on Grange for a yard loss. Later, Brown stopped him for no gain. Oosterbaan, protecting the flank, hit Grange. Again no gain.

It was clear that 1924 was not to be repeated. Illinois tried to pass, and Molenda picked off another. Deep into the second period Earl Britton, in kick formation, threw a pass downfield, but Oosterbaan made the interception at midfield. Michigan immediately drove the ball to Illinois' 18-yard line. The Illini line held, and on fourth down Friedman kicked a field goal from the twenty-four.

That was all the scoring. Molenda ran his total of interceptions to five. Each team used only eleven players during the 60 minutes. Grange ran the ball from scrimmage 25 times, gained 65 yards, and lost 9 yards. Yost was elated and in talking

Michigan's Bennie Oosterbaan, a sophomore, and Illinois' Red Grange, right, met before their game in 1925.

about the 3-0 victory he often said, "The 'Old Redhead' didn't gain enough ground to bury him in, y'know." Yost would pause, then add, "Not even if they buried him head down!" It was not a tactful appraisal by Yost, but it did reveal what that game meant to him.

For Bob Brown it was a second chance to "meet him at the crossroads," and the Michigan captain met Grange there, ten times.

Confidence mounted among the Wolverines. With Friedman tossing three touchdowns and dusting off "Old 83" for Bill Herrnstein to score, they rolled over Navy, 54-0.

Then, on November 7, Michigan traveled to Chicago to play underdog Northwestern. It was raining when their train arrived on Friday. Saturday, Soldier Field was covered with mud and several inches of water. A driving rainstorm held the

Benny Friedman, one of Michigan's greatest passers, also played defense extremely well. Here he intercepts a pass against Minnesota.

crowd to 40,000. Never before had a football game been played under such adverse conditions, wrote one Chicago sportswriter.

With running virtually impossible, the game settled quickly into a battle of punts. Yost had outfitted his team with rubber pants, but that did not help. He wanted to call off the game, but nobody listened. With less than five minutes played, Tiny Lewis, Northwestern's great sophomore fullback, exploded a punt inside Michigan's ten. The ball bounced to Friedman, who started to run, was tackled, and fumbled. Northwestern recovered on the four, and when Michigan's line held, Lewis had a chip-shot field goal from the 12, which he made.

Scoring was impossible from then on. In the third period Lewis, back to punt on his 10-yard line, decided to take an intentional safety. It gave Michigan two points, and allowed Northwestern to retain possession of the ball at its 30. The rule was changed the following year.

Michigan rebounded from that 3-2 loss to blank Ohio State, 10-0, with Oosterbaan catching two touchdown passes, giving him eight for the season, and Gilbert running 65 yards for another. Minnesota was buried, 35-0.

Michigan scored 227 points and allowed just 3 during the 1925 season, but those three points were decisive. Still, the Wolverines claimed the Big Ten championship, their tenth. Friedman and Oosterbaan were named all-Americans along with Tom Edwards, Harry Hawkins, and Bob Brown, who, like Goebel, became a regent of the university. There were no players who weighed more than 200 pounds on the team that Yost would call "the finest I ever coached."

"It's Touchdowns That Count"

The Twenties offered America its "Golden Era" of sports. Legends grew around Babe Ruth, Jack Dempsey, Bill Tilden, and Bobby Jones. In college football, out in the midlands, Red Grange, Benny Friedman, and Bennie Oosterbaan were idolized. Grange had left Illinois, and a pro football league would be built around his awesome talents.

Friedman, who threw an unbelievable fourteen touchdown passes in 1925, and Oosterbaan, who caught eight scoring passes, returned for the 1926 season. This pair generated unprecedented interest in football among Michigan students and alumni. Ferry Field, with a seating capacity of 45,000, could not accommodate the growing thousands who wanted to watch the Wolverines. Demands increased for a new football stadium, and in April of 1926 the university regents acted.

The regents passed a resolution approving a new stadium, but with the reservation that "70,000 seats would not be objectionable" and insisting that the construction be handled "as not to overdo it." The size of the new stadium had been a lively subject of debate on campus with faculty men favoring a smaller stadium and Yost seeking one of 80,000 or more.

The regents also established tighter faculty control of athletics by changing the composition of the Board in Control. Effective May 1, 1926, membership included nine faculty men, including the university president and athletic director, three alumni, and two students.

Yost had approval for his giant bowl, but another problem

confronted him for 1926—scheduling. He solved this in a novel way.

Michigan was winning, and if Minnesota was not winning, the powerful Gophers still liked to play bruising football. They blocked hard, and they tackled hard. Games were increasingly difficult to schedule for both teams. Yost and "Doc" Spears of Minnesota were sharing their problems of scheduling when Yost jokingly suggested, "Y'know, maybe we ought to play twice." The Minnesota coach thought about the proposal for a minute, then agreed. They would play October 16 at Ann Arbor, then close the 1926 season at Minneapolis on November 20.

When Yost told his quarterback about the unusual arrangement, Friedman was not enthused. Yost smiled and said, "It's all right, Ben, we'll outsmart them."

"That's okay for you, coach," Friedman replied, "but you don't have to play against those guys."

Yost figured that Michigan could play against any team. Returning with Friedman in the backfield were Louis Gilbert, another in a succession of great Michigan punters, Bo Molenda, and Wally Weber. Sid Dewey, Ray Baer, and Bill Flora, the end opposite Oosterbaan, were solid linemen.

Wally Weber, a tough fullback on Michigan's teams of 1925-26, served the Michigan athletic department for forty years as a coach and physical education instructor.

The Twenties had its sports heroes, and six of them met in New York. The group, from the left, includes Glenn "Pop" Warner

of Stanford, Knute Rockne of Notre Dame, Babe Ruth, Christy Walsh, T. A. D. Jones of Yale, and Fielding H. Yost.

The Wolverines overwhelmed Oklahoma A&M, coached by former Michigan all-American Johnny Maulbetsch, 42-3, in the opener. In that one Molenda scored three touchdowns and Friedman connected with Oosterbaan on a 10-yard scoring pass.

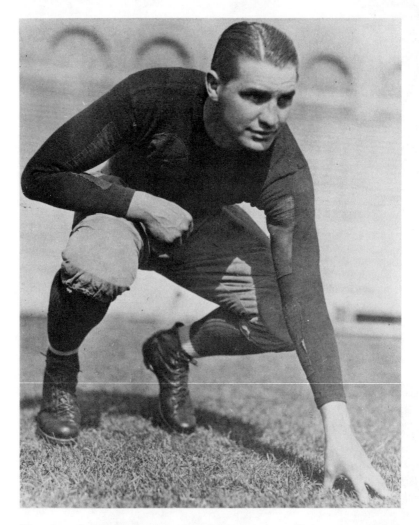

Bennie Oosterbaan was a three-time all-American end, 1925-26-27, the only Wolverine to achieve this honor. He was an all-American basketball player at Michigan and led the Big Ten in hitting in baseball, earning nine letters during three varsity seasons.

Next the "Bennies" hooked up on a 21-yard scoring pass as Michigan State fell, 55-3, and Gilbert's 42-yard touchdown run helped win the "opener" against Minnesota, 20-0. Friedman kicked two more field goals against Illinois in a 13-0 win, but Navy stopped the streak with a 10-0 victory before 80,000 in Baltimore.

The Wolverines were back on the track the following week against Wisconsin. It was the last game Michigan would play at Ferry Field and Friedman's last home appearance. He responded by catching a touchdown pass from Gilbert and lofting a 16-yard pass to Oosterbaan, who outjumped three Badgers in the end zone for the touchdown.

Next came two of the most dramatic victories ever recorded by a Michigan team—the first at Columbus and the second at Minneapolis.

A record crowd of 90,411 watched Ohio State shock Michigan with 10 points in the first 12 minutes. When Michigan took a timeout, Wally Weber turned to Oosterbaan and said, "Ben, at this rate they're going to beat us 40-0." Oosterbaan slapped his hand across Weber's shoulder pad and told his friend, "Dammit, Wally, we haven't had the ball yet."

When Michigan did get the ball moving, Friedman fired a pass to Oosterbaan on Ohio's 21. Then, using a place kick formation, the artful quarterback threw to Oosterbaan, who caught the ball alone in the end zone.

There were 30 seconds left in the half when Michigan again went into a place kick formation. As the Wolverines jumped into position, Oosterbaan waited a moment, then appeared to speak briefly with Friedman. As the husky end took his position on the flank, the once-stung Buckeyes yelled, "Fake, fake, watch Oosterbaan." The snap came back to the 43-yard line, and Friedman, without the pressure of a charging Ohio State line, kicked the ball through the uprights to tie the game at 10-10. When asked later what he said, Oosterbaan smiled and quipped, "I merely asked Louie Gilbert, who was the holder, 'Isn't this a long way to kick a ball, Louie?'"

In the fourth period Sid Dewey recovered a Buckeye fumble on their six, and Michigan had its break. Three running plays failed, then Friedman shot a pass over the middle to Leo Hoffman in the end zone for the touchdown. Friedman kicked

123

Louis Gilbert was an outstanding kicker and passer in 1925-26-27. He threw touchdown passes in the Michigan Stadium dedication game against Ohio State.

the extra point. Ohio State scored again, but the vital extra point attempt by Myers Clark failed.

That victory, however, proved just a warm-up for the Little Brown Jug battle the following Saturday. The Minnesota winter had moved in early, and the field was frozen. When Yost saw hay-covered Memorial Stadium on Friday, he had his team run through a special drill, grabbing the football off the ground. He reasoned that the frozen turf would be topped by a layer of mud by game time, and, "That ball might be hard to handle."

The doubts Friedman had expressed about playing Minnesota twice, however, appeared justified. The Gophers took complete charge of the game and marched 70 yards to score in the second quarter. Their relentless running attack continued. Michigan's defense bent, but did not crack. That was Yost's plan...wait for a break. It came in the fourth period as the Gophers drove to another first down on their 40.

The ball was snapped, but suddenly it was bouncing around in the Gopher backfield. Oosterbaan, charging in from his end position, grabbed the ball and took off, 60 yards to the Minnesota goal. A touchdown! Friedman kicked the extra point. The 7-6 lead stood up.

Yost's insistence on kicking had provided Michigan with victories on successive Saturdays. He also discounted figures showing that Minnesota had 18 first downs to 2 for Michigan and rolled up 307 yards rushing to 48 for the Wolverines. "You see," he explained, "Minnesota would grind out 50 or 60 yards and make four or five first downs. Michigan would kick the ball 50 yards or 60 yards, and that yardage counts just as much as all that hard work Minnesota did. It isn't the first downs that count, y'know, it's the touchdowns."

Who could quarrel with that philosophy? Michigan shared the Big Ten title with Northwestern, the fourth championship in the last five years. Friedman and Oosterbaan repeated as all-Americans, the first time a college passing combination had achieved this honor in successive seasons. And for the first time in the history of official all-American teams—those of Caspar Whitney, Walter Camp, and Grantland Rice—no player from the Big Three of Harvard, Yale, and Princeton was selected. Gross football receipts rose to $488,618, and a new stadium was being constructed.

125

But Friedman was graduating, and Yost had coached his last Michigan team. Except for the 1924 season Michigan had known no other coach since 1901. In twenty-five seasons his teams won 165 games, lost 29, and tied 10. They competed for the Western Conference championship fifteen times under Yost and won or shared ten of those titles. He came into the conference with four straight championship teams, and he left with four straight winners. Now he was turning over Michigan's football team to his top assistant, Elton E. "Tad" Wieman, for the 1927 season. Yost, the coach, would become Yost, the builder.

Michigan Gains A Stadium, Loses An All-American

Fielding Yost made it official in September: he would not coach Michigan's 1927 football team. Yost strongly hinted, however, that there was a possibility of returning to coach later. Tad Wieman, a Phi Beta Kappa and former Michigan football captain, took charge of the Wolverines.

Yost had plunged into his duties as director with the same verve that gave him the "Hurry Up" label. His vision? Building the finest athletic complex in the nation, and the showcase project was completed in 1927—Michigan Stadium. It was to stand as a glowing testimonial to Yost's talents as a builder, politician, and businessman. He secured the property, sold bonds to finance the giant bowl, and battled the idea of a super stadium over faculty objections. Debate raged over the size, but an acceptable figure of 70,000 or so was reached.

Michigan sold 3,000 bonds at $500 to raise funds for expansion of "athletic and physical education" programs. Those who bought stadium bonds were entitled to purchase two reserved tickets for the next ten years. The actual cost of the stadium was slightly more than $950,000.

The new stadium was listed originally as seating 72,000, but, when the demand for tickets in 1927 mounted, Yost secured permission from President Clarence Little and the faculty deans to add 10,000 "temporary" wooden seats around the concrete rim. His bowl shape design easily accommodated this type of expansion. In 1949 the "temporary" wooden stands were replaced by steel stands, increasing the stadium

Tad Wieman replaced Yost as football coach in 1927 and compiled a two-year record of 9-6-1.

capacity to 97,239. This figure was raised to 101,001 in 1956, and with more modernization in 1973 the capacity stood at an imposing 101,701.

Yost was called a visionary when he campaigned for the super stadium. His critics might have been more vocal had they investigated the actual stadium construction plans of Yost. When the steel stands were added in 1949, engineers reported that the footings were so deep they could easily support a second deck around the stadium.

Formal dedication of the largest college-owned football stadium in the nation was scheduled for October 22 against Ohio State. The first game, however, on a dark, rainy Saturday, brought in Yost's old school, Ohio Wesleyan. Yost not only had coached the Ohio team to a 0-0 tie with Michigan in 1897 but played in the game. Ohio Wesleyan could have used the extra help thirty years later as Louie Gilbert staged one of the greatest offensive shows in Michigan history before a crowd of more than 50,000.

The 159-pound halfback from Kalamazoo passed 28 yards to LaVerne "Kip" Taylor to officially record the first touchdown in the stadium. Later, Gilbert dazzled the Ohioans on a 25-yard punt return to score, passed 24 yards to Leo Hoffman and 47 yards to Ben Oosterbaan for two more touchdowns, and capped off his show with a 90-yard scoring run.

Gilbert scored a touchdown to trigger Michigan's 21-0 win over Michigan State, and at Madison, Wisconsin, the following Saturday "Old 83" set up a touchdown in a 14-0 win. This gave Michigan three straight victories entering the dedication game with the Buckeyes.

June temperatures and a sky barren of clouds prevailed for a record 84,401 fans. Governors of Michigan and Ohio walked across the field with Yost, who drew a stirring ovation. The "Old Man" was still very much in charge.

Ohio State had seen its dedication plans ruined by Yost's famed reverse play, and now, five years later, the Wolverines had another trick or two in their bag. They pulled it out in the second quarter with the ball near the sidelines on Ohio's 45. Oosterbaan shifted into the backfield from his end position. Bill Flora remained on the opposite sideline following a wide sweep. Oosterbaan quickly took the ball, faked a long pass to Flora, and threw to Gilbert coming out of the backfield, and he scored with ridiculous ease. Michigan came back in the third period, again shocking the Buckeyes on a 39-yard Oosterbaan to Gilbert

From 400 To 101,701 Seats

For the first quarter century Michigan played football at Regents Field (top photo). The original stands seating 400 were expanded gradually through the years but still could not accommodate the demand by students and alumni. Ferry Field was opened in 1906 (photo, lower left), and its capacity was finally increased to seat 45,000 with the completion of concrete stands at the south in 1914. Giant Michigan Stadium (lower

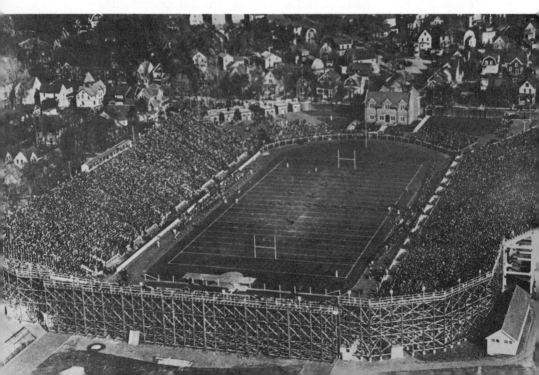

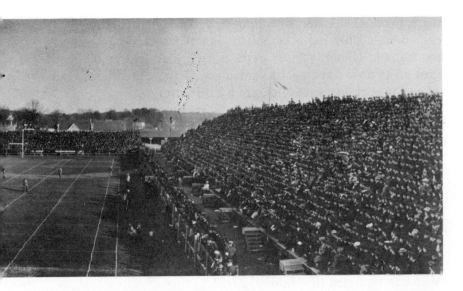

right) was completed in 1927, and with temporary wooden stands around the top of the bowl, crowds of 83,000 were recorded in the late 1920s. The stadium capacity was increased to more than 97,000 in 1949 and then to 101,001 in 1956. The final count of 101,701 was achieved in 1973 when box seats were removed and regular bleacher seats installed. Michigan Stadium is the largest college owned football structure in the nation.

touchdown pass. Later, operating more like a halfback than an end, Bennie shoveled a lateral to Gilbert who scored his third touchdown. Gilbert's three extra points, kicked over the new goal posts now standing 10 yards deep in the end zone instead of on the goal line, gave Michigan a 21-0 victory.

The following Saturday Illinois, cashing in on a blocked punt and fumble, defeated the Wolverines, 14-0, as Gilbert missed the game with an elbow infection. The setback was temporary. Oosterbaan pitched a lateral to Gilbert from five yards out for one score and then hauled in a 40-yard pass from Gilbert for another in a 14-0 win over Chicago. A shivering crowd of 87,000 in Michigan Stadium was treated to an Oosterbaan-Gilbert show against Navy. Bennie's lateral pass started the little halfback on a 23-yard touchdown run, and later Oosterbaan moved into the backfield to score on a short run as Michigan trampled the Middies, 27-12.

Oosterbaan closed out an incredible football career by grabbing a 23-yard touchdown pass from Bill Puckelwartz, but Minnesota and its all-American fullback, Herb Joesting, stormed back to win, 13-7, and reclaim the "Little Brown Jug" for the first time since 1919. A 3-2 conference record put Wieman's team in third place behind undefeated Illinois and Minnesota.

Oosterbaan, Michigan's captain and most valuable player, was named all-American for the third successive year, a feat not accomplished before or since by a Michigan player. He completed the school year by earning all-American honors in basketball and leading the Big Ten in scoring, then captured the conference batting championship. During his career he led the conference in touchdowns, baskets, and hits, the only athlete ever to accomplish this. Oosterbaan had nine letters and offers from professional football and baseball teams. He rejected all of them to remain at Michigan as an assistant football coach where his accomplishments would be equally as impressive. Bennie Oosterbaan would make the Michigan tradition very personal for hundreds of athletes.

The "Golden Years" Return

Ticket Manager Harry Tillotson was a busy man after the 1927 season. Michigan's new stadium had not proven big enough for the games against Ohio State, Navy, and Minnesota, and $35,000 in ticket refunds had to be processed. Tad Wieman's first season as coach produced a solid 6-2 record, and his job appeared secure, especially with a surprise announcement at Michigan State. The Spartans hired Harry Kipke to coach football.

Once regarded as the "heir apparent" to Yost, the former Michigan all-American settled in East Lansing with a three-year contract. But reports of a rift developing between Yost and Wieman persisted. The rumors and speculations, mainly over coaching methods, were vigorously denied by them.

Little Ohio Wesleyan, however, stoked the fires anew by handing Michigan its first opening-game loss since 1888, 17-7. The 1928 season never got much better. Indiana, Ohio State, and Wisconsin ran the Wolverines string of defeats to four before Joe Gembis' 35-yard field goal shot down Illinois. It was the third time in seven years the Illini had lost a 3-0 game to Michigan. A satisfying 6-6 tie with Navy and another 3-0 victory, this one over Kipke's Spartans, took some of the pressure off Wieman. When little Alvin Dahlem sprinted 19 yards for a touchdown that tripped favored Iowa, 10-7, the improvement was obvious.

But 1928 had been a strange season. A 3-4-1 record included a victory over conference champion Illinois. The best

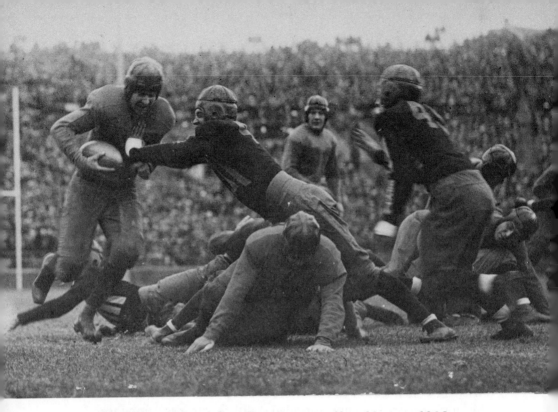

Michigan halfback Joe Gembis runs off tackle in a 1928 game.

Michigan player was Otto Pommerening, a quick tackle from Ann Arbor who played every minute of every game and was picked on Grantland Rice's all-America squad. He led a defense that allowed just 62 points, but the Wolverine offense scored just four touchdowns all season.

The coaching situation at Michigan had been confusing all season. Yost waited until October 4, 1928, the day before the opener, to announce *officially* that Wieman would remain as coach. Still, "Hurry Up" did not divorce himself entirely from the team. The situation dragged on through the winter and into the spring; then Yost, on May 16, 1929, told Wieman his services as head football coach "would be terminated at the end of the summer session."

Wieman replied, "It is not my desire or intention to voluntarily sever my connection with...Michigan." Later, he was assigned to a counseling position. A year later Fritz Crisler, building a football power at Minnesota, hired Wieman as his chief assistant.

Yost quickly announced that Kipke would coach the Wolverines in 1929. Extremely popular at Michigan, Kipke had secured a release from Michigan State of a contract that had two years remaining. Cappie Cappon replaced Wieman as assistant athletic director and assistant football coach.

While Michigan was hiring its fifth football coach of the century, the Western Conference suspended Iowa for one year, effective January 1, 1930. Reports indicated that the violations centered around subsidizing athletes, a charge Iowa denied.

Kipke immediately put Michigan on the road to recovery. The Wolverines won five games, lost three, and played Iowa to a scoreless tie. The 14-12 win over Harvard was their first in history over the Crimson, while the Little Brown Jug returned to Ann Arbor on a 7-6 decision over Bronko Nagurski and

Harry Kipke began his coaching career at Michigan in 1929 and during the first five years his teams lost only four games.

Minnesota. Sol Hudson ran 80 yards to score in a rewarding 17-0 victory for Kipke over Michigan State and its new coach, Sleepy Jim Crowley, the former Notre Damer of "Four Horseman" fame.

If 1929 proved to be a step in the right direction, the following season had the Wolverines vaulting to prominence. Kipke was grooming a rollicking, confident band of athletes who wanted to play football...for 60 minutes. Maynard "Doc" Morrison and Bill Hewitt were returning, and a new passing combination was joining the varsity—Harry Newman and Ivy Williamson. And waiting in the wings as freshmen were Ted Petoskey, Francis "Whitey" Wistert, Chuck Bernard, Stan Fay, and Herman Everhardus. Five of these players were destined for all-American honors as Michigan "Punted, Passed, and Prayed" their way through four seasons of championships. They lost only once during that period and brought Michigan two national championships. The "Golden Years of Football" were never brighter at Michigan.

Rose Bowl? No, Thanks

Several sportswriters were kidding Harry Kipke about his legendary kicking exploits, and the Michigan coach was noticeably irritated. Suddenly he walked over to the sideline of the practice field and dropped a handkerchief. He continued on upfield until he was nearly 40 yards away. He turned, took three steps, and drove his foot into the ball. The ball arched high, seemed to hesitate at its highest point, then dropped out of bounds at the sidelines, just a foot beyond the handkerchief. Kipke walked slowly back to the writers and said, "Gentlemen, you have seen my last punt. There's work to do."

The work consisted of long hours of practice. Defense, passing, and kicking were Kipke's football staples, and he wanted his teams to excel at all three. It was evident that the passing would be no problem. Kipke had a special drill for his passers. There was a series of four holes in a canvas, and each quarterback, upon signal, had to fire passes in succession through the holes. In 1929 a skinny freshman from Detroit Northern was hitting the holes eight out of every ten times he threw. Harry Newman would do just nicely as Kipke's quarterback, though he would wait three games for his chance just as Benny Friedman had done.

Michigan opened the 1930 season with victories over Denison and Michigan State Normal, then was surprised by Michigan State in a scoreless tie. The Spartans had not defeated Michigan since 1915, scoring only three points on the Wolverines over that period. Michigan met a favored Purdue team the

137

next week, and Newman was still on the bench. The Boilermakers took a quick 13-0 lead before passes were needed. Newman was called. He proceeded to toss a 40-yard touchdown strike to Norm Daniels, set up another score with a pass, and kicked both extra points as Michigan won, 14-13.

Newman was just starting. His two touchdown passes and extra point accounted for a 13-0 win over Ohio State. He kicked a field goal as Illinois fell, 15-7. A Newman-to-Hudson touchdown pass dumped Harvard, 6-3. Shutout victories over Fritz Crisler's Minnesota team and Chicago wrapped up an undefeated season and gave Michigan a share of the conference championship with Northwestern.

Michigan had allowed just two touchdowns and two field goals the entire season. During the next three seasons the defense grew stronger, and pride became ingrained in the Wolverines. Ted Petoskey, twice an all-American end, spoke of that pride:

"We were never afraid to give the other team the ball. We always figured when we wanted the ball, we could take it from them. We took pride in holding our opponents for negative yardage. We never considered missing practice. It just never crossed our minds. We had a job to do that we loved, and we loved to do our job."

It was a team of twenty-five men. A bond existed. In the postseason game of 1931, Michigan, leading 13-0 over Wisconsin, had the ball on the Badger 30. A time out was taken, and Roy Hudson, the captain, said, "Hey, fellows, you know I've played three years and never drop-kicked a point. How about it?" Michigan went into a kick formation, and Hudson drove the ball squarely through the uprights.

Against Illinois, Kipke sent in a rangy, sophomore tackle. Francis Wistert would become an all-American, but in his first Big Ten game he was frightened. Wistert recalled that moment vividly. "Stan Hozer, our senior right guard, who was built like a tank, recognized my symptoms and gave me the confidence and reassurance I needed. 'Look, kid,' he ordered, 'all you have to do is lean against me on every play and keep that Illinois guard from falling off my shoulder when I block him.'"

Wistert was one of six children. His father, a Chicago policeman, was killed by a holdup man when Wistert was just

Ted Petoskey, Michigan's all-American end in 1932-33.

Francis Wistert, the first of three brothers to become all-Americans at Michigan in 1933.

15. He never played high school football, but neither did his brothers, Albert and Alvin. They came to Michigan and became all-American tackles. They all wore number eleven, a jersey that, fittingly, was retired when the last of the brothers, Alvin, was selected as an all-American in 1949—at the age of 33.

The season opener of 1931 featured a Michigan Stadium doubleheader against Central State Teachers and Michigan State Normal (Eastern Michigan University). Neither team scored a point as Kipke's reserves stopped CST and the varsity beat the Ypsilanti school.

Louis Westover started at quarterback against Chicago, but Newman had to set up both touchdowns with passes in a 13-7 win. The following Saturday nothing went right for Michigan, and a fired-up Ohio State team of considerable talent won, 20-7. Those were the last points any team would score on Michigan the rest of the season. The Buckeyes, in fact, waited until 1934 to score another point on Kipke's teams.

Bill Hewitt moved from end to fullback, gained 104 yards, and Michigan's defense throttled Illinois with a minus two yards in total offense en route to a 35-0 victory. Sophomore Stan Fay sprinted 40 yards on a fake field goal and rushed for 100 yards as Princeton fell, 21-0. After a 22-0 win over Indiana, the Wolverines were ambushed in the mud by Michigan State as 32 punts produced a scoreless tie. Hewitt's 57-yard run gave Michigan a happy homecoming against Minnesota, 7-0, and a 7-1-1 record that was impressive enough to receive an invitation to the Rose Bowl. It was declined in keeping with Big Ten regulations on postseason games.

The Depression, however, was tearing at the nation, and the Big Ten approved five postseason games for charity. Northwestern, with five straight victories, was upset by Purdue, while Michigan, with a 4-1 mark, toppled Wisconsin rather easily, 16-0. A three-way tie for the championship was created among Michigan, Northwestern, and Purdue.

Doc Morrison, the center and linebacker, was named to the all-America team. Hewitt might have made it but had to play two positions on offense, end and fullback.

For Newman his junior season of 1931 was not a vintage year. He had momentary flashes of his former brilliance, but an ankle injury kept him on the bench most of the season. After the Wisconsin game he very nearly packed his bags and went home. He decided, however, to stay and a year later was named the finest football player in America.

A Touch Of Class

Harry Newman had come back, but one last hurdle remained. It stood challengingly, 25 yards away at the base of the Minnesota end zone. The football season for Michigan came down to a field goal. Three points! So much had been accomplished, yet a final touch was needed to complete the work.

Michigan's seven straight victories in 1932 had made not only the Big Ten title but a national championship possible. Only Minnesota stood in the way, and the Gophers appeared ready to ruin it all. No Kipke team in the previous three seasons had scored more than a touchdown on the Gophers. A field goal might do it this time.

Chuck Bernard had provided Michigan with the break it needed, recovering Jack Manders' fumble on the Gophers 24. Newman quickly moved the Wolverines inside the ten with short passes to Stan Fay and Ivy Williamson, but Minnesota stiffened. Thirty seconds were left in the first half, and Michigan called time. Newman would try the field goal from the 14. Fay would hold. The snap was perfect, Michigan's line held, and Newman kicked, the ball sailing straight and true for the three points.

Sub-zero weather clung to Memorial Stadium. The brass instruments in the band froze and were useless. There was not a hint of a score the rest of the way as both teams played overpowering defense. In the locker room after the game, Michigan celebrated the 3-0 victory, and the head cheerleader was Fielding Yost. With his battered hat, a severely chewed

Harry Newman was an all-American quarterback for Michigan in 1932 and later a professional star with the New York Giants.

cigar in his mouth, and wearing a heavy overcoat, he charged into the shower room, throwing his arms around as many players as he could reach.

Michigan's first undefeated, untied season since 1923 had opened easily with a 26-0 victory over Michigan State. Northwestern became the first of only two teams to reach the Wolverine end zone, but Fay scored on two short runs and Newman kicked a 24-yard field goal to turn back the Wildcats, 15-6. Then Newman fired a short, fourth-down pass to sophomore John Regeczi and a 22-yarder to Williamson for two touchdowns as Michigan stopped Ohio State, 14-0.

Injuries began to mount among the Wolverines, but they could not be slowed. With Fay out and Jack Heston, the son of Willie Heston, on the sidelines, Ted Petoskey moved to fullback. On his first running play he exploded for 57 yards to score against Illinois, and Newman threw two touchdowns to Williamson, for 35 and 27 yards, as the Wolverines rolled, 32-0.

Michigan fans received a preview of what future Wolverine teams would be doing under Fritz Crisler when Crisler, who had left Minnesota after just two seasons, brought in his Princeton team. Using the single wing with fullback spinners and short passes, the Tigers surprised everyone by taking a 7-0 lead. But Regeczi's long punt was fumbled and kicked into the end zone, and when Jack Bales of Princeton attempted to run it out, sophomore Willis Ward, a track sprinter, nailed him with a diving tackle for two points. Later Newman threw 14 yards to Ward for a touchdown, and Bernard recovered a blocked punt to score. Michigan won, but Crisler's Ivy Leaguers shattered some overconfidence among the Wolverines, who still found the "Punt-Pass-Prayer" technique to be effective.

Newman slipped over the goal on a quarterback sneak in a 7-0 win over Indiana, then he returned a punt 78 yards and ran 27 yards from scrimmage to account for all the points in a 12-0 victory over Chicago and Amos Alonzo Stagg, in his final season of coaching the Maroons at the age of 70.

Eight straight victories, six of them shutouts, brought Michigan the National Championship. For Harry Newman it also meant a personal triumph, a vindication of his ability after living with disappointment and the frustration of sitting on the bench much of his junior year. That justification came dramatically in the Douglas Fairbanks Trophy as the most valuable player in intercollegiate football, just a few years before the mold of John Heisman came to symbolize players

A family tradition of the Hestons: Willie Heston talks with his two sons, Jack, left, and Willie, Jr., right. Jack lettered in 1929 and 1930, while his brother earned letters in 1931-32-33. Their father was an all-American in 1903 and 1904.

like Harry Newman. The Big Ten selected him as its most valuable player, and the determined little all-American went on to become the premier passer in the National Football League, leading the New York Giants to a championship in 1934.

Bernard replaced Doc Morrison as center on the all-America team. His selection again in 1933 gave Michigan three straight seasons of filling this mythical position. Petoskey, who played end and fullback, was named all-American end. He would repeat in 1933.

Williamson, called by Kipke, "The smartest player I've coached or ever hope to coach," and destined for fame as Wisconsin's football coach, had played his final season. So, too, had Newman, but Michigan's abundant football success continued in 1933. The defense under Kipke seemed to grow stronger, more effective each season. Herm Everhardus became the bread-and-butter runner along with Captain Stan Fay, and they provided much of the offense. Michigan won seven games in 1933, but again Minnesota's defense proved troublesome. It was a classic battle of defenses with neither team gaining a yard with the forward pass. They combined to punt the ball for 1,252 yards in the 0-0 tie.

Michigan State, Illinois, and Iowa each scored six points on Michigan; that was it. Illinois gained just 66 yards rushing, as Michigan pulled out a 7-6 decision. The key game on Michigan's schedule, other than the traditional "Jug" game with Minnesota, involved Ohio State.

It was the third game of the season, and a capacity crowd in Michigan Stadium came to watch the two undefeated teams. Ohio State with Sid Gilman, Joe Gailus, and Regis Monahan was a slight favorite. The Detroit papers carried such glowing accounts of the Bucks, many Michigan players, including Whitey Wistert, found it hard to believe Ohio State would not win. He remembers the atmosphere in the Michigan locker room just before the game:

"Our 1933 team was such that coaches seldom found it necessary to indulge in pep talks. For this one, however, they too must have felt the impact of the sportswriters' stories, and we were set up for a pep talk. About five minutes before the kickoff all the coaches except Cappie Cappon left the dressing room. He called us down to the end of the dressing room

Ivy Williamson, called by Harry Kipke the smartest player I have ever coached or hope to coach, was an outstanding end for Michigan and later a successful coach and athletic director at Wisconsin.

nearest the door. We sat on benches with our helmets on the floor at our feet. In three short minutes he managed to raise us to an emotional pitch that was unbelievable. I glanced at Chuck Bernard next to me. His tears were falling into his helmet. I dared not look around any farther. I was sure the rest were as dewy-eyed as I. When Cappie finished and shouted, 'Let's go,' we almost tore off the dressing room door. The impact of bodies on the opening kickoff was unbelievable."

Michigan handed Ohio State its only loss of the season that Saturday, 14-0. The Buckeyes gained just 24 yards in 34 rushing attempts.

Michigan extended its unbeaten string of games to 22 with a final, 13-0, decision over Wisconsin as Everhardus kicked a field goal for his sixty-fourth point to lead the conference. The victory gave Michigan its fourth straight Big Ten championship and second straight National Championship. Kipke's record over the four years was a remarkable 31-1-3. Bernard and Petoskey, who repeated as all-Americans, were joined by Wistert. That summer Wistert, selected as the Big Ten's most valuable baseball player, signed a professional contract with Cincinnati. He was called up late in the summer and got his only major league start, a 1-0 loss to the Chicago Cubs. That run came on a home run by a 17-year old rookie, also playing in his first major league game, Phil Cavaretta.

With the closing of the 1933 season, all-Americans, like football victories, would become increasingly scarce at Michigan.

Willis Ward, a track sprinter, played end on Michigan's teams of the mid-1930s and later became a probate judge for Wayne County, Michigan.

No Cheers From The Alumni

Harry Kipke knew that Michigan football strength had declined. He predicted that his Wolverines probably would lose three games in 1934.

Michigan State, figuring it had one coming, defeated Michigan for the first time in 19 years, 16-0. Chicago and Jay Berwanger followed this up with its first victory over the Wolverines since 1919, 27-0. Ferris Jennings, a 138-pound sophomore quarterback, ran 66 yards with a punt that beat Georgia Tech, 9-2. It was all downhill from there. Illinois finally was on the winning end of a place kick against Michigan, 7-6.

Next came Minnesota, and the scouting reports left little doubt the Gophers would be the finest team Michigan would meet all season. They were a running team, a fact that particularly concerned Jerry Ford.

Six-foot-two and a deceptive 198 pounds, Ford was Michigan's linebacker and center. His prime assignment on defense was to contain Minnesota's all-American, Pug Lund, and the new sophomore sensation at fullback, Stan Kostka. The Gophers were unbeaten and driving for the Big Ten championship. They had not defeated a Michigan team at home in 41 years, and Minneapolis was alive with the battle-cry, "Mangle Michigan." A record crowd of 60,000 responded at Memorial Stadium to watch the Gophers avenge those many seasons of defeat.

Michigan's defense, however, seemed to regain its cracking effectiveness of former years. With Ford and his linebacking

150

Jerry Ford was Michigan's most valuable player in 1934. He coached at Yale and after World War II entered politics, rising to the position of President of the United States.

mate, Cedric Sweet, playing inspired football, Michigan continually stopped the powerful Gophers' running attack. Surprisingly the half ended scoreless.

"I knew how good they were," recalled Bennie Oosterbaan, Michigan's assistant coach who had scouted the Gophers. "They were heavy favorites, something like four or five touchdowns. And when I walked into the dressing room at half time, I had tears in my eyes I was so proud of them. Ford and Sweet played their hearts out. They were everywhere on defense."

Minnesota came out in the second half and wore down the Wolverines with raw power, winning 34-0. The Gophers went on to claim the Big Ten championship with Ohio State and were named National Champions.

That cold November afternoon in Memorial Stadium, however, remained very special for Ford, even after he became President of the United States. "During 25 years in the rough-and-tumble world of politics, I often thought of the experiences before, during, and after that game in 1934. Remembering them has helped me many times to face a tough situation, take action, and make every effort possible despite adverse odds. I remember how Michigan students and people in Ann Arbor met us at the train station that Sunday. There was a rousing parade, and this was a meaningful tribute to the fight the Wolverines had put up against Minnesota."

His teammates also paid Ford a meaningful tribute that season when Michigan won just one game. Ford was voted the most valuable player by his teammates. "They felt Jerry was one guy who would stay and fight in a losing cause," offered one assistant coach.

That was Kipke's first losing season, and the Michigan coach announced that the Wolverines would "be trying for the title" next season. They looked anything but title contenders in the 1935 opener as Michigan State rolled up 245 yards and won 25-6. Michigan rebounded to defeat Indiana, 7-0, but Yost remarked, "I never saw such a game. So many mixed up plays, such a variety."

Bill Renner, who first entered Michigan in 1930, was finally healthy against Wisconsin, and the "senior" quarterback tossed three touchdown passes in a 20-12 victory. Columbia and

Penn were handled, but a late season collapse set in. Illinois won on a field goal, the seventh time in fifteen years that this bitter rivalry was decided by a kick. Minnesota promptly stormed to a 40-0 triumph, and despite a pep rally of 5,000 students on Friday, Michigan was routed by Ohio State on Saturday, 38-0.

Renner was named Michigan's most valuable player, then followed Ivy Williamson and Jerry Ford to Yale as an assistant football coach.

These were the "Get Michigan Years," and 1936 was the ideal season for it. Michigan State captured its third win in a row over "M" and Indiana won for the second time ever. Minnesota held the Wolverines to a net 23 yards rushing and won, 26-0. The Wolverines beat Columbia, but that was it—one win and seven defeats. After Michigan's loss to Penn, the *Michigan Daily* ran a story pointing out how well the band did. It was not a good year for Michigan football, and the *Daily* started a campaign to legalize the training table (nightly meals at the Union finally came back in 1939). Two football players did leave campus, claiming they did not get enough to eat.

A change was needed, and, if a training table could not be obtained, then maybe more coaching could help. Hunk Anderson was brought in to coach the line, and several promising freshmen enrolled at Michigan. Despite the lean years WWJ radio in Detroit signed to broadcast the Michigan games for the fourteenth straight season with Ty Tyson and Doc Holland. Yost had made Tyson buy a ticket to broadcast his first game, the first play-by-play account of a college football game, October 25, 1924. Now they received press passes.

Still, 1937 was not a year for alumni to cheer. Michigan State, Minnesota, and Ohio State continued to whip the Wolverines, and without Stark Ritchie and Freddie Trosko the season might have been a complete disaster. Trosko beat Iowa with a place kick, 7-6, and the next week threw a 39-yard touchdown pass and kicked the point that defeated Illinois, 7-6. Ritchie scored twice as Michigan rallied to beat Chicago and fired the touchdown pass that toppled Penn.

The even split in eight games gave Kipke ten wins and twenty-two losses for the last four seasons. It was evident that a coaching change would be made and, accordingly, Kipke's contract was not renewed by the Board in Control. His replacement for the 1938 season was Herbert Orin "Fritz" Crisler of Princeton.

The late 1930s were lean years for Michigan, but Stark Ritchie (33) was one of the Wolverines' stars. He is on his way to a forty-yard touchdown run against Chicago in 1937.

A Touch Of The Ivy League

There is a special rivalry among Ivy Leaguers. Flowing with tradition and accomplishment, it is shared internally; and so it was on the Friday evening when representatives of Harvard and Princeton, prestigious men of varied interests, gathered in a festive mood to talk football. Fritz Crisler spoke first about his Princeton team, and in closing he offered: "May the best team win." A Harvard dean could not let that pass, reminding the *graduate of Chicago,* "You mean the better team, don't you, Coach Crisler?"

"No," Fritz said softly. "I plan on playing all three of my teams tomorrow against Harvard...and may the best team win."

Fritz Crisler always commanded a situation. Articulate, able to see beyond athletics itself, he knew the rules and he knew the stakes. He wrote many of the rules by which football is played. When Michigan began its search for a new football coach, Crisler could not be overlooked. President Alexander Ruthven immediately dispatched Michigan's faculty representative from the Law School, and chairman of the athletic board, Ralph Aigler, to determine if the Princeton coach would be interested in Michigan.

They met in New York City in Room 1107 of the Statler. After a warm and frank discussion about Michigan, Crisler thanked Aigler, but said, "I have no desire to move from Princeton." Aigler returned to Ann Arbor and a week later called Crisler for another meeting, this time in Room 711 of the Statler. "I remember the room because I'm very superstitious,"

Fritz Crisler began his coaching career at Michigan in 1938.

Crisler recalled. "Ralph told me there had been new developments, and now the opening was not only for a football coach but for an assistant athletic director who would become athletic director upon the retirement in three years of Mr. Yost. Again, I declined, but Ralph said, 'Fritz, would you outline what you feel the position for a football coach and athletic director should be in a university?' I agreed and a few days later sent him the outline."

Crisler then received a telephone call from Ruthven who asked him to come to Ann Arbor. A meeting followed at the home of Yost who had proposed that Tom Hamilton of Navy be hired to coach Michigan football. Later Crisler joined Ruthven at the president's home. "We accept the provisions of your outline and would like you to become our coach," Ruthven said. "I'm not familiar with athletics and would only ask that you keep me informed on what your aims and objectives may be so I can support you."

Crisler told Ruthven he would call him when he returned to Princeton, and a day later he called and accepted the position. He would be the football coach, assistant athletic director, and when Yost retired, he would become athletic director and chairman of the Board in Control of Athletics. Michigan thus became and remains the only major university in the nation where the athletic director serves as chairman of the board. He had full faculty status as head of the physical education and intercollegiate athletic departments and, like department deans, enjoyed tenure.

Crisler's football credentials were impeccable. He played and coached for Stagg at Chicago. He was Minnesota's football coach and athletic director for two years before accepting the Princeton football position in 1932. Under Crisler, Princeton football showed a 35-9-5 record in six seasons. His 1933 and 1935 teams were undefeated.

Crisler's career at Michigan lasted thirty years and, in a sense, moved in the same productive direction as Yost's. Both made dramatic changes in Michigan's football program and compiled almost identical winning percentages—Yost winning 85 percent of his games and Crisler 82 percent. Under Yost, Michigan built a field house, and when Cazzie Russell brought unprecedented popularity to basketball to Michigan, Crisler built a new All-Events arena. The mammoth intramural building went up under Yost's direction, while Crisler gave the women a $1 million swimming pool. Yost built a championship golf course and Crisler added a club house. Yost's football stadium

Fielding H. Yost retired in 1941 after serving 20 years as athletic director.

of 1927 with 85,000 seats was modernized in 1956 for more than 100,000 spectators. Both Yost and Crisler retired after winning championships.

Yost, however, had always wanted to coach. Crisler became a coach by accident.

Crisler came from the rich Illinois farmlands surrounding Earlville. Weighing not much over 100 pounds, he never played athletics at Earlville or at nearby Mendota. He earned an academic scholarship to the University of Chicago, and it was only a chance meeting with Stagg that sent him into athletics.

"One day in 1917," recalled Crisler, "I thought I'd take a look at that football stuff I'd been hearing about. The freshman and varsity were scrimmaging, and on a wide end sweep Stagg tried to get out of the way and backed into me. We both fell down.

"Mr. Stagg said rather angrily, 'If you're going to play football, why don't you put on a suit?' Maybe I was still dazed from my contact with the great man, but, anyway, wanting to see the inside of the gym I went in and drew a uniform."

Crisler was not an immediate success and, after forty minutes of scrimmage, he decided the game was not for him. A week later Stagg was riding his bicycle across campus when he stopped in front of a rather startled Crisler and snapped, "What happened? Weren't you out for football?"

"Yes, sir, I quit," replied Crisler.

"I'd never have picked you for a quitter." Then the famous coach pedalled away.

"That made me so mad I went right back and demanded my suit again," said Crisler. He went on to earn nine letters in football, basketball, and baseball. During one practice session Crisler had disrupted three successive plays with mistakes, and Stagg finally halted practice, and in his dry voice said: "Crisler, you are 'Fritz' from now on (after the master violinist), but I want you to know it's from contrast of any ability, not from any similarity."

Crisler graduated in 1922 with 146 honor points, two more than required for Phi Beta Kappa, but his mandatory chapel attendance had been lax, and he lost four points and thus was denied his key. With just a year remaining for his medical degree, financial problems arose, and Crisler had to accept an assistant coaching position under Stagg. "He paid me too much, but I thought it would be temporary until I had enough money to finish my medical studies," Crisler said.

The temporary job in athletics became permanent in 1924 when Chicago named Crisler baseball coach and assistant athletic director. Offers began to arrive from other schools, including Minnesota. Crisler asked Stagg for his advice. "Fritz, you're not ready to fly yet," offered Stagg.

In 1930 Minnesota repeated the offer to coach football and also to become athletic director. Crisler accepted this time and left with Stagg's advice, "Fritz, you are now ready to fly, but no matter what happens, don't worry. Never let the job get bigger than you are."

Crisler's appointment at Michigan was announced February 9, 1938. He was given a complete "free hand" with football and immediately hired as assistants Earl Martineau of Minnesota, Campbell Dickson from Chicago, and Clarence "Biggie" Munn, who had played for Crisler at Minnesota. Tad Wieman, who coached with Crisler at Minnesota and Princeton, was named head coach of the Tigers and recruited Cappie Cappon from Kipke's old staff. Bennie Oosterbaan remained on the Michigan football staff but also was named head basketball coach. Crisler named the loquacious Wally Weber to direct the freshman football program. A new era of Michigan football was beginning.

A Near Miss

Harry Kipke's legacy to Michigan was tripartite: a brilliant player, a championship coach, and an electric personality that drew many athletes to Michigan. It was his latter talent which offered hope for Michigan football success in 1938.

First indications that Michigan had a special group of future players appeared during the 1937 season when the varsity was experiencing unusual difficulties with the freshman team. In one long scrimmage these yearlings led 21-0. The workout was extended into the darkness of Ferry Field, but the score failed to change.

A year later Paul Kromer, a 160-pound halfback from Lorain, Ohio, and Kiski Prep; Howard "Jeep" Mehaffey, also from Kiski Prep; guard Ralph Fritz; Forest Evashevski from Detroit Northwestern; Tom Harmon and his buddy from Gary, Indiana, Ed Christy; and Ed Frutig from River Rouge, all moved up to the varsity.

That freshman group also contained an unusual quarterback whose kicking once defeated Michigan. Dave Strong two years previously had kicked the field goal in Illinois' 9-6 victory over Michigan. He had entered the game only when Illinois' regular quarterback was injured, and when it came time for the field goal Strong decided to try it himself. It was the first time he had kicked a ball for Coach Zuppke. Strong played in five straight games for Illinois but was not happy. His father had attended Michigan, and that is where he always had wanted to go. Strong transferred to Michigan and played with the freshmen group, waiting for his chance. Crisler would give it to him.

Michigan entered its opener against Michigan State with a record of four straight losses to the Spartans. Crisler was cautious, refusing to predict immediate success. He had a talented but untested group of sophomores and some extremely capable veterans, led by Captain Fred Jahnke, guard Ralph Heikkinen, center Archie Kodros, and halfback Norm Purucker. Michigan State offered its all-American halfback, Johnny Pingel, and he was cause for concern. Pingel the year before led the nation in punting, completed nearly half his passes, and averaged six yards every time he carried the ball.

Crisler keyed his defense on Pingel, shifting his defense to anticipate a run or pass. An all-veteran team started, except Evashevski, a sophomore who played linebacker and quarterback. The Spartans were heavily favored, but Crisler believed victory could be attained if "we outcharge their line and maintain control of the line of scrimmage."

The plan worked. Michigan's aggressive defense forced Michigan State into two fumbles and four interceptions and held its rushing to 25 yards. Kromer was inserted into the game at tailback and scored two touchdowns. Harmon at wingback had runs of 22, 15, and 13 yards as Michigan pulled off a 14-0 upset.

Harmon started the following Saturday against Clark Shaughnessy's Chicago team and sprinted 59 yards to score. Strong, making his "second debut" in the Big Ten, passed for a touchdown and ran 14 yards for another score as Michigan won 45-7.

The Gophers continued to perplex Michigan, however, winning their fifth straight over the Wolverines by recovering a Harmon fumble and moving in to score. An extra point decided it, 7-6. Jerry Ford, the former Michigan center, scouted that game for Yale, and returned very impressed with the Wolverines despite their defeat. His glowing reports did not impress the Yale team. The Ivy Leaguers took a 13-2 lead over Michigan the following Saturday, but Harmon came out throwing in the second half, setting up two touchdowns. The deciding score in the 15-13 game came on a short Evashevski pass to John Nicholson.

The reunion of Fielding H. Yost (left), Germany Schulz (center), and the legendary Willie Heston during a Michigan football game.

Illinois was the next loser, 14-0, as Harmon scored from 13 yards out and passed 23 yards to "Evy" for the other. The Penn-Michigan game was billed as a duel between Harmon and the Quakers' triple-threat sophomore, Francis X. Reagan, but

little Paul Kromer starred in the 19-13 Michigan victory. He gained 92 yards in 13 carries as a little reserve guard from Muskegon Heights, Milo Sukup, cleared the way. Kromer also caught a touchdown pass, while Harmon rested on the bench most of the game.

Northwestern then surprised Michigan with a 0-0 tie as Freddie Trosko, who kicked the Wolverines to successive victories the previous year, missed a field goal from short range. A win would have provided Crisler with a share of the championship in his first season. Michigan completed the year with an 18-0 win over Ohio State, the first success after four straight defeats to the Ohioans. Harmon ran for one touchdown and passed to Ed Frutig for another.

Michigan was 3-1-1 in the conference with Minnesota's 4-1 mark earning the championship. Heikkinen, the "vest pocket" guard on Crisler's single wing, was everybody's all-American, and for the second straight year he was voted Michigan's most valuable player. A 6-1-1 record, however, was just a near-miss for the Wolverines.

Harmon Of Michigan

Thomas Dudley Harmon was an authentic sports hero in the years when America was overstocked with athletes to cheer. Before he won the Heisman Trophy or the Maxwell Trophy or the Washington Touchdown Trophy, his considerable talents landed the Michigan halfback on the cover of *Time* magazine. The number "98" across the back of his jersey became as familiar as the "double sevens" of Red Grange.

Perhaps more than any player of his time Harmon was involved in the dramatics of college football. He did not just score touchdowns, he created them. His career from 1938 through 1940 was strung together with the spectacular. His run against Penn, when he retreated 25 yards toward his own goal, then twisted, cut, and ran his way some 150 yards to score as every player on the Quaker team had two shots at him, remains a classic in college football.

There was the Saturday he scored all Michigan's 27 points against Iowa. The day against California when he so dazzled the Bears and their fans that one of them, a fan, staggered out on the field and tried to tackle Harmon on an 86-yard touchdown run. His luck was no better than California's.

Harmon's first honor came in Gary, Indiana, where he won the city's "Bubblegum Championship" while in grade school. At Horace Mann High he earned fourteen varsity letters and won the national interscholastic football scoring championship with 150 points. His coach, Doug Kerr, who once was on the Michigan football team, directed Harmon to Michigan. Harmon,

To Fritz —
In sincere appreciation for all you have done — my best wishes always to not only the greatest coach in the world but also the greatest guy — ole "98" will take you as the all american coach every day — Sincerely
Tom —

Tom Harmon was a 60-minute player for Michigan.

168

years later, said of that decision, "I am sure that hundreds of football players have enjoyed the experience of wearing the Maize and Blue, but none has enjoyed it more, or appreciated it more, than this very lucky Irishman."

Harmon was a talkative six-footer with a powerful physique and a yen for swing music. Newpaper and radio reporters, photographers, and newsreel film crews were his constant companions while he ate, walked to class, or was on a date. Crisler had a rule, however. Harmon was available for ten minutes before practice, then he would tell an assistant, "Go fetch the prima donna." It was said lightly, but it served the team well. Harmon never forgot he was part of a team.

Forest Evashevski, mature, articulate, with a biting sense of humor that always hinted at the truth, did his part to keep Harmon on an even level. He never let the halfback forget who threw the blocks. They became close friends. When it was assumed that Harmon would be Michigan's captain during his senior year, Tom went out and campaigned for Evashevski's election. "Evy" was named captain.

Michigan was a winning football team, but the headlines went to Harmon. It is a tribute to him that players, writing about those seasons years later, always pointed out their respect for the "Hoosier Hammer." He was a 60-minute player whose dedication to football was as evident in his last game as it was in his first.

When writers called him the best since Grange, Yost would say, "The best since Heston." Crisler said, "I always thought Tom was a better football player than Grange because he could do more things. He ran, passed, punted, blocked, kicked off, and kicked extra points and field goals, and was a superb defensive player." Crisler played Harmon at the wingback position his sophomore year, "because Kromer was an excellent runner, too, and Tom had the strength to play right half where more blocking was required."

Harmon was eventually switched to the tailback position, but at the start of the 1939 season he was still at right halfback in Crisler's explosive offense. Michigan scored four touchdowns in the first half and dumped Michigan State, 26-13, in the opener as Bob Westfall and Evashevski supplied the running thrust. Then Harmon exploded for all Michigan's points, one touchdown coming on a 95-yard pass interception, in a 27-7 victory over the great Nile Kinnick and Iowa. Crisler kept his regulars on the bench for all but sixteen minutes and used guards to run the ball in an 85-0 romp over Chicago, where football was in its final season. He scored 21 points against Yale. He gained 203 yards from scrimmage and amazed a Franklin Field crowd with a criss-crossing 63-yard touchdown run in the much publicized duel with Reagan of Pennsylvania. Reagan was brilliant, too, but it was Harmon's day as he scored twice and passed for a third touchdown in Michigan's 19-17 win.

Michigan lost only two games in 1939. Illinois, a decided underdog, shocked the Wolverines, 16-7. Michigan's Dave Strong threw a touchdown pass against his former teammates, a flat pass that Harmon carried 45 yards. Coach Bob Zuppke of Illinois took advantage of Crisler's "missing bugler" to cement the victory with a "sleeper" play. The "sleeper" play, where a player lines up along his own sideline and blends in with his teammates near the bench, was a popular trick of the time. In Michigan Stadium, Crisler would have a bugler high up in the stands looking for a "sleeper" with instructions to "sound the alarm" when he found one. "We didn't take him on road games, and Illinois pulled the 'sleeper' play and it went for a touchdown," Crisler complained. Illinois had waited until it recovered a fumble and immediately, without using a huddle, threw a pass to the "sleeper."

Evashevski, injured early in the Illinois game, missed the next battle with Minnesota, and the Gophers won, 20-7. The Wolverines rebounded to defeat Penn, then 81,000 turned out in Michigan Stadium for the final game of the 1939 season against Ohio State. The Buckeyes took a quick 14-0 lead as Freddie Trosko had a pass intercepted to set up the first OSU touchdown, and his fumble led to the second. Going into the game, the 154-pound senior had been discouraged because of several other misfortunes. He was down, and Crisler knew it. Crisler had called him to his room at the Barton Hills Country Club where the team stayed on Friday nights and said, "Freddie, I still have supreme confidence in you."

Crisler's confidence might have been shaken in the first quarter against Ohio State on Saturday, but he stayed with him.

170

The famed running-blocking combination of Michigan: Harmon, the runner, and Forest Evashevski, the blocker.

Michigan battled back. Harmon scored on a brilliantly executed play coming off the buck-lateral series. Then Harmon fired a touchdown pass to Evashevski, who made a sensational catch with three Buckeyes surrounding him in the end zone. The game was tied, 14-14.

Now there were 50 seconds left, and Michigan was in field goal range. The ball was on the Ohio State 23. The play? A fake field goal with the holder running. The holder was supposed to be Freddie Trosko. Crisler sent him in, again telling him, "Freddie, nothing has changed." Trosko took the center snap and Harmon executed a perfect fake kick as the Ohio State end charged in to block it. Trosko jumped up and sprinted down the

Crisler with his 1939 backfield of (left to right), Forest Evashevski, Bob Westfall, Tommy Harmon, and Fred Trosko.

sidelines to score easily. Harmon's extra point made it 21-14. Trosko came out of the game as a thunderous ovation rose in Michigan Stadium for the young man from Flint.

Despite the loss Ohio State captured the conference championship. Michigan finished in a fourth-place tie with a 3-2 record (6-2 overall). Harmon, rushing for 884 yards, passing for 488, and leading the nation in scoring with 102 points, became Michigan's first halfback to be named to the all-America team since Harry Kipke.

Harmon, Evashevski, Fritz, Frutig, Kromer, Joe Rogers, and Ed Czak would be back in 1940. The impressive sophomores, Davey Nelson, Bob Ingalls, and Bob Westfall, would be joined by a second Wistert and a quarterback destined for stardom at Michigan, George Ceithaml. Another wild season was building.

A Birthday Present
On The Coast

The travel itinerary for the opening game of the 1940 season called for stops at Des Moines, Denver, Salt Lake City, and San Francisco. The Michigan football team was headed west to play California, and for the first time in intercollegiate history the trip would be made by airplane. Three United Airlines DC-3s were chartered for the two-day trip. A stopover in Salt Lake City was scheduled to allow the Wolverines a day of practice.

Every player under 21 had to receive permission from his parents to make the trip. Attendance for the trip was perfect. A few passengers became sick, but the party of 53, including 35 players, arrived without incident.

A crowd of 54,000 in Berkeley turned out to watch the Bears of California and the highly regarded Wolverines. Just prior to the kickoff Forest Evashevski waved Tom Harmon away and huddled the rest of the players near the goal line. Michigan was receiving, and "Evy" told them, "This is Tom's twenty-first birthday. Let's give him a present by everybody knocking somebody down."

The kickoff soared high and deep to Harmon on the five. He started upfield, cut slightly, and broke through the first wave and into the open as Evashevski delivered the key block. Harmon had his birthday present, a 95-yard touchdown run, but he had only begun. Later he returned a Cal punt 70 yards to score. Again he shook free on an end sweep from his own 14, and was in the open near the goal line when a spectator darted

One of three chartered planes Michigan used to become the first college team to fly cross-country in 1940. The Wolverines defeated California in a memorable afternoon for Tom Harmon.

out of the end zone and dived for the legs of the Michigan halfback. He missed, and Harmon had an 86-yard touchdown, his third. In the second half the "Ace" scored on a 7-yard run and threw a touchdown pass to Davey Nelson. Harmon also kicked five extra points in the rousing 41-0 victory.

Harmon scored all of Michigan's points the next week in a 21-14 win over Michigan State. Then the Wolverines traveled to the East coast and blanked Harvard, 26-0, with Harmon accounting for another 20 points. Illinois and Pennsylvania, with Reagan gaining just ten yards, fell. The next one was scheduled in Minneapolis, and once again the Gophers were

176

blocking Michigan's road to a championship.

Every Michigan player had pointed to the game. Twice the Gophers had ruined their hopes for a title. Unbeaten, untied, and physically awesome, they had an extra weapon going for them. It came about 2 a.m. Saturday morning as the rolling sound of thunder woke Evashevski, the captain and quarterback. Harmon, his roommate, also awoke, and the two listened as the storm built. Evashevski began to study Michigan's game plan, wondering if a wet field would break down a plan that appeared foolproof on a dry field. When Michigan arrived at the stadium Saturday, Evashevski knew the game plan based on

Besides being an exceptional passer and runner, Tom Harmon (98) was also a great punter, often getting Michigan out of trouble with his long, booming kicks. Blocking for Harmon in the 1940 Minnesota game is another all-American, fullback Bob Westfall (86).

speed and deception would have to be abandoned. Michigan would have to play straight, power football...the game played best by the Gophers.

The Wolverines took charge of the game immediately. Crisler's single wing outgained the Gophers and Bruce Smith three yards to one. Four times they drove inside Minnesota's ten and never scored. Michigan received a break in the second period when Bill Daley fumbled on his five and Bob Westfall recovered. Unable to gain on the muddy field Harmon switched gears and tossed a short pass to Evashevski for the touchdown. The extra point kick by Harmon sailed a little to the right.

Minnesota continued its plodding attack of power and stone-wall defense until another Michigan drive died at the end of a fumble. The Gophers took over at their 20 and on first down a power play to the short side sent Bruce Smith, the all-American, off tackle. He broke through, and Michigan's secondary defenders, moving in quickly, overshot him. Smith was free, running 80 yards to score. On the extra point the center snap rolled back on the ground, but little Joe Merick got his foot on it and drove it perfectly over the uprights. That 7-6 lead stood up the rest of the game.

On the long train ride back to Ann Arbor dejection set in among the Wolverines. Northwestern and Ohio State remained to be faced, but a third straight loss to Minnesota had its toll. When they got off the train at Michigan, however, several thousand students were there cheering. Evashevski recalls, "They had a portable mike, had members of the team say a word, then hoisted us bodily onto a hay rack, and the freshmen pulled us up the long hill to campus. When they all broke into 'The Victors,' it hit a crescendo I couldn't believe. Life had a new meaning."

Westfall rambled for 92 yards, and Michigan rebounded to defeat Northwestern. The following Saturday Michigan traveled to Columbus and blew the Buckeyes out of the stadium as Harmon packed all his brilliance into one last effort. Michigan exploded for 20 points in the first half and won, 40-0. Harmon rushed for 139 yards, completed 11 of 22 passes for 151 yards, ran for two touchdowns, and passed for two more. He kicked four extra points, averaged 50 yards with his punts, intercepted three passes, returning one for his third touchdown. Kromer,

180

courageously battling back from a severe knee injury suffered as a junior, returned a punt 80 yards for a touchdown in his final game. With 15 seconds left, Crisler pulled Harmon from the game, and the Buckeye fans gave him an ovation that a visiting player had seldom received in Columbus.

Michigan won seven of eight games, but finished second to the undefeated Gophers, who won the 1940 national championship.

Harmon's three touchdowns gave him a career total of 33 to break Red Grange's record. In three years he gained 2,134 yards rushing (averaged 5.4 yards per carry) and passed for 1,304 yards. He is the only player in modern college football history to win successive scoring titles as his 117 points in 1940 gave him a three-year total of 237.

Harmon, a two-time all-American, was voted the top award in college football, the Heisman Trophy, and in an Associated Press poll was named the outstanding male athlete in the nation, gaining nearly three times as many votes as runnerup Hank Greenberg of the pennant winning Detroit Tigers.

A war was approaching, and Harmon and his teammates would become part of a new team. They never won a championship, but they never ran from adversity, either.

A Trip To South Bend

Fielding H. Yost retired as athletic director in 1941. The last tie with Michigan's pioneer football years was gone...to his home on the hill in Ann Arbor where he could relive with pride 40 years of accomplishment.

At 70 he was entitled to remember Benny Friedman as a junior, when he took the young passing wizard to old Ferry Field, an arm around his shoulder, his other hand pointing to the 20-yard line near the sidelines. "Right cheer, Ben, we pulled off 'Old 83' to beat them...And right cheer we...," Yost would recall another play, another Michigan victory.

Yost brought a unique color to college football. "Athletics," he would say, "is the Golden Rule in action." He pronounced it "Meeshegan" with a West Virginia accent that never left him, but he knew what Michigan meant. After Yost died in 1946, his wife was going over the hundreds of notes he scratched on bits of paper. One read, "I want to rest where the Michigan spirit is warmest."

Rockne was gone. Pop Warner was gone. Yost's old rival and friend at Illinois, Zuppke, had one year left of coaching. Stagg was nearing the end of his historic career. The giants of college football were fading, but a new command had arrived— Frank Leahy of Notre Dame, Earl Blaik of Army, and Michigan's Fritz Crisler.

Michigan's football outlook in 1941, however, was not encouraging. Harmon, now broadcasting U of M games with Harry Wismer, and his companions had departed after winning

19 games, losing 4, and tying 1. Sophomores like Tom Kuzma from Gary, Indiana, and Paul White from River Rouge, were backfield replacements. Julius Franks from Hamtramck and Merv Pregulman from Lansing, two more sophomores, appeared ready to take over in the line. Captain Bob Westfall and quarterback George Ceithaml gave the backfield some experience, while Al Wistert, Bob Kolesar, Reuben Kelto, and Bob

Tom Kuzma was a triple threat halfback for Michigan, leading the Wolverines to a victory over Notre Dame in 1942.

Ingalls returned in the trenches. Still, three or four defeats were predicted for Michigan.

When the season was completed, Crisler could look back at one of his finest coaching efforts. Four straight victories at the start, including a tough 14-7 upset win over Northwestern and Otto Graham, had the Wolverines flying. Next came Minnesota, in the process of repeating its national championship, and again the Gophers pulled out a 7-0 victory. Michigan rebounded with two more victories as Westfall, a magnificent leader who had played in the shadow of Harmon, scored two touchdowns against Illinois and three more against Columbia.

In the final game Paul Brown's Ohio State team was giving Michigan problems. The Bucks had just scored to open a 20-14 lead when Westfall gathered his teammates just prior to the kickoff. "Gentlemen," he said, "I and we have no intention of losing this game." Michigan took the kick and launched a

Julius Franks, Michigan's all-American guard, was switched for the 1942 Notre Dame game because he was "too fast."

13-play drive that tied the game. Bill Melzow, who had converted 12 of 14 extra points, just missed with his last kick. That tie gave the Wolverines a 3-1-1 record and a second place finish, while their 6-1-1 overall record enabled them to repeat their fifth place national ranking.

Westfall, the husky fullback from Ann Arbor, who had played in every game from his sophomore year on, earned all-American status. He gained 688 yards, and his three-year total stood at 1,864, just 270 less than Harmon's. Kuzma led Michigan in total offense, passing, and punting. Kelto, who turned in an outstanding season at tackle, was named the most valuable player.

When the 1942 season opened, a world war was gripping the nation, and college football appeared to be a luxury. Crisler and Ralph Aigler were sent to Washington by the Western Conference to argue the cause of college football before the armed services. The Navy and Air Force immediately approved the continuing of football, and the Army later relented as the values of leadership and physical training for young men entering service proved vital. Michigan's schedule began to include service teams.

The Wolverines had the feeling, "We can go all the way," and their opener against Great Lakes Naval Training, a team featuring all-American Bruce Smith and eight pros, indicated that. Crisler opened up the attack, and Michigan threw 24 passes in a 9-0 win. One touchdown pass came off the arm of Bob Chappuis and a field goal was produced by Jim Brieske, two sophomores Michigan fans would come to know after the war.

After an easy victory over Michigan State, Michigan ran into a tidal wave of talent as powerful Iowa Pre-Flight, using a Wolverine quartet of Forest Evashevski, Whitey Fraumann, Butch Jordan, and Bob Flora, romped 26-14. Recovery was instant. Wistert tipped an Otto Graham pass, and Merv Pregulman picked it out of the air and ran 65 yards to score as Northwestern fell 34-16, but the next week it was the old nemesis from the north, Minnesota.

Typically, the game was close. Just seconds before the half ended and with the clock stopped, the Gophers' Bill Garness managed to kick a field goal. It was a hotly disputed play, and

185

while many argued that the clock was illegally stopped, Crisler never complained publicly. Michigan lost, 16-14.

Illinois and Harvard offered no problems, and the Wolverines had five victories in hand when they traveled to South Bend for a long-awaited battle with Notre Dame. They had not met since 1909. There was no doubt, this one was special as Crisler called an unprecedented indoor practice on Monday. The gates were locked, and even Ken Doherty's track men in Yost Field House were suspect. Crisler put in twelve new defenses. "Red Dog" joined their football vocabulary after Oosterbaan, who scouted the Irish, noted a flaw in their pass protection. The intensity of practice was electric.

Saturday in South Bend was cold, but 57,000 fans enjoyed brilliant sunshine. Notre Dame took the opening kickoff and quickly drove in to score on a pass from Angelo Bertelli to Bob Dove. It was after this touchdown that a Notre Dame lineman caustically asked, "Where's that great Michigan line I've heard so much about?" None of the Wolverines replied, but a resolve moved through their ranks. They were called the "Seven Oak Posts" as 60-minute players, and pride was never in shortage. Michigan stormed back with the kickoff to score on a short plunge by George Ceithaml, then recovered a fumble and threatened again. Notre Dame held, however, and the field goal team of kicker Jim Brieske and holder Don Robinson was sent in. Robinson knelt on the eleven, the ball was snapped back, and the little halfback jumped up and scooted around his left end for the touchdown. Notre Dame, refusing to crack, came back to score again just before half time to gain a 14-13 lead. It was anyone's game.

The Wolverines met quietly in the dressing room at half time. Confidence still prevailed. Crisler went over the game plan, then announced, "We'll kick off to start the half." Immediately the disappointment showed on the face of Ceithaml. Marty Martineau, an assistant coach, noticed it and walked over to the Michigan quarterback. "What's the matter, George?" asked Martineau.

"We'd like to receive. We think we can score," replied Ceithaml.

The team left the dressing room, and on the way to the Michigan bench Ceithaml approached Crisler. "Could you

Merv Pregulman, one of Michigan's finest guards and an all-American in 1943.

Michigan's fake field goal scores against Notre Dame. This play triggered a 32-20 victory over Notre Dame in 1942 as Don Robinson (46), the holder for "Automatic" Jim Brieske, darted

around left end to score. There are four Michigan all-Americans in this photo—Al Wistert (11), Merv Pregulman (67), Julius Franks (63), and Elmer Madar (right corner).

change your mind about kicking off, coach?" he asked.

"Why?" demanded Crisler.

"I think we can go."

"Do the rest of the players feel the same way?" Crisler asked.

"Yes, they do," answered the Michigan captain.

"Let's take it, then," Crisler said.

The kickoff came to the Wolverines, and they immediately marched 51 punishing yards to score on a short run by Paul White. Michigan quickly recovered another Notre Dame fumble, and Kuzma scored. Then White intercepted a Bertelli pass, and Kuzma scored again. Three touchdowns in eight minutes and Michigan had a 32-20 victory.

It was a masterful coaching job, executed by an inspired team. Crisler, fearing that Notre Dame Coach Frank Leahy would take advantage of Julius Franks' great speed with trap plays, had shifted him to right guard. Notre Dame immediately came pounding at the left guard spot, occupied by Bob Kolesar. Crisler watched him take a battering for an entire quarter, then yelled, "Bob, grab the grass and hold on."

Playing next to Kolesar was Al Wistert, who could not be trapped or blocked that day. After the game his teammates lifted the "Ox" on their shoulders and carried him to the dressing room. He was named all-American in 1942, much of the recognition coming from that Saturday in South Bend. His teammates selected him as Michigan's most valuable player.

Michigan suffered a letdown the following week and lost to a fine Ohio State team, 21-7, but rebounded and finished with a 28-14 victory over Iowa. The Wolverines had a surprising 7-3 record as Ohio won the title. Franks, a junior, joined Wistert as all-American linemen.

But 1942 was just the beginning of those hectic war years when coaches would not know their starting lineups from week to week. Out of the confusion would come Michigan's first championship in a decade.

When Albert Wistert reported to football practice at Michigan, equipment manager Henry Hatch asked him, "How would you like your brother's jersey?" He was the happiest player in camp with number eleven, and like his brother, Francis, became an all-American tackle in 1942. A third brother, Alvin, wore number eleven before it was retired.

The Years Of Lend-Lease

Elroy Hirsch had nearly led Wisconsin to the Big Nine football championship during the 1942 season but now was packing his bags. The Marine Corps had assigned him and a group of other Wisconsin students to the Ann Arbor campus under the war-time V-12 training program, and he had doubts about how his group would be accepted by the Michigan students. "I wondered if we'd be considered a group of service men cluttering up an already crowded campus?" Hirsch recalled.

It would not take long for Michigan fans to show their approval of the blond, crew-cut halfback with the hitch in his stride, the guy they called "Crazy Legs." They would approve, also, of another V-12 student, a fullback from Minnesota and a Marine trainee named Bill Daley.

There were in 1943 new arrivals weekly, and departures. Captain Paul White left for service duty. Bob Chappuis went to the Air Force. Tom Kuzma and Julius Franks could not play because of illnesses. When Kuzma recovered he entered the Army and became an infantry sergeant. Michigan athletes, past and present, were involved in the war. Tom Harmon commanded headlines again, first when his plane went down over South America, and he walked out of the jungle. Then his plane crashed in China. Again he was rescued.

Hirsch and Daley were among the 1,300 sailors recruited and sent to Michigan for their education prior to becoming officers. Hirsch was one of eleven Badgers on "lend-lease" to Michigan. Others came from Michigan State, Idaho State,

Toledo, and Western Michigan. They were housed in West Quad, known as "The Ship." During the fall of 1943 more than 4,000 men in uniform were on the Michigan campus.

Hirsch and Daley provided the championship spark in 1943, but at times it was an uncertain spark. Daley powered his way to touchdowns of 37 and 64 yards, and Hirsch scored from the 3 as Michigan stung Northwestern with three touchdowns in seven plays.

Hirsch was injured for the Notre Dame game, and Crisler had to alter his backfield. Leahy had his T-formation working perfectly as Creighton Miller exploded on a quick opener 66 yards to score. The result was a 35-12 win for ND. The following week "Crazy Legs," on the first play of the game, sprinted 61 yards to score and added two more touchdowns in a

Bill Daley, a lend-lease all-American at "M" from Minnesota in 1943.

Paul White was named captain of the 1943 team, but left for military service before the season opened. He returned and played after the war with his brother, J. T. White.

49-6 rout of Minnesota, the first Michigan win over the Gophers after ten long years of frustration.

After Michigan ran over Illinois, 42-6, Daley and tackle Merv Pregulman left for service. Daley gained 817 yards in six games, averaging nearly seven yards per carry. Pregulman played tackle, guard, and center. After the season both were named to the all-America team. The Wolverines had enough left to defeat a growing football power at Indiana, 23-6, but Hirsch sustained a shoulder injury and missed playing against his old teammates the following week at Wisconsin. He had a bet that he would score, so the ex-Badger put himself into the game and kicked the final extra point. Hirsch's replacement, Bob Nussbaumer, gained 113 yards in Michigan's 27-0 win. Michigan then nailed down the championship with Purdue by bombing Ohio

State, 45-7.

Football was the start of a near-perfect athletic season for the Wolverines. They won eight of the nine Big Ten titles in 1943-44, missing only in basketball. Hirsch, playing basketball, baseball, and competing in track, became the only athlete in modern Michigan history to earn four letters in a single school year.

As a fitting tribute to the Wisconsin great, equipment manager Henry Hatch arranged for a small party to honor him. Hirsch was surprised and thrilled when Hatch presented him with an "M" blanket containing four stars, an award always reserved for seniors.

Hirsch departed, and two all-Americans of 1943, Daley and Pregulman, were in the service as Crisler tried to regroup his

Fred Negus, one of eleven players assigned to Michigan from Wisconsin in 1943.

forces for the 1944 season. Bob Wiese, the captain and most valuable player, was returning along with Nussbaumer and Bill Culligan. That was the extent of veteran players at Michigan. Joe Ponsetto was the starting quarterback as a 19-year-old sophomore. Several freshmen, who would play vital roles on Michigan's post-war powerhouses, were pressed into starting positions.

One of them, Dick Rifenburg, caught two touchdown

Elroy "Crazylegs" Hirsch scores on a 61-yard run, the very first play of the game, in the 1943 rout of Minnesota.

passes in his first game against Iowa Pre-Flight to account for Michigan's 12-7 victory. Ben Oosterbaan, who noticed a flaw in the Sailors' defense, came down from the press box to improvise the new plays for "Rife," and Culligan hit him twice on scoring passes.

With Michigan State off the schedule for the second straight season (the Spartans dropped football for one season in 1943 because of the war), the Wolverines toppled Marquette,

14-0, then lost 20-0 to Bob (Hunchy) Hoernschemeyer, who had received a surprise discharge from the Navy, and a "bunch of civilians" at Indiana. "I guess Bo McMillin found a lot of 4-Fs, but they sure the hell could play football," offered Crisler. Michigan then won three straight, but, after defeating Purdue, Wiese and Nussbaumer received their sailing orders. The pair had rushed for 275 yards against Northwestern and 244 yards in the Purdue victory. Don Lund and Ralph Chubb stepped in to fill the vacancies.

Rifenburg, just turning 18, left for early induction into the U.S. Maritime Service, and manpower became critical. It provided a chance for one courageous athlete who had first enrolled at Michigan in 1937. Howard "Jeep" Mehaffey, an outstanding fullback from Kiski Prep, had been a sophomore with Tom Harmon's group, but osteomyelitis set in and cut his career short. During the 1944 season he was attending school and working a full shift at the Willow Run bomber plant, but his chance had come. Now a guard, "Jeep" returned to football and played.

Once proud Penn bowed by 22 points. Illinois, two years away from a title and with Buddy Young in the backfield, lost. Culligan ran 85 yards and Lund 55 yards to account for the touchdowns that beat Wisconsin. The victory put the Wolverines into a title game with Ohio State. Culligan scored twice to give Michigan a 14-12 lead over Ohio State, but with three minutes left, Les Horvath, the Heisman Trophy winner, led a game-winning scoring drive as the Buckeyes captured the championship.

There were no all-Americans in 1944, but Ponsetto and Milan Lazetich, a strong lineman, were Michigan's representatives on the all-Big Nine team.

Finding experienced players in 1945 would continue to plague Crisler. Two freshmen, Rifenburg and Gene Derricotte, joined the service rolls. Bruce Hilkene, voted captain for 1945, was transferred by the Navy. Lund, the team's most valuable player, graduated. It would be the year of the "fuzzy-cheeked kids," and with national champion Army looming on the horizon Crisler had to pull something out of the hat. He did!

Elroy Hirsch earned four letters during the 1943-44 season, the only Michigan athlete ever to accomplish that feat.

"M" Platoon Meets Army

Fritz Crisler liked to attend coaching conventions. The free and informal exchange of ideas, innovations, the camaraderie with his colleagues, he thought, were worth the trip to New York. When Earl "Red" Blaik turned the conversation to scheduling, Crisler's attention sharpened. Several Ivy League teams had dropped football because of the war, and Blaik was complaining about the growing problems of arranging a schedule for his Army powerhouse. Navy's coach, sitting at the table, agreed. Nobody wanted to schedule a certain defeat.

Crisler listened for several minutes. As Michigan's athletic director, he, too, faced scheduling problems of a different nature. He needed attractive teams to fill those 86,000 Michigan Stadium seats, and, of course, he always wanted at least one team from the East on Michigan's schedule. What better attraction than Army and Navy? Finally Fritz said, "Michigan would like to play your team next season, 'Red,'" and turning to Oscar Hayberg of Navy, "and yours, too." Both coaches were surprised. "You understand," Crisler said, "I have no illusions about beating you this season, but I'd like a four-year contract. I'm betting the war will be over, and we'll be able to compete with you then."

Both Army and Navy accepted Crisler's offer. Michigan would play Army's national champion team in New York City in 1945, the fifth game of the season. Navy was scheduled for the eighth game at Baltimore. Michigan and Army would meet again in Michigan Stadium the following season, and the two

200

remaining games were to be finalized later.

That conversation in New York would produce a landmark game in college football, though. The prospect of facing the finest college team of the day, perhaps of all-time, remained heavily on Crisler's mind throughout the summer months and into fall practice. It was obvious to Crisler when he greeted his varsity candidates for the 1945 season that Michigan did not have the experience or talent to play with The Black Knights of the Hudson.

Joe Ponsetto, a sturdy and effective quarterback, was back with Howard Yerges behind him. Fullback Jack Weisenburger and halfback Bob Nussbaumer fortified the backfield, while Art Renner, an end in 1943 and 1944, had his discharge from the Marines. But, mostly, it was a collection of 17-year-olds fresh out of high school who would provide the playing talent as the ban on freshmen had been temporarily suspended because of the war.

Michigan, facing one of the most demanding schedules in its history, opened with a 27-2 win over Great Lakes. Wally Teninga, whose last game had been played at Morgan Park High in Chicago, passed for one touchdown and ran for another. Gradually the talents of other freshmen, Dom Tomasi, Scotty McNeill, Stu Wilkins, Len Ford, Dan Dworsky, and Pete Elliott, commanded attention. Michigan lost to Indiana but followed up with victories over Michigan State (their first meeting in three years) and Northwestern. The next date was October 13— Yankee Stadium.

Army, unbeaten and unscored upon, drew a crowd of 70,000 on a bright, clear day in New York. The Cadets, four or five touchdown favorites, had Blanchard, Davis, Tucker, Gerometta, Foldberg, Coulter, McWilliams, a team that averaged nearly 23 years of age. The New York writers immediately tabbed Crisler's Wolverines "The Fuzz Kids."

It might have been the unrealistic innocence of youth with its boundless energies, or Michigan tradition, or a talk Crisler had with his team before boarding a bus at Ferry Field when he asked, "Is there anyone who believes victory cannot be achieved?" Whatever the reasons that enable football players to rise to the heights, Michigan possessed them. The Wolverines took the opening kickoff and drove hard for 80 yards, but the

Army held. As his Cadets took possession, Blaik watched in amazement as eight Wolverines trotted off the field and eight more came in to replace them. Michigan's defense checked the first Army assault, and, again, eight Wolverines were switched. Platoon football had made a dramatic entry!

Army was not to be denied, however. In the second period the Cadets drove 67 yards with Shorty McWilliams scoring from the one. Just before the half ended, Doc Blanchard powered his way 69 yards, and Army had a 14-0 lead.

Still, Crisler had his Michigan team believing they could win, and it was evident they were not going to run and hide as the second half opened. Teninga took the kickoff and started to his right. First Tomasi, then Wilkins, then Harold Watts cut down tacklers. Teninga, at full speed now, was nearing midfield along the sidelines with only one defender to beat—Blanchard. Seeing the big Army fullback closing in, Teninga put his head down and rammed his 179 pounds into Blanchard as the young freshman strained for a few extra yards. The ball and Teninga both sailed out of bounds, in different directions. As he was struggling to his feet, Teninga, eyes dazed and staring up at Ben Oosterbaan, said, "Coach, I'll bet he felt that one." Oosterbaan glanced over at the Army all-American who had never left his feet, smiled, and said, "Okay, Wally, let's move it in."

Michigan did move, to Army's nine-yard line in thirteen plays. Then Teninga shot a pass toward the end zone. The ball glanced off an Army lineman's helmet, seemed to hit another defender, and sailed directly into the hands of end Art Renner for a touchdown. Joe Ponsetto's kick made it 14-7. Army had been scored on.

Army did not score the rest of the period. Crisler had devised a four-man line with three linebackers. Their orders were to stunt and blitz. Michigan was throwing a seven-man charge at the Cadets. It was dangerous, but Crisler said, "When you have a dime and the other guy has $1,000, it's time to gamble."

Blaik's forces kept hammering. The offense was based on power, and it had an effect. Early in the fourth period Blanchard again scored. Several minutes later Army had the ball again when a mixup occurred in Michigan's new defenses. Glenn Davis responded by bolting 70 yards to score the final

Joe Ponsetto, a 17-year-old quarterback during the war years, later was a Michigan captain.

touchdown in a 28-7 victory. Davis and Blanchard were forced to carry the ball forty times against the Michigan defenses that held Army to 14 points for more than three periods.

Crisler's phone began ringing Sunday night and continued all week. Coaches from coast to coast wanted to know what happened. Platooning players was to become a way of life in college football. Crisler would begin to fully exploit it the following year.

"Three little words, 'at any time,' gave me the opportunity of using separate teams for offense and defense," Crisler explained. "The substitution rule was changed in 1941. Until that time players could not reenter a game in the same quarter they had left. This restriction was removed, and all that remained was the provision allowing a player to enter the game at any time the clock is stopped.

"I knew our boys could not stay with that great Army team for 60 minutes. Our only hope was to play our best tacklers on defense and our best runners and blockers on offense. We tried to keep as many fresh players in the game as possible. I don't think anyone had used the four-man front before, and this helped. Only our halfbacks and safetyman were left in the game to play offense."

Michigan completed the 1945 season with victories over Illinois, Minnesota, Purdue, and Ohio State, losing only to Navy, another of the nation's finest teams, and Big Ten champion, Indiana.

Crisler had only one returning regular entering the 1945 season, Bob Wiese, yet these young Wolverines, who averaged 19 years and 2 months, won seven of ten games and finished second in the conference. A year later his problem was to sort through a post-war tidal wave of football talent at Michigan. It would not be an easy task.

The Year Of People

The hot Michigan summer lingered punishingly on the crowded practice field as Bob Chappuis strained to make muscles respond the way they had four years before. He remembered his sophomore season of 1942, his chance to play when the regular tailback was injured, the touchdown passes against Great Lakes and Iowa Pre-Flight, the victory over Notre Dame.

He remembered, too, the bombing missions which followed. Twenty-one times over Europe, until finally the last one when his plane went down. Months of hiding, in homes of Italian partisans, on farms, then reaching the British lines. Then back to Michigan, back to football. He had thought, "I really don't give a hoot whether I play football or not." He did not know if he could play football after three years in the Air Force.

The six-footer with thick, black hair and wide, powerful shoulders had come back. And, as he flicked the ball, 10, 15, then 20 yards downfield, he could feel an old spark, a desire return. Pete Elliott, the redheaded sophomore from Bloomington, Illinois, and Gene Derricotte, lithe, strong, with the legs of a sprinter, were throwing with Chappuis. They, too, had scored touchdowns for Michigan.

The photographer finished taking Coach Crisler's picture with his captain, Art Renner, then the veteran end walked over to rejoin his group. As Renner looked at the parade of receivers waiting their turn to run downfield, he wondered if he would be

Bob Chappuis, one of the greatest halfbacks ever to play for Michigan, resumed his career in 1946 and was an all-American in 1947.

a "playing" captain. Dick Rifenburg, a freshman starter in 1944; 6-foot-5 Len Ford; Bob Mann, who looked like he could outrun a small gale; Elmer Madar, once a member of Michigan's famed "Seven Oak Posts"; Scotty McNeill, a starter at end with Renner just the year before—they were all back. Crisler had told him that Bruce Hilkene was being shifted to tackle. A fine end in 1944, Hilkene was elected captain for 1945, but his transfer by the Navy came before the season opened.

Bump Elliott had played halfback on Purdue's undefeated team of 1943. He was listed as the sixth wingback. Paul White, Michigan's captain in 1943, and Don Robinson, an ex-bomber pilot who had scored a touchdown against Notre Dame on a fake field goal, were ready to battle for the position.

Players stood four and five deep at every position. It was the year of people—the fall of 1946. The war was over and GIs were returning. Stars on Michigan's teams of 1942, 1943, and 1944 were back. So, too, were those youngsters who had battled the long odds against Army and Navy; now a year older, more mature.

Crisler began his sorting process. There was an astounding total of 125 varsity candidates. Crisler wondered how many could regain their former talents, their timing. Would their legs respond to the demands of football? "Our plan for the season was to stress passing," Crisler recalled. "Naturally, Chappuis would play a large role in the offense, and we were delighted to see he was the same competitive athlete we had known as a sophomore. So were the others."

Michigan went into the season favored to win the Big Nine championship. The opener against Indiana, however, was a raggedly played game. Derricotte passed 11 yards to White for one touchdown, returned a punt 53 yards for another, and Pete Elliott hit Len Ford with a 17-yard scoring pass to account for the 21-0 win. The next week Chappuis came off the bench to score twice and pull out a difficult 14-7 win over Iowa.

More than 85,000 fans filled Michigan Stadium for the third game, a rematch with Army, still boasting the fearful Blanchard and Davis combination. The Wolverines promptly jolted the Cadets with a 41-yard touchdown drive. Chappuis, facing a fourth down situation at the 13, pitched a short pass to Howard Yerges for the score.

Glenn Davis again staged a brilliant performance against Michigan and by half time had Army in front 14-7. Davis ran 57 yards for one touchdown and passed 31 yards to Bob Folsom for the other.

Michigan, using fullback spinners, reverses, and Chappuis' passing split the Army defense for 83 yards and a touchdown in the third period. White made the final six yards on a reverse. Army, undaunted, came back to move 76 yards with Doc Blanchard finally scoring on a short plunge for a 20-13 lead. Late in the fourth period the Wolverines put together another drive, this one carrying down to Army's eleven. Hopes of an upset died behind a penalty and a pass interception.

Crisler had bet that his Wolverines could compete with "Red" Blaik's powerhouse and almost won. Unfortunately the next meeting between these two teams would not come in 1947 or 1948 but in 1949.

The Army game, as always, had been emotional, and in the aftermath Northwestern took advantage of it the next week against Michigan. The Wildcats broke in front 14-7 and appeared headed for victory until Bob Wiese intercepted a jump pass on the Michigan 15. He shot out to the right and was near midfield when a Northwestern defender moved in for the tackle. Suddenly, he heard the yell, "Cow, Cow." Without thinking, Wiese immediately lateralled the ball back. Bump Elliott picked it out of the air and sprinted down the sidelines for the touchdown. The play covered 85 yards and was executed precisely as Crisler had hoped.

Michigan's intricate offense also included downfield laterals, but Crisler needed some way of attracting the runner's attention to the trailing man. "Cow, Cow" was picked. Elliott, whose sensational catch of a Chappuis pass earlier had produced Michigan's first touchdown, was in the right spot to score the second. He seemed always to be in the right spot and Michigan pulled out a 14-14 tie.

Still, it was evident Michigan had not put it all together, and looming ahead was dangerous Illinois. The game took on title proportions, and tension among the Wolverines was obvious. Nothing went right for Michigan on Saturday. Frenzy replaced timing on offense, and the result was twelve fumbles, mostly on ball handling. Hilkene blocked a punt and nearly had

Bruce Hilkene was elected captain of the 1945 Michigan football team, but missed the season due to military service. He returned and again was elected captain of the 1947 team.

a touchdown, but the ball rolled out of the end zone. Michigan gained 352 yards to 151 for Illinois and had twice as many first downs. Touchdowns, not first downs, win football games, and Illinois received one from Sam Zatkoff on a 57-yard pass interception. Illinois pulled off a shocker, 13-9.

The following week practice took on the freshness of a new season. The pressure that had been mounting left. Minnesota was the first to see the "new" Wolverines. Elliott scored twice, and when Crisler left his defensive backs in the game after a turnover, Derricotte immediately passed 43 yards

Elmer Madar, a member of the 1941 Michigan team, came back as a 26-year-old veteran in 1946 to win all-American honors as an end.

to Bob Mann for a touchdown. That 21-0 win was the start of a victory streak that extended into the 1949 season.

Chappuis scored three times and Michigan gained 500 yards in a 55-7 blitz of Michigan State. Mann scored on two pass receptions against Wisconsin and came back to score twice more as Michigan demolished Ohio State 58-6. Chappuis was superb, completing 13 of 21 passes for 244 yards, but it was a field goal by Jim Brieske from the 12-yard line with 96 seconds left in the game that would fester in the football blood of Columbus. "On Ohio, Fifty-Eight To Six" would become a rallying cry of the Buckeyes.

Michigan had won five conference games, lost one, and tied one. Illinois on the final Saturday defeated Northwestern, 20-0, and claimed the title and a trip to the Rose Bowl. Strangely, there had been reports earlier in the season when the conference approved the historic five-year Rose Bowl pact, on a vote of seven-to-two, that Illinois and Minnesota were the only universities voting against the post-season appearance. Still, the Illini went, though the West Coast was up in arms over the selection. "We want Army" reverberated throughout Southern California. Unwanted, Illinois promptly stormed over UCLA, 45-14.

Four straight victories lifted Michigan to a 6-2-1 record. Madar, the 26-year-old veteran end, was honored as an all-American. Chappuis, called by Crisler "the finest passer I've seen in 16 years of coaching," broke Otto Graham's total offense record by moving Michigan 1,038 yards with his running and passing. The 180-pounder was named Michigan's most valuable player.

Hilkene, for the second time elected captain of a Michigan football team, stood before Michigan alumni at the annual football bust in Detroit and told them, "Illinois is going to the Rose Bowl this year, but next year we will be going." It was not an idle boast.

The Perfect Season

Fritz Crisler cautioned his teams on occasion: "Michigan's tradition is to win. Don't expect our followers to be exalted by our triumphs."

There is a soundness of truth to that, but 1947 would be an exception. Even the freshmen who had failed their sixth grade music classes would be humming "The Victors."

They called them Michigan's "Mad Magicians." Writers pulled out all the adjectives. One author of sports prose wrote of Bob Chappuis, Bump Elliott, Jack Weisenburger, and Howard Yerges, "A backfield full of pervasive shadows that flit about like wraiths."

Crisler wanted none of it. He knew that field goals, even those with some question of legality, could tumble the greatest hopes and destroy the wraiths. He knew of the Minnesota mud, the Illinois spirit. He would take no chances.

Crisler had 125 varsity candidates in 1946. A year later his squad numbered a workable 59. Twenty-seven had earned football letters. He went to work perfecting the complete extension of the buck-lateral series, the full spinners, the reverses, and all the passes which would come off those plays. He designed a complete platoon of teams with one exception. Bump Elliott would play both ways. The first-string offense was the second-string defense. The defensive starters were first-line replacements on offense. Michigan was a team of interchangeable parts, a complete team.

The opener was against Michigan State and its new coach,

212

Michigan's "dream" backfield of 1947 was (left to right) Bump Elliott, wingback; Howard Yerges, quarterback; Jack Weisenburger, fullback; and Bob Chappuis, tailback.

Clarence "Biggie" Munn. Crisler's former assistant had left Michigan in 1946 to coach Syracuse and now was in charge of the Spartans. Chappuis scored three touchdowns, Crisler sent thirty-seven players into the game, and Michigan won, 55-0. Dick Kempthorn, a sophomore who scored a touchdown in his first varsity game, was leading the locker room cheers for Michigan's victory when Ben Oosterbaan put a hand on his shoulder and said, "Big boy, they won't all come that easy."

It appeared, however, that Crisler had created an unstoppable machine of precision. Chappuis fired a 60-yard scoring pass to Bob Mann, and the Wolverines exploded for four touchdowns in the first 8½ minutes against a bewildered Stanford team. They worked the identical play the following

Michigan's 1947 national champions lined up as follows, left to right: Linemen: Dick Rifenburg, Bill Pritula, Joe Soboleski, Dom Tomasi, J. T. White, Captain Bruce Hilkene, Bob Mann. Backs are Bump Elliott, Jack Weisenburger, Howard Yerges (behind center), and Bob Chappuis.

week against Pitt, this one going 70 yards, and Michigan won by 69 points. Notre Dame had beaten this same Pitt team by 34, so the nation's sports editors made the Wolverines No. 1 in their poll. Delighted with the recognition, Michigan rolled over Northwestern, 49-21, but then victories did become harder.

Hilkene thought he detected an overconfidence taking hold of the team, and with Minnesota coming up the next week that attitude could prove fatal. So the Michigan captain called a

team meeting at the Union to "straighten everything out." The meeting was serious, almost grim. Before leaving, Hilkene asked if any one had any comments. Rifenburg stood up and with a straight face said, "I'm not getting enough publicity. The reporter from *Time* was out to interview Chappuis and never even asked for my material." Rifenburg had a way of replacing tension with laughter.

Though the Gophers were not impressive on offense, their

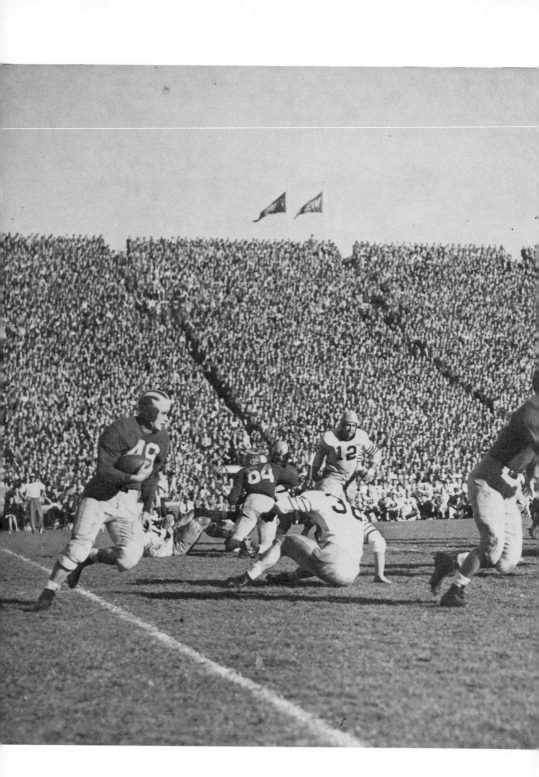

The definitive power sweep: Bob Chappuis (49) follows a wall of Wolverine blockers as the single-wing attack explodes.

Bump Elliott's seventy-four yard punt return for a touchdown helped defeat Illinois in 1947. Michigan devised a punt return formation in Fritz Crisler's early coaching years, and it drastically changed the kicking game. Blockers charged downfield, circled, and set up a wall along the sideline for the runner to use, creating a clear path toward the goal.

defense of Leo Nomellini and Clayton Tonnemaker was intimidating. Kempthorn had injured a knee against Northwestern, and J. T. White, a center, faced the prospect of playing 60 minutes against the huge Gopher line. White had played two seasons at Ohio State, but after the war transferred to Michigan and joined his brother, Paul. The 26-year-old veteran did not wait long to prove he could play defense. Minnesota's early touchdown had put Michigan behind for the first time, but on the extra point White and Len Ford crushed in to block the kick. That 6-0 lead remained menacingly on the scoreboard until deep into the second period.

Michigan, struggling with an offense that was held to a minus five yards, had the ball on Minnesota's 40 with less than a minute remaining in the half. Yerges called time and reminded his teammates they had not gone into the second half trailing all season. Then he called the longest pass play Michigan had, Chappuis to Bump Elliott. Chappuis, hampered by a pinching Minnesota pass rush all afternoon, was worried. He turned to Elliott and asked, "I don't have much time to look for you, do you have any idea where you might be?"

"Just throw it toward the corner, and I'll see if I can get there," Bump answered.

Chappuis took the snap, faded back, and as he looked downfield he saw that both Nomellini and Tonnemaker had broken through. He immediately threw the ball toward the right corner. As Chappuis lay on the ground, the heavy roar of the Michigan crowd told him that Elliott had "gotten there." It was a 40-yard touchdown play, and Jim Brieske's extra point gave Michigan a 7-6 lead. Michigan added a touchdown in the second half when Derricotte cut inside Nomellini's charge and raced 21 yards. The 13-6 victory dropped Michigan to second place behind Notre Dame, but Chappuis found himself on the cover of *Time Magazine*.

Illinois was next, and Crisler added a twist. He changed his punt return formation, and that was the difference. Michigan had returned punts to the wide side of the field all season, but Crisler set up the blocking to the short side for Illinois. In the first period Dike Eddleman boomed a long punt to Elliott on his 26. He started to his left, feinting to the wide side, but then came back and headed up the sidelines. The play went 74 yards for the touchdown.

Illinois struck back to tie the game, but Chappuis passed to Elliott for 52 yards to set up the winning touchdown by Hank Fonde. The 14-7 victory did not move Michigan up in the national ratings, but it did stir Rose Bowl talk in Ann Arbor. Crisler, however, forbade the word "Rose Bowl" among his players. After Chappuis had fired three more touchdown passes and Elliott scored twice in hammering Indiana, 35-0, even ticket manager Don Weir became involved in the Rose Bowl. While Crisler was holding the line on anticipation among his players, Weir sent out a mailer to the thousands who had requested Rose Bowl tickets, explaining that no tickets were available now and that an announcement would be made later.

Michigan then traveled to Madison where the matter of the Rose Bowl could be decided, but Saturday morning Crisler was worried. Rain, sleet, and snow turned Randall Stadium into a field of mud and offered perfect conditions for an upset. Crisler told his quarterback, Yerges, "Play it safe; don't take any chances. It's muddy on both sides of the line, and we'll wait for our breaks."

Michigan scored quickly and minutes later was back on Wisconsin's four. Under orders to play it safe and with the sleet still pelting the field, Chappuis recalled the situation, "We anticipated the call for Weisenburger up the middle or perhaps a straight handoff to Bump. Yerges stepped into the huddle and called a pass play. We all thought Howard had been hit on the head. We broke the huddle without saying anything, however. I got the ball and threw the pass. Right to Yerges, who caught it for a touchdown."

From that point nothing was impossible for Michigan. Chappuis tossed three touchdown passes, two of them to Yerges. Derricotte returned a punt for 77 yards down the sidelines to score. Elliott averaged 6.6 yards running, completed two passes, and caught two passes. The offense, operating in mud, was near perfect.

After the 40th point was scored and Michigan huddled for the kickoff, Dick Rifenburg asked his teammates, "Do you think it's okay now to mention," he spelled out "R-o-s-e B-o-w-l."

The 40-6 win cemented the Big Nine title, and in the dressing room Fritz told reporters, "I'm so damn proud of this team I feel like crying." But quickly he cautioned his team that a vote had not been taken on the Rose Bowl representative, and Ohio State remained to be played.

Michigan's Gene Derricotte intercepts a Wisconsin pass as everything went right for the Wolverines in a 1947 victory over the Badgers that wrapped up the Big Nine title. Pete Elliott (45) also was on the spot.

Wes Fesler told a Friday night pep rally of 4,000 that his Buckeyes would win. Fesler's team had not had a good season, and losing to Michigan was not the way to close it. Francis "Close the Gates of Mercy" Schmidt lost a 40-0 decision to Michigan in 1940 and was not around the next season. After the 58-6 defeat in 1946 to the Wolverines, Paul Bixler left.

Ohio State with only two victories was a heavy underdog, but the Buckeyes played extremely well against Crisler's powerhouse. Michigan, however, had too many weapons and capped the perfect season with a 21-0 victory.

Michigan won nine straight games, scoring 345 points to 53 for the opposition. When the Big Nine selected the Wolverines as its Rose Bowl representative, there were no objections from Southern California this time.

Recount After The Roses

The Big Nine championship was not the end of the 1947 season at Michigan, and Fritz Crisler immediately started to remind his players of that extra game as the honors and praise began to build for the Wolverines.

Chappuis and Bump Elliott were named all-Americans. Chappuis led the conference in total offense for the second straight season and was runner-up to Notre Dame's Johnny Lujack in the Heisman Trophy balloting. Behind his running and passing from the tailback spot, Michigan led the nation in total offense, averaging 412.7 yards a game. The Wolverines also boasted the best passing average of 173.9 yards.

Elliott, the only two-way player on Crisler's platoon forces, led the league in scoring with 54 points and was voted Michigan's and the Big Nine's most valuable player.

Crisler was voted Coach of the Year, and about the only honor not afforded Michigan was the national championship which went to Notre Dame. Michigan, however, would have something to say about that championship.

Crisler told his players, "You are going out to California to play a football game. Southern Cal is a good team, so don't underrate it. You will be praised and told how good you are. I only hope you men will properly evaluate this praise and not let it go to your head. Flattery is lethal."

Michigan left December 18 on the *Mercury* to Chicago and there boarded the *Santa Fe Super Chief* for the trip to California. Special cars were assigned to the party of 104,

including 44 Michigan players. A final touch was added by Santa Fe Company officials who ordered a piano in the lounge after learning that Dan Dworsky was an accomplished pianist.

When the train arrived in California, Hilkene told reporters, "We are not here for a joy ride." Still, Crisler was concerned over the mental attitude of his team, a solid 15-point favorite over the Trojans. Crisler's spirits were not lifted when Chappuis tore a leg muscle jogging in practice.

Michigan's players attended a rehearsal with Bob Hope; they met Charlie McCarthy and Edgar Bergen, Loretta Young,

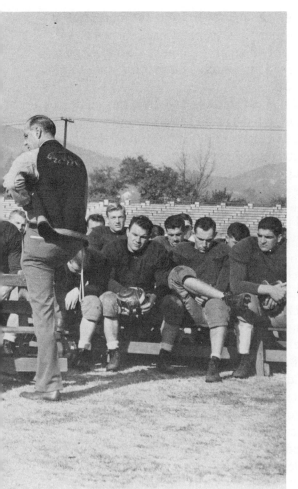

Crisler was worried about his team's attitude for the 1948 Rose Bowl game, and here he has the final meeting with his players.

Marlene Dietrich, and toured the studios. Bump and Pete Elliott played golf with Bing Crosby. Pete, who earned four letters in golf at Michigan, shot a 44, Bump a 39, and Crosby came in with a 37.

Finally, Crisler called a team meeting. Serious, somber, he reminded them of the season, of the final game remaining. Rifenburg made no comment. Crisler was fearful his team would not be ready. The players knew they would be.

A crowd of 93,000 sat in the hot California sun on New Year's Day, and after 60 minutes there was no doubt Michigan had come to play. It took nearly 10 minutes, but Jack

225

Weisenburger finally spun his way over from the one after a march of 54 yards. Michigan then stormed back on a 41-yard drive, and Weisenburger scored again. Chappuis, operating on a wounded leg, jump passed to Bump Elliott for the third touchdown of the first half.

Southern Cal could not get started. One drive carried deep into Michigan territory, but linebacker Dick Kempthorn came up with an interception. Michigan retained control of the game in the third period as Chappuis threw another touchdown pass, this one covering 18 yards to Yerges. Weisenburger scored his third touchdown at the start of the fourth period, then little Hank Fonde and Gene Derricotte combined on a 54-yard touchdown pass. Crisler had labeled it a "129 Pass," to be used only when Chappuis and Bump Elliott were in the game. It involved some intricate ball-handling as the fullback spun, faked to the tailback, then pitched to the wingback coming around on an apparent reverse. Instead of running, however, the wingback would pass to the tailback, who had circled to the left.

Pete Elliott, playing quarterback instead of Yerges, called "129 Pass" and Fonde, in the game on offense for the first time, pulled the play off perfectly.

When Yerges passed to Rifenburg for the final touchdown and Jim Brieske booted his seventh straight extra point, Michigan had a 49-0 victory—the identical score rolled up by Yost's first Rose Bowl team in 1902.

Chappuis completed 14 of 24 passes and ran for 91 yards. Weisenburger, on his destructive spinners, gained 95 yards as Michigan produced a record 491 yards on offense. It was a performance seldom seen in college football. Braven Dyer of the *Los Angeles Times* wrote, "Aw, well, it wasn't as bad as we expected; it was worse."

Red Blaik of Army noted, however, "The great backfield precision and ballhandling certainly is to be admired, but nothing can be accomplished without sound blocking and tackling, and Michigan excelled in both."

Bill Pritula, a veteran from the 1942 team; Dom Tomasi and Stu Wilkins, the freshman guards of 1945; center J. T. White; and the captain, Hilkene, had their finest hour on offense. Al Wistert, the 32-year-old Marine veteran, Len Ford, Joe Soboleski, Quent Sickels, and linebackers Dan Dworsky and

Dick Kempthorn led a defensive charge that held the Trojans to 133 yards in total offense.

In a special Associated Press poll after the Rose Bowl game Michigan was voted the national championship by a wide margin (226 to 119). The season was complete...almost.

Crisler Retires,
The Single Wing Remains

The Rose Bowl hoopla had cleared, and as a final touch to the 1947 season Fritz Crisler in March announced his retirement from coaching. His successor as Michigan's head coach was Bennie Oosterbaan, "The one man who could retain our single wing, and the finest football mind I know," Crisler said.

Retiring as a champion is the ideal way to go, but Crisler had other thoughts—recruiting, building programs, administration. All these weighed heavily on his decision.

"I knew the door of recruitment of college athletes was opening," Crisler said. "It was only a matter of time before the college would seek the man, instead of the man seeking the college. And, personally, I would never be able to recruit.

"I realized we had been making a great deal of money, and nothing had been done to improve our athletic plant since Yost built the field house and stadium. There was a pressing need for expansion in this area. I felt my entire energies should be directed toward building projects and the pressure of administrative duties.

"I knew we had a fine group of players returning, well-drilled in the single wing formations. I guess with the T-formation becoming so popular, it would have pleased a great many of our alumni if we had hired someone with that type of background, but that would not have been fair to the men coming back. There was only one man, in my judgment, who could preserve everything we had built and also was an outstanding coach, Ben Oosterbaan."

228

Bennie Oosterbaan took over as Michigan's head football coach in 1948 and guided the Wolverines to a national championship his first year.

There had been dramatic attendance increases at Michigan. In 1941 a total of 6,958 season tickets were sold to non-students. This increased to 20,293 in 1947. Season tickets to students totaled 10,639 in 1941 but jumped to 21,304 in 1947. During the 1946-1947 seasons Michigan drew nearly a million paying customers. With money in the bank, Crisler went to work.

The possibility of a second deck on Michigan Stadium was investigated. The footings to support such an expansion had been provided by Yost, but the cost averaged out to $90 a seat. Crisler decided to replace Yost's "temporary" wooden stands that rimmed the top level of the stadium with permanent steel stands at a cost of $11 per seat. This increased the seating to 97,239. A modernization of the stadium, including the press box in 1956, hiked the capacity to 101,001.

Crisler's building projects included a varsity swimming pool, a $1 million pool for women, an athletic administration building, and a golf club house, all financed with athletic department funds. And, finally, before he retired in 1968, a new all-events building would be completed. One of his former players, Dan Dworsky, would design it, and the Regents would appropriately name it Crisler Arena.

Crisler took care of the building projects, and Oosterbaan took care of the single wing, that precision philosophy of football that Crisler had been developing since 1930. Crisler first used the buck-lateral while at Minnesota against Northwestern as his fullback Jack Manders received the ball, drove into the line, and handed off to the quarterback, who pitched or lateralled to the wingback coming around. That play went for a touchdown the first time he used it.

He used Manders on a half spin into an unbalanced line, then at Princeton put in the full spin for the fullback. The deception was growing. Coming to Michigan in 1938, he saved the full spin until the final game of the season when a little known fullback, Wally Hook, had an outstanding afternoon in an 18-0 win over Ohio State.

The full development of the spin and buck-lateral evolved with the addition of three or four new plays each season. Blocking became identical on all the various options. Perfection was achieved, Fritz recalled, "when the fine artist Jack Weisenburger came along and the spin and buck-lateral were combined. Weisenburger would fake to the tailback, then to the wingback on a spin, go up and do the buck-lateral with the quarterback. Any back could end up with the ball. It provided a combination of three separate and distinct maneuvers with the same blocking.

"After my second year at Michigan, the balanced line and short punt were discarded. In 1942 the man in motion was added together with the unbalanced line and 'Alumni T.' Only a few plays were introduced from the T, enough to lead the alumni to believe we were progressing when everybody was adopting the T."

230

That was the Michigan system Bennie Oosterbaan knew so well and the system he would use to lead Michigan to another championship.

Ben's National Champions

It was an unusually calm day in the Pacific, and Alvin Wistert was walking on deck when an officer approached him.

"Say, aren't you the Wistert from Michigan?" he asked, enthusiastically shaking Wistert's hand.

"No sir, those were my brothers. I never attended college," Wistert replied.

The officer looked at the 6-foot-3, 220 pounder for a moment, turned abruptly on his heel, and walked away.

That shipboard incident in 1945 was the start of a startling football career for Al Wistert, a high school dropout. He did not want to walk in the shadows of his older brother, Francis, a Michigan all-American, or his younger brother, Albert, another Michigan all-American. He spent five years in the Marines, but following his discharge Wistert passed a series of tests and entered Boston University. He had never played high school football, but as a 30-year-old freshman he became Boston U's first string tackle in 1946. A year later he transferred to Michigan and played on Michigan's 1947 Rose Bowl championship team.

He had been a good player but not an all-American. That was the goal for 1948, the third Wistert to earn all-American honors at Michigan.

Wistert was one of twenty-one Michigan lettermen returning for Oosterbaan's first season as head coach. The entire starting backfield had been lost, including Bump Elliott, who

232

was ruled ineligible by the Big Nine despite strong protests by Ralph Aigler, Michigan's faculty representative. Elliott played three games in 1943 and six games in 1944 for Purdue, but all the games came during the one school year he was assigned there by the Marines.

The single wing attack was left in charge of Pete Elliott at quarterback, Gene Derricotte at tailback, Wally Teninga at wing, and Tom Peterson at fullback. Two sophomores, Chuck Ortmann and Leo Koceski, were moving up from the freshmen team. Rifenburg, Tomasi the captain, Wilkins, McNeill, Soboleski, Sickels, Ralph Kohl, and the linebacking combination of Dworsky and Kempthorn were all back.

Michigan took a 14-game winning streak into the 1948 opener at Michigan State, and Oosterbaan was determined to add to that record. He devised a series of three plays for the opening series. The third was called "six points." MSU's great halfback, Lynn Chadnois, played the right side defensive corner, and Oosterbaan wanted to take advantage of his great desire to tackle the ball carrier at the line of scrimmage.

Derricotte returned the opening kick to Michigan's 45, and Oosterbaan's "six point" series began. Peterson hit at right tackle for a couple of yards. On the second play Elliott lateralled to Peterson who swung to his left for good yardage as Rifenburg blocked Chadnois. The ball was now on State's 41. Peterson again swung to his left on an apparent repeat of the previous play, and this time Rifenburg faked a block on Chadnois and turned up-field. Peterson stopped and fired a pass. Rifenburg was completely alone and took the ball for the "six points," just as Oosterbaan had diagrammed it.

The Spartans of Biggie Munn fought back to tie the game at 7-7, but Michigan began moving in the fourth period. Derricotte was injured early, and Ortmann, responding to the pressures of his first college game, fired two key passes, to Irv Wisniewski and Leo Koceski. Peterson finally took the ball in from the five. The 13-7 win was not impressive.

Derricotte was on the shelf the next week, and Ortmann had to match passing talents with Norm Van Brocklin of Oregon. Ortmann and Rifenburg teamed up on a 61-yard scoring pass in the second period, and, after Ortmann was injured, Chuck Lentz tossed a key 35-yard pass to Pete Elliott.

233

This set up a short touchdown run by Peterson. Van Brocklin, who Michigan's freshman coach Wally Weber said, "has the accuracy of a Swiss watch," completed 13 passes for 194 yards, but the Dutchman was not enough as Michigan prevailed, 14-0.

Michigan then put it all together against Purdue, winning 40-0. Rifenburg, on his way to all-American honors, caught one touchdown pass from Ortmann and made a diving catch on Purdue's five to set up another score. Northwestern became Michigan's third straight shutout victim, 28-0, as Koceski scored three times. Two of them came less than a minute apart on passes, one from Teninga and one from Ortmann, to break open a tight game.

The next week Leo Nomellini fell on a fumble to score first for Minnesota, but Michigan stopped the Gopher rushing attack with 22 yards and posted a 27-14 win. Teninga passed 14 yards to Peterson for one touchdown, and Sickels recovered a blocked punt on the one-inch line to help Peterson to his second touchdown. The Gophers came back to take a 14-13 lead before Michigan could break it open with the most spectacular play of the season. Peterson fired a long pass that appeared to be intercepted by Minnesota's Ev Fraunce, but he batted the ball in the air. Rifenburg came down with the ball, took two strides toward the end zone, and fumbled. Trying to retain possession he literally dribbled the football to the goal line for the touchdown, as Harry Allis threw a block that cut down five players, including two of his own teammates. Rifenburg then threw the key block to spring Koceski loose, who caught a pass from Ortmann and ran 64 yards to score.

Illinois had thoughts of an upset the following Saturday as an unheralded junior, Bernie Krueger, hit 12 of 21 passes for 216 yards. Rifenburg caught another scoring pass to break a 7-7 deadlock, but Ortmann had to hit Allis with a 45-yard touchdown strike to cement the wild 28-20 victory.

Michigan next handed Navy its first shutout of the season, 35-0, with Ortmann scoring his first collegiate touchdown. A 54-0 thrashing of a weak Indiana team gave Michigan a chance for an undisputed Big Nine title. Only a victory over Ohio State in Columbus was needed.

Thoughts of championships usually created some tension, and it was evident the Michigan players were concerned over

Dick Rifenburg, one of the finest pass catchers in Michigan history, earned all-American honors on the national championship team of 1948.

their final game of the season. Rifenburg, however, was quick to remind them there was nothing to get excited about, "After all," he dead-panned during the bus trip to the stadium, "it's only 22 wins in a row, you know."

Michigan had to come from behind for No. 23. Ohio State took a quick 3-0 lead, but Ortmann unloaded a 44-yard touchdown pass to Allis. After Ortmann was injured, Teninga stepped in to direct a final, 57-yard scoring drive, the payoff coming as Peterson scored his ninth touchdown of the season from the Ohio three. The final was 13-3.

There was no doubt about it this time, Michigan's Wolverines with a 9-0 record were No. 1 in the nation, and a

Chuck Ortmann (49) scores the first Michigan touchdown on this 10-yard run in the 1949 battle for the Little Brown Jug,

trip to the Rose Bowl was not required to earn the national championship. Northwestern, finishing second to Michigan, made the trip and defeated California, 20-14. It was the first time the "no repeat" rule kept the conference champion at

236

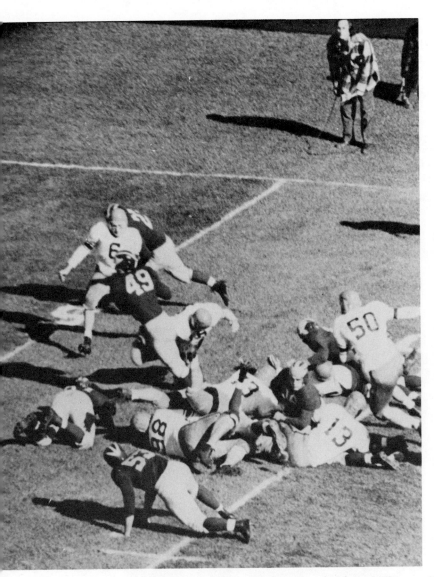

won by the Wolverines 14-7. Al Wistert (11) and Harry Allis (88) clear the way.

home on New Year's Day.

The 41-year-old Oosterbaan was voted Coach of the Year in his first season. Never before had different coaches at the same university been accorded this honor in successive seasons.

Michigan broke Big Nine records for defense against the rush, yielding only 70.2 yards per game, and shattered its own conference passing record with a 151-yard per game mark as ten different players contributed to the aerial act. Allis, the end and placekicker, won the scoring championship with 40 points.

Rifenburg, Wistert, and Pete Elliott were named all-Americans. Tomasi was voted the team's most valuable player and the 20-year-old guard from Flint then turned his captaincy over to the 32-year-old "third" Wistert for 1949. The "old man" with number eleven on his jersey would be back for another season, another championship.

Dom Tomasi played as a 17-year-old freshman in 1945 and later captained the Wolverines.

A Premature Burial

Bill Putich, a third-string quarterback, sat nervously on the bench. The sidelines were alive with shouts and yells of encouragement to the Michigan defense. He tried, as best he could, to join in. Then suddenly Michigan Stadium seemed to shake as nearly 100,000 fans erupted into one, vast roar. Dick Kempthorn's murderous tackle on Michigan State's Frank Waters had stripped the big fullback of the football. Lloyd Heneveld had it on State's 25.

It was the opening game of the 1949 season, and everything seemed so unreal for Putich, a stocky, 165 pounder, who was dressing for his first varsity game. He held a faint hope that he could play, but that was unlikely. The Spartans had taken a 3-0 lead, and halfway through the second quarter the Wolverines were still scoreless. Coaches in Ohio had told him he was a little too small to play, but now he was with a team that had won twenty-three straight games, the defending national champions. The tension was real.

Putich watched as Don Dufek powered down to State's 15. The Spartans tightened. Three assaults at their defense were turned back, and Michigan, facing a fourth and six on the eleven, called time out. Then he heard it, "Putich, Putich." Coach Bennie Oosterbaan wanted him. Putich reached for his helmet, fumbled it, got it. "God knows, I almost missed the train," he thought.

Oosterbaan looked at his sophomore. "Right half at 6 pass;" his voice had a sharpness, a confidence that Putich

239

understood.

Putich made the long run from the bench to the huddle. It was his first play, a T-formation play. He took the snap from Bob Erben, faked a pitchout to Dufek going left, and Chuck

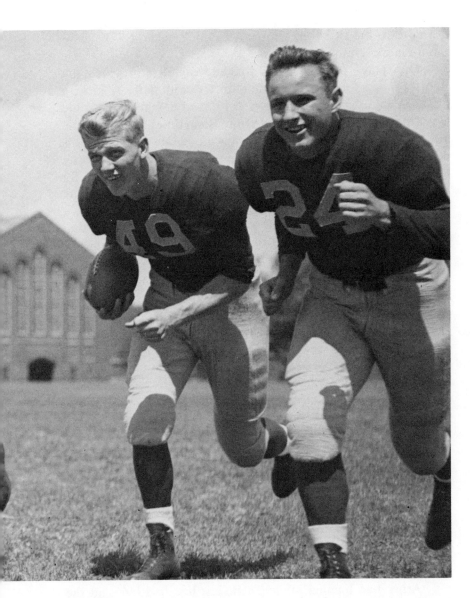

Michigan's 1950 backfield of Leo Koceski, Don Dufek, Chuck Ortmann, and Bill Putich.

Ortmann hit the defensive end with a resounding block. On the other side Irv Wisniewski, using a block and delay pattern, slipped down the right sidelines unnoticed. Putich saw him and floated a soft, arching pass. Wisniewski grabbed it, and easily

241

trotted into the end zone. Harry Allis' kick made it 7-3. There was no more scoring in the game.

One play, 10 seconds, a touchdown. That provided the tipoff for a football season that drifted with fate. A kick, a punt, an injury would decide victory...and defeat. For Bennie Oosterbaan, his exacting preparations sometimes seemed futile, but often from adversity rose a new hope. He had based his offense in 1948 on the considerable talents of Gene Derricotte. His injury in the first game ruined these plans and brought a sophomore into prominence, Chuck Ortmann. Now he had gone to his third-string quarterback and achieved victory.

The following week under a blistering California sun, Michigan made it twenty-five in a row with a 27-7 conquest of Stanford. The heat and a leg injury to captain Al Wistert left Michigan with a tired, battered club to face another strong Army team.

Oosterbaan watched in despair as Michigan's chances for victory all but disappeared. Ortmann, carrying the ball on the second play of the game, went down, and a foot accidentally struck his head. He was carried from the stadium on a stretcher with a mild concussion. With Ortmann gone Michigan's passing game became a shambles. The Wolverines threw twenty-three times and connected on only three. Four of them were intercepted, including one damaging Army theft in the fourth period. The Wolverines, trailing 14-7, had driven to Army's 16 and needed a yard for a first down when the pass was picked off.

Quarterback Arnold Galiffa directed the Cadets 89 yards for their first touchdown, and they used a pair of Michigan fumbles to generate two more in the 21-7 victory. College football's longest winning streak in a quarter century stopped at twenty-five.

Army had handed Michigan its last loss in 1946, and the following week a still stunned Wolverine team had met Northwestern and escaped with a tie. They were not as fortunate this time. The Wildcats and Michigan each scored three touchdowns, but the three extra points by Eddie Nemeth provided the difference for the Wildcats, 21-20. This, too, was Michigan's first Big Nine loss since 1946.

The *Detroit Free Press* headlines stated, "The King Is

Dead!" and sportswriter Tommy Devine wrote under an Evanston dateline: "Michigan fell with a dull thud into the ranks of football's also rans."

If the previous two weekends were wrought with problems, the future loomed even darker. Out of the northlands, their thoughts on the conference championship and the Rose Bowl, came the Golden Gophers of Minnesota. Undefeated and boasting the finest line in football, short of the Chicago Bears, the Gophers were two-touchdown favorites. When Koceski and Erben were ruled out of the game, it appeared that Michigan's homecoming should be postponed.

A capacity crowd of 97,239 jammed Michigan Stadium with hopes for the impossible. They were not disappointed. Michigan turned to defense, hard, bruising defense, and pulled off a stunning 14-7 upset. A pass interception by Chuck Lentz triggered Michigan's first touchdown. Ortmann, in a dazzling performance of running and passing, hit Allis for 19 yards, and eventually the blond tailback scored from the four. After Dufek had intercepted another Minnesota pass, Ortmann again connected with Allis for 22 yards. Don Peterson, Tom's younger brother, scooted to the 13. Oosterbaan sent in Putich, and he passed to Wisniewski at the 5. Putich stayed in for a *second play* and passed to Teninga at the one. Teninga then crashed in for the touchdown.

Minnesota scored when an abortive Michigan punt attempt hit a Gopher lineman and was recovered in the end zone. Linebacker Dick Kempthorn was overpowering on defense as a team that averaged 5 yards a play settled for 67 yards on the ground and waited until the fourth quarter to earn a first down by rushing. Ortmann completed 9 of 17 passes for 92 yards and rushed for 115. The upset ranked among the finest in this classic rivalry for the Little Brown Jug.

The load did not become lighter the following week. It was Bob Zuppke Day in Champaign, the 25th anniversary of the stadium dedication and Red Grange's historic five-touchdown afternoon. Illinois, unbeaten and once tied, had visions of the Rose Bowl, and it had a modern version of the "Old Redhead"–9.9 sprinter Johnny Karras.

Michigan was not impressed. Ortmann, working from the Michigan 49, fired a long pass to Allis, who tipped the ball with

Halfback Leo Koceski (18) sprints around end in the 1948 Northwestern game won by the Wolverines, 28-0. Chuck Ortmann (49) helped spring Koceski on this run.

one hand, caught it, and raced for the touchdown. Later, Teninga's punt, which rolled out on Illinois' six, helped set up a short drive for Michigan's other score. Karras gained 122 yards, but when he did break free and had the chance to go all the way, Michigan end Bob Hollway ran him down from behind. It was a 13-0 shutout.

Michigan now was in good shape for a run at the title. Purdue offered its great running star, Harry Szulborski, but Michigan had numbers. The Wolverines, leading 7-6, started to move on an 82-yard kickoff return by Ortmann. Don Peterson scored on the next play. Lentz then came up with his seventh interception of the season, and Michigan drove quickly to the 12. Oosterbaan sent in Putich, and the sophomore specialist fired a touchdown pass to Allis.

That 20-12 win over Purdue and a follow-up 20-7 victory over Indiana stirred title thoughts in Ann Arbor. Again the decision would rest on the game with Ohio State, also possessing a 4-1 record in the Big Nine. The Bucks were considered to possess a better offense, Michigan a sharper defense.

The Wolverines did not waste time. The second time they had the ball they moved 31 yards to the Ohio 15. Trapped in a fourth down situation Teninga flipped a touchdown pass to Koceski, playing his first game since his injury against Northwestern. Midway through the final period Ohio State marched 80 yards to score. Jim Hague's first attempt at the matching point was wide to the right, but an offside penalty against Michigan gave him another chance. He made this one, and the game and the championship ended in a 7-7 deadlock.

Because Michigan had been to the Rose Bowl within the two-year no-repeat period, the "electoral college" of the Big Nine sent its other co-champion, Ohio State. A similar situation would arise 24 years later when these two teams would play to a tie and share the title. Only the rules of selection would change, and again Ohio State would travel West.

Michigan, with a 6-2-1 record, finished sixth in the final Associated Press poll. For their six home games, the Wolverines averaged a record 93,892 fans—an incredible figure that may never be equalled in college football.

Ortmann won his second straight conference total offense

The all-American Wistert brothers of Michigan—Alvin (1948-49), Albert (1942), and Francis (1933). Alvin, at the right, was the middle brother in age, but spent five years in the Marines before attending Michigan. After he graduated, jersey number eleven, worn by all three brothers, was permanently retired.

title, picking up 768 yards, and Al Wistert, at 33, did his brothers one better. He was picked for the second straight season as an all-American, and his jersey, number eleven, was retired as a tribute to the three Wisterts of Michigan. He passed along his credentials as captain to another all-American tackle that season, Al Wahl. Among the fourteen seniors leaving Michigan football after 1949 was Dick Kempthorn. He had teamed with Dan Dworsky in 1947 and 1948 as one of the strongest linebacking combinations in Michigan history. Ignored by the all-American selectors, he stood as a giant among linebackers in 1949.

The "Snow Bowl"

The two athletic directors, Fritz Crisler of Michigan and Richard Larkin of Ohio State, had three choices: call the game off, postpone it, or play it. Never before had a Big Nine game been cancelled, and 85,000 tickets had been sold. They tried to contact Commissioner Tug Wilson by phone to learn his feelings. He could not be reached. They decided to go ahead, play the game.

Ohio's worst blizzard since 1913 had covered Columbus with six inches of snow. Winds of 30 miles per hour whipped through the open end of the horseshoe stadium, stacking six feet of snow in the corner. The canvas covering froze on the turf. Playing conditions would be impossible.

But it had been an impossible football year for Michigan, anyway, starting with the opener against Michigan State. Michigan lost to the Spartans for the first time in 13 years, and in the process lost tailback Chuck Ortmann with an ankle injury. He was not needed in the second game, a 27-7 win over Dartmouth. Lowell Perry, a sophomore end, caught one touchdown and intercepted three passes.

Leo Koceski was injured the next week against Army. It was a game the Wolverines had pointed to, and after 44 minutes there was hope the Cadets' string of victories would stop at twenty-two. Army then broke the 6-6 tie with three touchdowns in less than six minutes as everything went wrong: a pass interception, a blocked punt, a dropped pass at the Army five. Army won this last of the four-game series, 27-6, and, strangely, it was accomplished with the manpower of two platoons against the young Wolverines, most of whom played both ways.

Michigan bounced back to defeat Wisconsin, 26-13. Ortmann, showing his former form at tailback, ran 16 yards for one touchdown and fired a 28-yard pass to Bill Putich for another, while Don Dufek scored twice. Any thoughts of a championship or a Rose Bowl, however, appeared gone after a 7-7 tie with Minnesota and a 7-0 loss to Illinois in the freezing snow of Michigan Stadium. Michigan was a step from complete elimination.

Oosterbaan had used four wingbacks but was forced to go even deeper the next week against Indiana. He came up with 5-foot-6, 155-pound Wes Bradford. The little speedster responded by rushing for 105 yards in 15 carries, including a 41-yard touchdown run off a reverse. The 20-7 triumph had Michigan back in the bowl picture...just barely.

Ortmann scored twice and Dufek barrelled his way through the Northwestern line for 110 yards as Michigan dumped the Wildcats, 34-23. When the report came that Illinois had upset Ohio State, the nation's top-rated team, 14-7, the season finale took on more importance. The possibilities were puzzling, but real. Ohio State, a 17-14 victor over California in the Rose Bowl the previous season, could not repeat under conference rules. The Bucks could, of course, earn their second straight championship with a tie or victory over Michigan.

Illinois' upset win over OSU put the Illini directly on the Rose Bowl path. They needed only a win over Northwestern to make it. Wisconsin even held out hopes. Victories by OSU and Northwestern would send the Badgers to Pasadena.

This wild, unpredictable season was nearly behind Michigan. Because of the slim chance of everything fitting into place—a victory over heavily favored Ohio, an upset by Northwestern over Illinois—Oosterbaan's players were relaxed. Tensions had long since passed. When their special train pulled in alongside Ohio Stadium, they amused themselves watching fans tumble, slip, and fall trying to walk up the ramp leading into the stadium. Oosterbaan was concerned and snapped, "Let's get our minds on the game."

The game was delayed more than 30 minutes while work crews and volunteers literally ripped the frozen canvas off the field. The snow was picking up force. Temperatures were near 10 degrees.

During the pre-game "warm-up" assistant coach Dick Kempthorn noticed that Ortmann was having trouble handling the center snap. He walked over to Ortmann and said, "Here, Chuck, try these."

The former Michigan linebacker handed Ortmann a freshly cut pair of deer-skin gloves. "I just got them from Colorado," Kempthorn explained.

Ortmann nodded thanks and went back to his punting. It would be a game of punts.

Early in the first period Ortmann dropped back to punt from his own eight. He never had a chance as a Buckeye rushed in to block it. Bob Momsen of Ohio State, the brother of Michigan's linebacker, Tony, chased the ball down at the six. Three plays later Ohio was back on the 21 with fourth down. Vic Janowicz then drove the ball into the teeth of the gale, straight over the cross bar for a field goal.

Late in the first period Michigan slashed into Ohio's lead. Ortmann floated a punt out at the four, and Janowicz immediately went deep into the end zone to punt on first down. Wahl charged in and blocked it, and Al Jackson chased the ball down. The officials ruled that the ball had left the end zone before Jackson could grab it and awarded Michigan two points.

The game remained stalemated as the ball changed hands eight times in the second quarter before Michigan took a weak Janowicz punt on Ohio's 28. Ortmann drove to the 22. Dufek was stopped. Putich barely missed connections with Perry at the goal line. Allis then tried a field goal which sailed to the left.

Janowicz immediately punted from his 20, and Ortmann punted back to Ohio with 48 seconds left in the half. Oosterbaan had said, "Having the ball today is a liability."

Ohio tried to run it out and could not. The seconds ticked down. Michigan called time out. Ohio would have to punt. Michigan's plan called for stacking the right side of the line, hoping to get one man through. The ball was snapped, and as Janowicz's foot hit the ball, so, too, did Tony Momsen. The 210-pound linebacker scrambled after the loose ball and grabbed it in the end zone. It was the seventh time during the season that Momsen had blocked a kick, but these six points might send Michigan to the Rose Bowl. Allis' extra point put the Wolverines in front 9-3.

Visibility dropped to zero in the second half. Ortmann and Janowicz traded punt for punt.

Late in the game Koceski entered the huddle and said, "Northwestern upset Illinois." That was all the incentive needed. The "Snow Bowl" ended with Ohio throwing desperately from somewhere around midfield, no one could tell exactly where. Ortmann punted a record twenty-four times. Ralph Straffon, playing for Dufek who was injured in the first half, was the game's leading rusher with fourteen yards in twelve carries. Michigan never made a first down in the game.

For Oosterbaan, it was a coaching gem. He held a team together through severe adversity. He brought them back when all appeared lost. His offense was not intimidating, but Michigan's defense, for the fourth straight season, was the best in the Big Nine. Wahl repeated as an all-American.

But the year of the impossible dream was not complete.

"Victory Is Still Ours"

For those who were wagering, it was about even money—the 1951 Rose Bowl game. California appeared stronger on its season record. Lynn "Pappy" Waldorf, the old Northwestern coach, had come to the West Coast and produced three championship teams. His latest team had won nine games, tied Stanford, and was rated fourth in the nation.

Michigan offered a paradox. The Wolverines came west with the worst record (5-3-1) of any conference team in the past five years. Still, they had players who could not be overlooked. Chuck Ortmann could sting any team with his running and passing. Don Dufek, his team's most valuable player, was one of the best fullbacks in the midlands. Al Wahl, the team captain, was an all-American on defense, and it would be defense where Michigan might have an edge on the Golden Bears.

The West Coast had seen its last four Rose Bowl teams rocked by members of the Western Conference, but California appeared to have the best chance of reversing that record. It was probably that hope which drew 98,939 fans into the Pasadena bowl, and the Bears were ready and capable of doing the job.

Michigan kicked off, and on the second play of the game little Pete Schabarum turned to his left and raced 73 yards to the end zone. As the play started, however, a flag was thrown and the touchdown nullified by an illegal motion penalty. The Bears kept hammering at the Michigan defense, though, and early in the second period they had their break, an interception of an Ortmann pass. Jim Marinos then threw a 41-yard

253

Don Dufek scored both touchdowns and was named the outstanding player in Michigan's 14-7 Rose Bowl victory over California in 1951.

touchdown pass to Bob Cummings. He slipped by Dufek, caught the ball on the four, and carried the Michigan fullback with him into the end zone. Les Richter's kick for the extra point was wide.

Just before the first half closed, California was on another drive and moved to Michigan's eleven with a first down. Johnny Olszewski slammed to the six, Schabarum carried to the three. Jim Monachino lost one. On fourth down Schabarum was sent at Michigan's tackle fortress and was stopped three yards short with a minute and a half left in the half. Michigan ran out the clock.

California had rolled up 192 yards and held Michigan to 65. The Bears had an imposing 10-2 edge in first downs. In the Michigan dressing room a visitor might have thought these figures were reversed. It might have been the goal line stand. It might have been the 1950 season when they had fought back against all odds to get to the Rose Bowl. Whatever the reason, the confidence among the Wolverines was obvious.

Bill Orwig and George Ceithaml, two of Oosterbaan's assistant coaches who were handling the phones in the press box, suggested some defensive adjustments. In an attempt to counter the quick offensive charge of the Bears, Michigan's linemen had been playing a yard or so off the line. They were brought up to the scrimmage line. Trap plays and screens were ordered.

Then Oosterbaan told his squad, "Victory is *still* ours." It was an attitude of Michigan football, Michigan tradition, and Oosterbaan knew that his players shared it.

Michigan's new defensive alignment closed down Cal's running, and Ortmann, who had thrown only two passes in the first half, started to throw. The score remained at 6-0 until early in the fourth quarter when a California punt sailed into the Michigan end zone, and the Wolverines went to work from their 20. There were 12 minutes left in the game. Ortmann passed to Fred Pickard for 15 yards. He hit Pickard again for nine. Dufek rammed for a first down on the 45, but two running plays left Michigan with a vital third and seven. Putich called the screen. Ortmann waited until Dufek slipped by the Cal right end, then threw. A first down on the 37. Dufek barreled to the 27, then Ortmann connected with Lowell Perry on the 15. Another pass, Ortmann to Allis, gave Michigan a first down on the four.

Dufek hit the Cal line once, twice, a third time. Still inches away. Putich called the identical play a fourth time, and the stocky fullback, driving close to the turf, squeezed into the end zone. Allis converted and Michigan led 7-6.

Michigan scored its first touchdown on a fourth down plunge by Don Dufek to tie California in the 1951 Rose Bowl game as the Wolverines bench explodes.

When Cal elected to pass on fourth down and missed connections, Michigan drove in to score again. This final touchdown came on a trap play with Pete Kinyon pulling from his guard position and leveling a perfect block on Richter, the Cal all-American. Dufek easily scored his second touchdown as the Wolverines produced the most dramatic reversal in Rose Bowl history. After Cal had dominated the first half, Michigan had a 15-2 edge in first downs and a 226-52 advantage in total offense during the final two periods.

Michigan rushed the ball 39 times in the game and Dufek handled 23 of those rushes. He gained 113 yards and was named the game's most valuable player. Ortmann had a dazzling 15 completions in 19 attempts for 146 yards.

The Michigan locker room was ecstatic, and no one was happier than Fritz Crisler. He put an arm around Oosterbaan and said, "Ben, I enjoyed this one more than mine in 1948."

"I liked yours more, Fritz," Bennie replied, then added, "but maybe, I haven't had time to enjoy mine yet."

The Changing World Of Football

The "cribbing" episode at West Point and the basketball scandals brought the critics of college athletics out in full force. Recruiting was intensifying. As Fritz Crisler had cautioned, "The boy must seek the colleges." Now the colleges were seeking the boys.

One writer charged that "College athletics are rotten to the core." Crisler, an articulate spokesman for the game, responded immediately. "I can't go along with that," he told the Football Writers Association. "A system that produces a Nile Kinnick, an Elmer Gedeon, who gave their lives for their country, or kids like Bob Chappuis, like Pete and Bump Elliott, or Chuck Ortmann at Michigan—is not 'rotten to the core.'"

He might have added Dick Kempthorn to the list. The big linebacker, who had served as an assistant coach for Oosterbaan in 1950, left after the Rose Bowl for active duty with the Air Force in Korea. Kempthorn had been on sixty missions and was in a group ferrying planes from Korea to Japan. At Itazuka Air Base one of the planes piloted by Lieutenant Henry Rock collided with a second plane on the runway. The second plane came to rest over Rock's Mustang, jamming the cockpit. Fire broke out. Kempthorn landed his plane, sprinted 200 yards to Rock's burning plane, and ripped off the canopy with his bare hands. The gunsight mounting still prevented Rock from escaping, and Kempthorn ripped that away. Minutes after Rock was freed the plane exploded.

At home Allan Seager, an English professor at Michigan

Dick Kempthorn, one of the strongest linebackers ever to play for Michigan, used his great strength to save the life of a fellow pilot during the Korean War.

Marcus Plant has been Michigan's faculty representative since 1955. He has served as president of the NCAA.

and a novelist who twice was an all-American swimmer, suggested banning varsity sports and added, "Grow flowers in the stadium."

The National Collegiate Athletic Association pressed for tighter enforcement of entrance requirements for athletes and for more control of all athletics by universities. The College Presidents Association decided to take a new look at control of athletes.

Bennie Oosterbaan, appearing before Michigan alumni and many high school seniors, told the young men, "We will not get into a bidding contest for you with any university. We'd love to have you at Michigan and hope you decide to come. But we will not lower the dignity of Michigan to get you. I swore I would uphold this tradition when I took the job."

At Ohio State, Wes Fesler had resigned after the "Snow Bowl" adventure, and Woody Hayes replaced him. Biggie Munn was preparing his Michigan State Spartans for entrance into the Western Conference. Their membership had been approved in May of 1949, but football scheduling problems would delay their participation for the championship until 1953. The Big Nine, however, had become the Big Ten.

The Rose Bowl pact was renewed for three years with the stipulation that no team could compete more than once in a two-year period. The Big Ten also enacted a war-time measure, allowing freshmen to compete in athletics.

Michigan had just completed one of the most successful periods in its football history. From 1938 through 1950 the Wolverines won 92 games, lost 21, and tied 5. That record includes five Big Nine championships, two national championships and two Rose Bowl titles. Oosterbaan, in his first three seasons, compiled a 21-5-1 record. But the days when young men sought out Michigan were fading. A new era of college football was beginning...and not just at Ann Arbor.

No Titles, But Compassion

The preseason ratings of the top football teams in the nation for 1951 listed Michigan seventeenth. "That's all right," quipped Bennie Oosterbaan. "The only reason we're that high is that we're Michigan."

After more than a decade of success, first under Crisler, then under Oosterbaan, the Wolverines were becoming a fixture in these early guessing games. Still, anyone connected with Michigan football could see troubled times ahead. Dufek, Ortmann, Wahl, Momsen, Koceski, and Carl Kreager, the fine center who snapped twenty-four times perfectly for Ortmann's punts in the historic "Snow Bowl" game, all were gone. Captain Bill Putich would lead an inexperienced team.

Freshmen were made eligible because of the Korean "conflict," but Oosterbaan was not counting heavily on them. He hoped some of the sophomores could fill glaring holes in the Wolverine lineup.

First indications that Oosterbaan's concerns were real came in the opener. Michigan State, building a national reputation in football, stopped Michigan's offense with a minus 23 yards rushing and only 29 yards in the air. Michigan suffered its worst defeat ever from the Spartans, 25-0.

Stanford made it two defeats in a row, before Michigan turned it around and won three straight. Putich hit Lowell Perry on a 43-yard scoring pass against Indiana. Iowa was blanked, then Michigan blew the cork of the Little Brown Jug. Perry returned a punt 75 yards to score and caught a Ted Topor pass

End Lowell Perry (85) makes a sensational one-handed stab of a Don Peterson pass in the 1951 win over the Hoosiers of Indiana.

for 71 yards and a touchdown. Wes Bradford, still awaiting his draft notice, scored twice, one coming on a 49-yard run. The 54-27 victory was the highest scoring game in the "Jug" history. Illinois, unbeaten in five games and heading for the Rose Bowl, brought the Wolverines back to reality the following week, connecting on a pass in the final 71 seconds to win, 7-0. It was a repeat of Illinois' 7-0 win the previous season, also achieved on a pass.

Cornell and Northwestern extended Michigan's winless

streak to three, before the unexpected, which was becoming expected, occurred in the season finale against Ohio State. The Bucks were favored, but Michigan staged its finest defensive show of the season to win, 7-0. The touchdown came immediately after the Ohioans figured they had recovered a Michigan fumble on their six. A referee's whistle had ruled the play dead, however, and Don Peterson promptly scored. In Columbus they referred to the game as the "battle of the fast whistles."

The victory lifted Michigan to a 4-5 record overall (4-2 in the Big Ten). It was the first time since 1936 that Michigan had a losing season. Perry, who caught 16 passes for 395 yards, was exceptional on defense and punt returns. The junior from Ypsilanti was named all-American.

Oosterbaan's reconstruction efforts were to continue in 1952. Putich and Peterson, the team's most valuable player, graduated, and Bradford was drafted by the Army, creating severe gaps in the backfield. Ted Kress, a talented, 175-pound junior from Detroit, took over at tailback, Topor was returning at quarterback, and Tony Branoff, a second semester freshman from Flint, began his superb career at wingback. It was to be a year of injuries as Ralph Stribe, a veteran guard, hardluck Frank Howell at wingback, fullback Bob Hurley all were lost at critical times.

After two games it looked like a repeat of 1951. Michigan grabbed a 13-0 lead over highly-favored Michigan State, but lost, 27-13. Stanford made it two in a row before the Wolverines came back to win three straight. Perry's two touchdown receptions helped sink Indiana, then Kress exploded for 218 yards in a cakewalk against Northwestern. He fumbled six times, however, and a "recount" of his efforts resulted in 32 yards being taken from his total, and this denied Kress a Big Ten rushing record. The Wolverines blanked Minnesota to remain undefeated in the conference, then the growing jinx against Illinois struck. Michigan had two punts blocked and did nothing right in the first half as Illinois exploded for 22 points and won, 22-13.

Michigan hammered Cornell with a total offense of 519 yards, then faced Purdue, undefeated in the league and carrying Rose Bowl thoughts. The Boilermakers took a 7-0 lead in the

Ted Kress cuts back away from a Northwestern defender in a 1953 game. He gained 218 yards against the Wildcats at Evanston in 1952, but lost a Big Ten rushing record when yardage was taken away because of several fumbles.

first period, after Perry fumbled the first punt of his career, and took a 10-7 lead into half time. Perry sat on an empty trunk in the corner of the dressing room, dejected, as Oosterbaan talked to the squad at half time. Just before they were to leave, the Michigan coach said, "This game has to be won, if for no other reason than one young man's peace of mind. He is not going to leave here thinking he cost Michigan a victory."

Michigan proceeded to dominate the favored Boilermakers. Kress hit Topor with a touchdown pass. Don Oldham intercepted a pass and Howell scored. Michigan won, 21-10, and set up a season finale with Ohio State that could mean a share of the championship.

November 22 in Columbus again proved a day for an upset. Ohio State rode three pass interceptions and a great running effort by Hopalong Cassady to a 27-7 victory, its first over Michigan since 1944.

Michigan repeated its 4-2 conference record and won five of nine games. It was a near miss again as Purdue and Wisconsin shared the title. The Badgers went to the Rose Bowl and became the first Big Ten team in seven years to lose in Pasadena as Southern Cal prevailed, 7-0.

For the first time since 1945 the all-American listings were devoid of a Wolverine. Perry finished his career by catching 31 passes for 492 yards. No receiver in Michigan history had accomplished more in one season.

Perry, however, had graduated a year too early. In 1953 the rulesmakers decided to put 60 minutes back into the game for each player.

Bennie Oosterbaan thought the decision wise, but his fellow coaches voted four to one against it. College football was back to one team. The platoon system was gone.

Fritz Crisler, the man who pioneered platoon football, made the announcement as chairman of the rules committee. Colleges were dropping football as costs of maintaining two separate squads, the recruiting expense, and coaching staffs were spiraling beyond their means.

The effect on college football in 1953 was profound. Players who were specialists now had to play both ways or ride the bench. At Michigan several starters of 1952 found themselves in just such a position: Tad Stanford, captain Dick O'Shaughnessy, fullback Bob Hurley, and Duncan McDonald, one of the finest passers to come out of the Michigan prep ranks in years. For a player like Gene Knutson, who had been a pass-catching end at Beloit (Wisconsin) High School, but played mainly on defense at Michigan, the new rule enabled him to play 60 minutes.

The rule stipulated that players removed from the game in the first or third periods could not reenter in those periods. It did leave room for some substitution, and Oosterbaan was ready to take advantage of it. Players could reenter the game in the final four minutes of the quarter, if they were pulled in the second or fourth periods.

Michigan unveiled a new 1953 backfield of Ted Kress at tailback, Tony Branoff at wingback, sophomore Lou Baldacci at quarterback, and fullback Dick Balzhiser. Behind that quartet and a forgotten quarterback the Wolverines jumped off to the finest early season showing since 1948.

The Wolverines won four straight, and it was a fourth-string quarterback, Duncan McDonald, who had an arm in two of them. The Flint junior fired the winning touchdown pass to Knutson that tripped Iowa and Forest Evashevski, 14-13. Baldacci kicked both extra points.

The next week Oosterbaan sent him in the game three times against Northwestern, and the skinny, 175-pounder engineered a touchdown each time with his passing. In a rarity Baldacci managed to complete a pass to himself. His toss bounced off a Northwestern lineman and rebounded directly into his hands for an eight-yard loss.

It was the year of the all-American halfback in the Big Ten, and Michigan felt the full impact of two of them. Paul Giel ran for 112 yards and passed for another 169 as Minnesota beat Michigan for the first time in a decade, 22-0. After a victory over Penn, J. C. Caroline rambled for 184 yards, and Illinois made it four in a row over the Wolverines, 19-3. Heavily favored Michigan State next won its fourth straight over Michigan 14-6, before the Wolverines turned it around against Ohio State.

Branoff, operating perfectly on reverses coming out of the single wing, gained 113 yards, more than the entire OSU backfield which included Hopalong Cassady, and the Bucks were never in the game. That 20-0 victory gave Michigan a 6-3 record, but all three losses were to Big Ten teams, including the one to "newcomer" Michigan State.

Illinois and Michigan State tied for the title on 5-1 records,

Duncan McDonald's perfect pass to end Gene Knutson (arrow) deadlocked Michigan with Iowa, and the extra point provided a 14-13 win in 1953.

but the Spartans received the Rose Bowl nod and produced a 28-20 win over UCLA. The vote to send Michigan State was six-to-four with Crisler casting a deciding ballot for the Spartans via phone from New York.

A Season For Upsets

Michigan represented one of the last bastions of single wing football power, but Bennie Oosterbaan was wavering. It was not any glaring weakness in the system that disturbed him, but the material to execute—the all-purpose tailback, the spinning fullback—was becoming more difficult to find. High schools were moving almost exclusively to the T-formation, and Don Faurot at Missouri was embellishing this explosive, quick-striking attack by featuring optional plays for the quarterback. The single wing as a primary offense at Michigan was in its countdown to retirement.

During the 1953 season Oosterbaan could not help but glance over at the freshman practice field and notice an imposing 6-foot-3, 215-pound end, who caught passes like he was stealing green apples off a neighbor's tree. It was evident Ron Kramer was a special athlete. Oosterbaan also thought of his young passer, Duncan McDonald, who had ridden the bench for most of two seasons. The slim senior was not equipped physically for the blocking and running demands of the single wing.

When fall practice opened, Oosterbaan and his staff had decided to install more T-formation plays. Michigan had only three starters returning for the 1954 season; quarterback Lou Baldacci, end Jerry Williams, and halfback Tony Branoff, the team's most valuable player as a sophomore. The football fortunes, Bennie thought, would ride with the sophomores—Kramer, Tom Maentz, Terry Barr, Charlie Brooks, Jim Maddock, Dick Hill, Mike Rotunno, and Marv Nyren. This group

271

Michigan's all-American tight end Ron Kramer (87) scored the winning touchdown in the 1954 Iowa game with this circus catch of a 29-yard Jim Maddock pass.

was the finest class to enter Michigan since 1945, possibly since Harmon and Evashevski in 1937.

Oosterbaan launched the most drastic series of changes since taking over for Crisler. Plays were designed to take advantage of Kramer's exceptional talents. McDonald was inserted as the starting quarterback. Baldacci was moved to fullback where his running and blocking abilities were more than adequate.

The opener against Washington was the first successful test of Oosterbaan's new design. Baldacci scored twice on runs, and McDonald completed 8 of 14 passes for 103 yards in a 14-0 win. Baldacci had to sit out the next game against Army with an injured shoulder as the Cadets romped to their fifth straight win over Michigan, 26-7. Branoff was hurt in the upset loss and joined Baldacci on the sidelines for the Iowa game.

Substitute quarterback Jim Maddock fired a 29-yard touchdown pass to Kramer—Michigan's only pass completion of the afternoon—and Kramer added his second extra point to pull out a 14-13 upset win. Wingback Ed Hickey, however, was added to the growing injury list. The Wolverines then slipped by an unimpressive Northwestern team, 7-0, when Ed Meads recovered a fumble and Dan Cline scored from the one.

The experiment with McDonald and the "T" was not producing the outstanding results Oosterbaan had expected, and, with a favored Minnesota team coming up, Michigan went back to the single wing. Branoff, expected to play only briefly, helped set up three touchdowns and scored a fourth. Kramer caught a 19-yard touchdown pass from Cline as Michigan amassed 443 yards in total offense in routing the previously undefeated Gophers, 34-0.

The victory staked the Wolverines to a 3-0 record in the conference and put them on the path to the roses. Their hopes received a severe jolt the following week, however, when an unheralded quarterback had Oosterbaan thinking about checking with the immigration authorities. Forian Helinski threw the winning touchdown pass and broke up a McDonald-to-Barr pass in the end zone as Indiana pulled off a real shocker, 13-9. The Hoosiers had won only one of their previous five games.

Branoff injured his knee in the Indiana game and had to

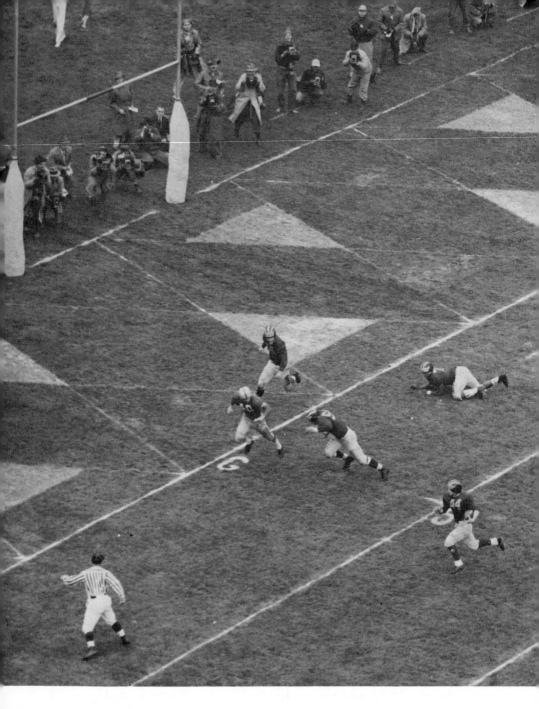

Michigan's famed "Old 83" scored again in this 1954 game with
Ohio State. With a fourth down and one on Ohio's seven,
fullback Fred Baer plunged into the line, and handed off to

*quarterback Lou Baldacci who lateraled to tailback Danny Cline
(44) who scored easily.*

undergo surgery, but his talents were not needed against Illinois. Michigan dusted off the old transcontinental pass as tailback Cline took a lateral from the quarterback and threw to Maddock on the right sidelines for a 21-yard scoring play. That pass broke a 7-7 tie and broke an Illini jinx of four years'

This was the key play in Michigan's loss to Ohio State in 1954 as fullback Dave Hill hits the Buckeye line and officials ruled he was stopped short. Ohio then drove ninety yards to score and won the game, the title, and the Rose Bowl trip.

standing.

It was strictly a band of Michigan opportunists against a fired-up Michigan State team the following Saturday. The Wolverines completed just five passes and gained only eighty-six yards on the ground yet won, 33-7. It was a game of opportunity and Ron Kramer. He helped set up the first touchdown on an end-around, then blocked a punt, grabbed it out of the air, and scored the second touchdown. After the Spartans had narrowed the count to 13-7, Cline passed 63 yards to Baldacci for a score. Kramer blocked his second punt to set Michigan in motion for its fourth touchdown. Three touchdowns in the last 12 minutes of the game broke it open and handed rookie Big Ten coach Duffy Daugherty his first loss in this long and intense rivalry.

The 1954 season came down to another Columbus classic with Rose Bowl bound Ohio State, undefeated in the Big Ten and favored to win. It appeared the game would take its normal upset course as Michigan drove 68 yards to score in the first period. It came on an adaptation of Yost's famed "Old 83." With a fourth down and one situation on Ohio's seven, fullback Fred Baer drove into the line and shoved the ball to quarterback Baldacci. After faking to the right, Cline took Baldacci's lateral and had nothing but grass in front of him as he sprinted down the left side to score. Michigan launched another 78-yard drive, but its destiny was a missed field goal by Kramer.

Ohio crossed the Michigan 48 only once in the first half. That came on an interception and set up a touchdown for the Bucks. Kramer then pressured Hubert Bobo into a weird punt that went straight up into the air, and Maentz recovered it on the Ohio fourteen. Michigan drove to the four and a first down. The next four plays decided the game.

Fullback Dave Hill was stopped for no gain. Cline lost one. Hill hit the line for two. On fourth down Hill rammed the massive Buckeye line again, but 248-pound Jim Parker stopped the Korean War vet a foot from the goal line.

Ohio State then drove ninety-nine yards, two feet to score and added an insurance touchdown for a 21-7 victory. The undefeated Bucks made it eleven straight with a 20-7 win over Southern Cal in the Rose Bowl.

It had been a strange year in the Big Ten. Illinois and Michigan State were preseason favorites. They won one conference game between them. Michigan, not considered at all, battled to the wire finish. Ohio State was rated a darkhorse at best.

Michigan finished with a fine 6-3 record overall and tied

for second place with Wisconsin on a 5-2 conference showing. Art Walker, the big tackle from South Haven, was deservedly named all-American, but in a year of stars Kramer, the sophomore, was overlooked. He would not be overlooked again.

Fifteen-And-Six,
Just Not Enough

College life at Michigan in the mid-1950s was relaxed. Excitement meant the J-Hop and the big bands in the intramural building, homecoming parades, and pep rallies on Friday night when students yelled, "roll them up," and the president of the university or Wally Weber would roll up his pant legs, then deliver a "Michigan will win speech."

Ron Kramer was part of this. He was part of Sigma Chi, along with many of his teammates, like the team captain, Ed Meads, Tom Maentz, Terry Barr, Ed Hickey, Marv Nyren, and John Morrow. Kramer was elected to the Board in Control of Athletics, gave speeches, and played varsity basketball. He was a psychology major, but liked Doc Losh's astronomy class.

When track coach Don Canham, figuring Michigan needed an extra point or two to win the Big Ten Outdoor Championship, asked Kramer to high jump, Kramer high jumped. He tied for fourth in the championship meet, and Michigan won it. Bennie Oosterbaan often would say, "No matter how badly I felt, when I walked on the practice field and saw Kramer and Maentz, I smiled. I was happy. They were the finest ends in college football, and both of them were all-Americans in my judgment."

Football practice in the fall of 1955 was in its second week, and Oosterbaan had only glanced at his kickers. A reporter asked him, "Coach, who's going to do the punting?"

"Kramer, of course," Bennie replied. "Why shouldn't he? He led the Big Ten in punting last year."

Ron Kramer, considered one of the greatest tight ends in football history, twice was named to all-American teams in 1955 and 1956.

"Then, how about the extra points?"

"Kramer made fourteen out of fifteen," Bennie reminded the writers.

"And kickoff, what about that?" the writer asked.

"Probably Kramer," Bennie said and then walked over to

his kickers.

Like Tom Harmon, Kramer was involved in the spectacular, the big plays. Like Harmon, he was part of a team. Maentz also could punt, and for the next two seasons he would lead Michigan in punting. The big end from Holland could catch the football with all the sureness of a Kramer, and Michigan would win games because of it. For 1955, Meads, a durable guard heading for a medical degree, was elected captain. The versatile Barr, and Dick Hill, a lightning-quick guard from Gary, Indiana, and Branoff, cheated from greatness by knee injuries, and Baldacci, who played where Oosterbaan asked him...these were players of unusual abilities.

Ticket sales at Michigan were up ten percent, and the 100th football edition of *Street and Smith* picked the Wolverines to win the 1955 Big Ten championship and go to the Rose Bowl. They were third-rated in the land. Oosterbaan said, "I just hope we're as good as everybody says we are."

Don Faurot brought in his split-T Missouri Tigers to open the season, and he left shocked and impressed. Kramer caught seven passes, three of them for touchdowns, averaged forty-one yards on his punts, converted five extra points, ran the ball twice for nine yards, and boomed kickoffs into the end zone. "He's the greatest end I've ever seen and I've seen a lot of them," Faurot said following a 42-7 Michigan victory.

They were not all that easy. Tony Branoff set up a touchdown with a pass interception against Michigan State, but the Spartans tied it. Michigan was struggling when Kramer blocked an Earl Morrall punt that resulted in the deciding touchdown, but the injury list continued to mount. Maentz, still on the sidelines with a back ailment, was joined by Baldacci, center Jim Bates, and tackle Bill Kolesar.

Oosterbaan was more concerned about his injuries than Army, but Barr handled everything. He caught Jim Maddock's pass for 40 yards and scored on the next play. The 175-pounder then dented the "Long Gray Line" with a dazzling 82-yard punt return to ignite an easy 26-2 win. Kramer, throwing a block at midfield on Barr's touchdown, suffered cracked ribs and missed the next two games. Michigan had to struggle, but won both. Barr's 46-yard scoring run was the difference against Northwestern, but it took a 62-yard punt "on the run" by Branoff

282

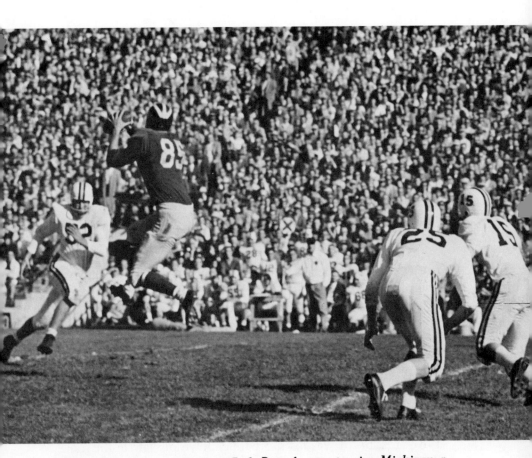

End Tom Maentz spears a Bob Ptacek pass to give Michigan a first down.

near his own goal line to hold off the Wildcats. Barr scored the first touchdown against Minnesota, and Maentz, returning to the lineup, caught the game-winner from Jim Van Pelt. It was Barr's block of a Gopher extra point attempt that provided a one-point win.

Michigan soared to the top of the polls, and Kramer returned for the Iowa game. The Hawks arrived in Ann Arbor with confidence and a couple of fine linemen, all-American Cal Jones and Alex Karras. They immediately rocked Michigan with fourteen points. Baldacci scored easily in the second half, then Branoff passed thirty-three yards to Maentz to bring the Wolverines within a point.

Iowa scored again, and in the press box Don Canham was busy taking pictures of the Hawks' secondary, then passing the prints along to the coaches. They detected a "weakness" and were calling for "passes, passes." Maddock responded by firing a 60-yarder to Kramer, and again Michigan trailed by one. There were just 3 minutes and 35 seconds left in the game with Michigan 91 yards away from the Iowa end zone. Maentz caught Maddock's pass on the 40. Then Maddock drilled a long pass down the sidelines to Maentz. He caught it on the Iowa 20, shook off a tackler, and went the rest of the way to score. The 33-21 victory represented one of the most sensational comebacks in Michigan history and again left Evashevski shaking his head in disbelief.

Illinois was next, and the trip to Champaign again brought frustration. Deadlocked 6-6 at half time, Illinois unwrapped a reserve halfback, Bobby Mitchell. The little sophomore speedster exploded for a 64-yard touchdown and gained 173 yards in just ten carries to stun the Wolverines. Michigan rebounded from that 25-6 upset, however, to blank Indiana and set up a showdown with Ohio State. The Big Ten championship and travel credentials to the Rose Bowl were on the line.

The Buckeyes had a strong defense and Hopalong Cassady, and they were enough for a 17-0 victory in the wildest finish of any football game ever played in Ann Arbor. Cassady gained 146 yards, but it was his short touchdown run late in the game that triggered the fireworks. He fumbled going into the end zone, and Michigan recovered. The officials ruled he had gone over the goal line before fumbling, making it a legitimate score. Michigan argued. Players were ejected; penalties on both teams followed as fans tore down the north goal posts. Snowballs were fired at the players.

Fritz Crisler sent an official apology to OSU officials.

Ohio State won the title, but runner-up Michigan State went to the Rose Bowl and tripped UCLA, 14-7.

The defeat was disappointing. Another near miss after a fine 7-2 record. Barr turned in a superb season on offense and defense and was named Michigan's most valuable player. Maentz, a third-team all-American, was elected captain of the 1956 team and Kramer was selected for every all-American team.

Tony Branoff's running punt saved the day for Michigan against Northwestern in the 1955 victory.

Crisler said, "The last game is unimportant, it's the next game that counts," and Michigan returned for the 1956 season with new hopes and a new look. Face bars and numerals were added to the winged Michigan helmet for the first time. Oosterbaan was grooming a new backfield of speed. Junior sprinter Jim Pace and Barr were the halfbacks; sophomore John Herrnstein, the third member of the Herrnstein family to play football at Michigan, took over at fullback. John's father played in the mid-twenties, and his great uncle, Al, was a halfback on Yost's "point-a-minute" teams.

Oosterbaan's eighth season at Michigan resulted in another

Michigan halfback Terry Barr (41) shows just how rough it can get with this 22-yard reception in the 1955 win over Army.

seven victory showing. The two teams which had denied the Wolverines a title the previous year—Illinois and Ohio State— were defeated. But Michigan State pulled out a 9-0 victory, and Minnesota won, 20-7. Those were Michigan's only two losses, but they were enough to force a second place finish.

The loss to Michigan State, before the largest crowd ever to see a Big Ten game (100,000), resulted from four damaging

End Ron Kramer (87) blocks the first of two punts in 1954 action against Michigan State. Kramer pounced on the loose ball at the Spartan five and scored to lift the Wolverines to a 33-7

turnovers. Minnesota rallied behind the passing of Bobby Cox for two touchdowns in the fourth quarter to pull off the upset. It was that close.

The rest of the season was all Michigan. Herrnstein scored two touchdowns, and Barr fired a 70-yard scoring pass to Kramer in a 42-13 rout of UCLA. Michigan slapped 48 points on the board before Army could score, as Barr again was

win. Also pictured are Fred Baer (30), Art Walker (77), Gene Snider (54), Ed Meads (76), and Ron Geyer (71).

brilliant, and Herrnstein scored on a 60-yard run. The big fullback tallied three more touchdowns in a high scoring win over Northwestern, and 26-year-old Mike Shatusky continued the dramatics against Iowa. The Hawks for the fourth straight season grabbed a two-touchdown lead, only to watch Michigan rally. Evashevski regrouped his forces, however, and they won the Big Ten title, then hammered Oregon State 35-19 in the Rose Bowl.

Pace, the 9.4 track star, began a rise to all-American status by gaining 120 yards against Illinois, while Bobby Mitchell was stopped with five yards in a satisfying win over the Illini. Barr scored three touchdowns in his final home appearance as Michigan stung Indiana. The following week he scored twice against Ohio State, one on a 21-yard pass from Van Pelt, in a 19-0 win that knocked the Bucks out of the championship and prompted Woody Hayes to remark, "Michigan was the best offensive team we have played all season."

Unnoticed Dick Hill was voted Michigan's most valuable player. Line coach Jack Blott called him one of the finest guards ever to play for Michigan. Kramer repeated as an all-American. Seldom playing without injury, he scored 203 points and caught 53 passes for 880 yards, an average of 16.6 yards per catch. He kicked 43 out of 51 extra points. Kramer brought a special intensity to athletics. He never just played sports, he absorbed them. His jersey, number 87, joined Oosterbaan's 47, Harmon's 98, and Wistert's 11 in permanent retirement.

The sophomore group of 1954 played in twenty Michigan victories and seven defeats. In the Big Ten the record was fifteen and six. But for a yard here, a touchdown there, the bounce of the ball...it could have been three golden years of championships.

A Definition Of Victory

Bennie Oosterbaan had been thinking of retiring from coaching. It had been nearly thirty years since he accepted his first coaching assignment under Tad Wieman. He mentioned his thoughts to Fritz Crisler, but the matter was dropped.

Speculation in the newspapers had Pete Elliott coming to Michigan, but the 30-year-old head coach of Nebraska instead accepted an offer from California. When Don Robinson resigned as backfield coach, Bump Elliott, Pete's older brother, was lured from Evashevski's staff at Iowa. He was immediately designated as Bennie's "heir apparent."

Recruiting continued to perplex educators and coaches. Michigan State in 1953 and Ohio State in 1955 were slapped with probation by the Big Ten for alleged infractions. A charge that Michigan collected $100,000 for aid to athletes brought prompt and vigorous denials from Crisler, who said he wanted to know the names of those persons providing all that money.

The Big Ten approved its ill-fated "need program" for athletic scholarships. Room, board, tuition, and books were provided student-athletes in relation to their financial need. Academic scholarships also were approved for those who qualified. The program contained many restrictions, and Phil Dickens, moving into Indiana as head coach for his first year, received a one-year suspension from coaching for reported violations. Dickens argued he did not know about the new regulations, and the program had not even been approved when he made his initial recruiting efforts.

Michigan's all-American halfback Jim Pace (43) finds the going tough against Ohio State in 1957 action. Despite losing to the Buckeyes, Pace, in his final game as a Wolverine, was brilliant as a one-man offense gaining 164 yards.

Each school was allowed a total of 100 scholarships for all sports under the new plan. Michigan sent out ninety applications for scholarships and received seventy-two acceptances. In football sixteen scholarships were granted on the basis of academic achievement and thirteen on the need factor. Crisler figured that the entire scholarship program covering seventy-two grants would cost $60,000 the first year. Michigan could afford the added expense after showing a profit of $566,171.57 for the 1956-57 school year on gross receipts of $1.4 million.

Oosterbaan had guided Michigan to the best football record of any Big Ten school over the previous nine seasons, 56-24-2, but when the reserves defeated the varsity in a scrimmage, prospects for success in 1957 did not appear bright. Michigan offered Jim Pace and Jim Van Pelt on offense, and a defense that would allow more points than any Oosterbaan team in ten years.

Michigan extended its victory string over nonconference opponents to six at the expense of Southern Cal and Georgia, but then ran into sharp-shooting Jim Ninowski, who triggered Michigan State to its biggest win ever over the Wolverines, 35-6. Van Pelt and Pace provided the big plays in victories over Northwestern and Minnesota. Then a series of misadventures struck.

Michigan rolled to a 21-7 half time lead over Iowa, but the Hawks finally reversed the trend of this dramatic series and tied the game at 21-21. Evashevski, remembering the comeback heroics offered by Michigan in past games, decided to run out the clock and preserve the tie. Two missed conversion points and Pace's injury produced Michigan's fourth straight loss in Champaign, 20-19. Pace returned to action the next week and gained 128 yards in a win over Indiana. He was even better in the season finale, rushing for 164 yards, but Ohio State, tuning up for the Rose Bowl, won rather easily, 31-14.

Pace, who led the Big Ten in rushing, was voted Michigan's most valuable player and was selected as the top player in the conference. Van Pelt topped the league in passing, but a reoccuring foot injury to Herrnstein took away much of Michigan's inside power. The Wolverines settled for a 3-3 mark in the league (5-3-1 overall).

Injuries had been a problem in 1957, and the following

season they were worse. Oosterbaan tried to develop more single wing plays to take advantage of his material, but by the end of the season every regular in the backfield had been on the bench with injuries.

Before the season opened, Fritz Crisler, as chairman of the NCAA Football Rules Committee, pushed through the first significant change in scoring in a half century. The optional two-point conversion was approved, and Michigan rode it to victory in the 1958 opener against Southern Cal, 20-19. The Trojans drove for a final touchdown, and, trailing by one point, decided to try for two points and victory. They failed. Bennie had constructed his offense around John Herrnstein, who had been injured most of the 1957 season, and the 215-pound fullback responded with two touchdowns and 144 yards rushing in the opener.

The brightest spot in the season came at East Lansing when Michigan reached into its historic past to battle the highly-favored Spartans of Michigan State to a 12-12 tie. A week later Oosterbaan was trying to pick up the pieces of a shattered offense after Herrnstein was accidentally clipped and lost for the season in a 20-14 Navy victory. Then Northwestern slapped the Wolverines 55-24. There was a brief respite as an injured Bob Ptacek came off the bench to score twice and Darrell Harper sprinted 58 yards for the deciding touchdown in a 20-19 decision over Minnesota. Tackle Willie Smith was injured in the game, and there just was nothing left. First Iowa, then Illinois jolted the battered Wolverines.

Two days before the Indiana game Oosterbaan announced his resignation as head coach, effective after the final game of the season. Bump Elliott was named to replace Oosterbaan, who had decided long before that 1958 would be his last season. Oosterbaan originally had wanted to announce his plans to retire at the start of the season, but Bump rejected the idea. "I agreed," said Oosterbaan. "We had no idea the season was going to turn out like it did."

Oosterbaan shared with Crisler a profound distaste for recruiting, and, rather than become totally involved in it, decided to step out.

Rain poured from the skies for Bennie's final game in Michigan Stadium, the stadium he helped dedicate so brilliantly

John Herrnstein was the captain of Michigan's 1958 football team, while his father, William, played on the 1923-24-25 teams. John's great-uncle, Al Herrnstein, was a star on Yost's teams of 1901-02.

32 years previously. The crowd of 31,000 watched the Hoosiers win in an upset, 8-6. A little of the past remained, however, as Harry Newman, Jr., son of Michigan's all-American quarterback of 1932, scored the Wolverines' only touchdown.

Bennie's 100th game in an eleven-year coaching career came in Columbus. The Buckeyes were favored, but Michigan very nearly pulled off an upset. The game, like the season, ended in frustration. Fred Julian completed the injury cycle in the backfield as he was forced to leave the game, and in the final seconds the Wolverines drove to Ohio's 4-yard line, only to

lose the ball on a fumble and the game, 20-14.

It was Oosterbaan's thirty-third defeat. His teams had won sixty-three games and tied four. His players carried him off the field on their shoulders. Oosterbaan left the way he came, with dignity and maintaining that victory is not always winning, "It's getting everything you can possibly expect out of a team, regardless of the score."

Oosterbaan, as an athlete, could have attended any school. He chose Michigan. Years before, when Bob Zuppke was leaving

Harry Newman, Jr., son of Michigan's former all-American, gains twelve yards against Indiana in 1958. Newman scored the final touchdown in Bennie Oosterbaan's final game as head coach in Michigan Stadium.

Illinois, they contacted Crisler about hiring Oosterbaan as their head coach. "Ben told me he didn't want a head coaching job, he just wanted to do what he was doing at Michigan," Crisler recalled. "I always said, Ben had the most creative mind in football. No one carried on the Michigan tradition better."

With his retirement from coaching Oosterbaan continued to serve Michigan as supervisor of public and alumni relations, a vital area in the athletic department, where he still was able to carry on "the Michigan tradition."

297

The Formative Years

George Van of the *Detroit Times* probably best captured the magnetism of Chalmers "Bump" Elliott. "Bump has a personality that would make most prep stars feel rude to say no."

At 33 Elliott was the youngest coach in the Big Ten. He had worked one spring in 1948 as an assistant at Michigan before joining former Michigan end Kip Taylor at Oregon. He moved to Iowa in 1952 and helped Forest Evashevski build a solid football program, but returned to Michigan in 1957 as Bennie Oosterbaan's backfield coach. When Bennie recommended the young blond as his replacement, Elliott knew exactly what the situation was at Michigan and said, "It will take three to five years to rebuild and win a championship." He was a year off. In six years the Wolverines would win a Big Ten championship and a Rose Bowl game.

It was evident Elliott was in charge. He brought in a coaching staff that looked like a young board of directors: Jack Fouts, 33, from Bowling Green; Jack "Jocko" Nelson, 31, from Colorado; and Hank Fonde, 35, a successful high school coach in Ann Arbor and a former teammate. Bob Hollway and Don Dufek remained. Elliott discarded the single wing entirely, installed his winged-T, and went searching for a quarterback to run it.

The 1959 season opened with losses to Missouri and Michigan State. Bennie McRae, a sophomore track sensation, scored a pair of touchdowns against Missouri, but the Tigers punched across a touchdown with two seconds left in the game

Bump Elliott, a former all-American halfback at Michigan, was named head football coach of the Wolverines for the 1959 season.

to win. Elliott was not impressed with Michigan's showing against the Spartans, saying, "The turning point was the opening kickoff," in the 34-8 loss.

Elliott's first coaching victory came at the expense of Oregon State, 18-7, but Northwestern kept him looking for a conference win with a 20-7 verdict. That first win came the next week against Minnesota as a pair of reserve halfbacks captured headlines. Darrell Harper returned a punt 83 yards and Fred Julian scored on a 42-yard run as Michigan won 14-6.

The rest of the season the Wolverines traded intercepted passes and victories with their opponents. They lost six interceptions and the game to Wisconsin, but a scrappy bunch of third-string defensive players, tabbed the "Raiders" by Hollway, captured the imagination of Michigan fans. Michigan did a reversal against Illinois and intercepted four passes in a 20-15 upset win. An unheralded linebacker, Jerry Smith, whose father had talked him out of quitting the squad, accounted for three of the interceptions.

Indiana intercepted four Michigan passes en route to a 26-7 win, but Michigan came back to upset Ohio State, 23-14, as Tony Rio, the team's most valuable player, took an eight-yard pass from Stan Noskin for one touchdown and plunged a yard for a second score.

The four and five record (3-4 and a seventh place conference finish) was not bad for a rebuilding year. Victories over Ohio State, Minnesota, and Illinois would have produced a championship a few years back, but the power structure appeared to be shifting in the Big Ten. The Pacific Coast Association, trying to weather out internal problems that had split the league, notified the Big Ten that the Rose Bowl pact agreement was being terminated after the January 1, 1960, game. The Big Ten on a 5-5 vote failed to authorize negotiations for the revival of the inter-conference pact but did not prohibit a member from playing in the Rose Bowl. Wisconsin, the 1959 champion with a 5-2 record, made the trip west and lost to Washington, 44-8.

A crisis in the Big Ten was developing as faculty men sought to increase their control of intercollegiate athletics. Angry athletic directors responded by leading a showcase move to ban all postseason athletics for all sports. A power struggle was on.

Michigan continued its improvement program during 1960 with a winning five-four record as an impressive group of sophomores—quarterback Dave Glinka, end Bill Freehan, tackle Joe O'Donnell, and halfback Dave Raimey—gave indications that, indeed, many prep stars were finding it difficult to say no

300

Bump Elliott talks with Bill Freehan, considered the best tight end prospect at Michigan since Ron Kramer. Freehan cut his football career short at Michigan to sign a bonus contract with the Detroit Tigers.

to Elliott.

Raimey and Bennie McRae provided Michigan with its greatest outside speed since the days of Harmon and Kromer. Raimey, a 9.8 sprinter, stung Oregon with a 25-yard touchdown run as Michigan won the opener. Dennis Fitzgerald ran a Michigan State kickoff 99 yards—the longest in Michigan history—but the Spartans pulled out a victory in the final three minutes. Raimey gained 114 yards, and Glinka passed for 111 more as Duke was beaten. A new star appeared and rescued a victory over Northwestern. Bob Johnson, who quit the Michigan Band after his freshman year to "give football a try," brought Michigan from behind when he caught a deflected pass and raced to the NU one. Michigan scored from there to win it, 14-7. Johnson accounted for the first touchdown on a 35-yard pass from Glinka.

The deflections went the other way against undefeated Minnesota. The Gophers recovered five Michigan fumbles and intercepted two passes in their 10-0 shutout. A week later Raimey scored twice against Wisconsin, but a late field goal by Jim Bakken gave the Badgers a 16-13 win.

At this point the 1960 season had been up-and-down for Michigan. The next game, ideally, would go right down the middle, at least for one charming mother who would watch her coaching sons compete for a football victory in the Big Ten.

"Woody Cut The Connection . . . 50-20"

Mrs. Norman Elliott at first was not going to attend the game but changed her mind. On Saturday, warmly clothed and holding a Michigan pennant in one hand and an Illinois banner in the other, she was hoping and praying for a tie game between her sons, Pete and Bump.

Pete Elliott was in his first year as head coach at Illinois and Bump in his second at Michigan. The classic encounter, brother against brother, was a first in the history of the Big Ten. Pete had coached for three years at California, taking his team to the Rose Bowl in 1958, and immediately after his appointment at Illinois the Michigan-Illinois game took on added significance.

Mrs. Elliott almost received her wish for a tie game. Both teams scored a touchdown, but Dennis Fitzgerald grabbed a Dave Glinka pass for two points after Michigan's score, and that was the difference, 8-7. The Wolverines followed this with a 29-7 thrashing of Indiana, then lost 7-0 to Ohio State.

Michigan's 5-4 record in 1960 was an improvement. Despite a league mark of two victories and four defeats, the Wolverines led the Big Ten in defense.

More scoring was the prime goal of Elliott and his staff for 1961. The Wolverines responded with 212 points and a fine 6-3 record overall, but still managed only an even split in six conference games. The prospects of a successful season were not helped when end Bill Freehan, after terrorizing Big Ten pitching in baseball, signed a bonus contract with the Detroit Tigers. The

303

big Detroiter was considered the finest athlete to attend Michigan since Ron Kramer. Then tragedy struck as Phil Garrison, a sophomore tackle, and Joe Sligay, a center, were killed in accidents. The team was captained by George Mans, and included a fiery guard, Frank Maloney. Both would return to Michigan as assistant coaches and later move on to head college football coaching positions.

Elliott experienced his finest start in three years as Michigan shot up to ninth in the polls after two non-conference victories. Ken Tureaud ran 92 yards with a pass interception against UCLA, and McRae scampered 47 yards to score against Army, which dropped its third straight to the Wolverines. It was back to reality the next week as powerful Michigan State prevailed, 28-0. After slipping by Purdue on a safety, Michigan blew a 20-8 lead against Minnesota. A fumble with three minutes left opened the gates for the Gophers, who received 304 yards from their quarterback, Sandy Stephens, and won 23-20.

Michigan rebounded with three straight victories. McRae's three touchdowns and Raimey's 116 yards crushed Duke. Bump made it two straight over Pete as Illinois fell heavily, 38-6. Paul Raeder, a leading member of the "Raider" squad, scored twice after McRae's 118 yards had softened up the Illini. It was Raimey's Saturday against Iowa, and the fleet 190-pounder rushed for 102 yards as Michigan rallied for victory.

Michigan closed the season against Ohio State, and Woody Hayes was looking for more ammunition in building his Bucks as the nation's No. 1 team. They locked the game away early, then continued to pull out all the stops to score more. After the final OSU touchdown, the Bucks drove across for two points to make it 50-20. It was not quite "58-6," but it would do. Sitting in a press box booth with a phone hookup to the Ohio State bench was a sturdy, intense assistant coach in charge of calling the plays, Bo Schembechler. He said, "After we scored 35, Woody cut the connection. He didn't want to take any more plays from me after that."

Ohio State won the 1961 Big Ten title and made it to the top in one national poll. The Bucks did not make it to the Rose Bowl, however, as their faculty turned down the bid and nearly ignited a riot on the Ohio State campus.

Minnesota had voted repeatedly against renewing the Rose Bowl pact but still accepted the "free lance" bid the year previously in 1960. Their faculty men apparently were impressed by that trip, and after the 1961 season Minnesota changed its vote, breaking the 5-5 deadlock in the Big Ten and enabling a new contract to be worked out. The runner-up Gophers then accepted their second straight invitation to Pasadena and posted a 21-3 victory over UCLA.

Bill Reed, former sports editor of the *Michigan Daily*, had taken over as commissioner of the Big Ten, and his leadership was impressive. The Rose Bowl question was settled, and the need factor was eliminated from athletic scholarships. Academic achievement remained as the sole criteria of financial aid to athletes.

At Michigan football progress had been noticeable. Elliott increased the Wolverine victory total from two, to four, to five, to six. Glinka and Raimey were returning for the 1962 season. Bob Brown, a name out of the past, was elected captain. His father, Robert, Sr., had captained the championship team of 1925. Then in rapid succession Michigan lost kicker Doug Bickle, fullback Bruce McLenna, and end John Henderson.

What appeared to be a promising season turned into a nightmare. First, Nebraska stunned the Wolverines in the opener. An upset victory over Army evened this out, but on successive Saturdays, Michigan State, Purdue, and Minnesota hammered the Wolverines. Michigan never scored a point! Glinka was injured in the Purdue defeat and was lost for the year. Bob Timberlake, a sophomore, took over, then Elliott tried Frosty Evashevski, Forest's son, then Bob Chandler, a senior who had been battling back from a serious knee injury. Wisconsin handed Michigan its fourth straight loss, but Raimey scored two touchdowns.

Deep into the season with no hope of rescue, Bump made it three in a row over his brother at Illinois, 14-10, as Chandler scored from the one in the fourth period. Iowa claimed the next victory, before Ohio State handed the Wolverines their fourth shutout of the season.

Michigan won two games and lost seven and finished dead last in the Big Ten with one victory and six defeats. Michigan had not found itself in such a position since 1936. The

Brother against brother on the coaching lines: With their mother looking on, Pete Elliott (right) led his Illinois team against Bump Elliott and Michigan in 1960, and it was nearly a draw. Michigan won 8-7.

Wolverines scored only ten touchdowns all season, and Dave Raimey accounted for five of them. He finished his career with nineteen touchdowns, a total exceeded only by Tommy Harmon.

It was the year of the Badger. An unknown quarterback, Ron VanderKelen, passed Wisconsin to the championship and the slender senior very nearly pulled out a dramatic victory in the Rose Bowl, but Southern Cal survived 42-37.

You Have To Start Somewhere

Two things were becoming clear about Michigan football. There would be injuries, and Bump Elliott's Michigan team would defeat Pete Elliott's Illinois team.

The season of 1963 at Michigan began with Rick Sygar breaking his leg and ended with the postponement of the final game with Ohio State following a national tragedy in Dallas. Between those two events Michigan would defeat Illinois, but that did not prevent Pete Elliott from taking his team to the Rose Bowl.

The Big Ten race was an open affair. The loosening of the substitution rule produced more confusion than substitutes. Players could enter rather freely on second and third downs, but their entry was restricted on first and fourth downs. Elliott at Illinois, Hayes at Ohio State, and Duffy Daugherty at Michigan State all had talented teams. Elliott of Michigan had material, too, but there was a greenness, an inexperience, there were holes to fill, and of course there were the injuries.

Bob Timberlake had a shoulder problem, and that put the spotlight on Frosty Evashevski as the starting quarterback. Sophomores were moving in: halfback John Rowser, Bill Yearby at tackle, and Tom Cecchini at center. Jack Clancy, less than sensational as a quarterback, was moved to halfback.

Captain Joe O'Donnell, switched from tackle to guard, had improvised a fake punt and run—with himself in the starring role—during fall practice, and the 240-pounder found the perfect spot to use it in the opener against Southern Methodist.

Michigan was at midfield in the second quarter and needed eight yards for a first down. O'Donnell took the center snap and turned the right end, racing 50 yards for a touchdown. "Nobody knew about it until I ran it," O'Donnell said. "I saw something earlier, the first time I punted, that made me believe it would work." The right end had retreated downfield after the ball was snapped, and O'Donnell was convinced, "I would at least get the first down and figured anything after that was gravy." Elliott was surprised but happy as his Wolverines won.

That was the kind of football season it would be at Michigan, prosperity or ruin. It was ruin the following week as Navy's Roger Staubach staged one of the most remarkable performances in the 36-year history of Michigan Stadium. He gained 94 yards running and completed 14 out of 16 passes, the first ten in a row without a miss, for 237 yards. Lost in Navy's 26-13 victory was Bob Chandler's passing brilliance of 9 out of 10 for 138 yards and John Henderson's 6 catches for 103 yards and two touchdowns. It was an exciting afternoon, and everybody from Michigan's players to Naval admirals had praise for Staubach.

Tempers flared and the tackling was heavy as Michigan and Michigan State battled to a 7-7 draw. Chandler tossed 15 yards to Henderson for the first touchdown, and this prevented the Spartans from registering an unprecedented fifth straight victory in a rivalry that recorded its sixteenth straight sellout crowd.

Then Purdue upended the Wolverines, who lost Tom Cecchini with torn knee ligaments for the season. Minnesota kept Michigan out of the victory circle for the fourth straight Saturday, before Timberlake, fully recovered from his shoulder problems, fired three touchdown passes in a 27-6 victory over Northwestern.

Bump maintained his perfect record over Pete and Illinois with a 14-8 upset of the second-ranked Illini as fullback Mel Anthony scored the deciding touchdown. He came back the following week to score all three in a 21-21 tie with Iowa.

Michigan's game with Ohio State was scheduled for November 23, but at 9:30 a.m. on Saturday, Crisler announced a week's postponement. The nation was mourning the death of President John F. Kennedy, assassinated during a motorcade through the streets of Dallas. The Illinois-Michigan State game in East Lansing, which would decide the Big Ten championship, also was postponed until the following Saturday.

The delayed game attracted only 36,424 fans on a cold day of swirling snow in Michigan Stadium. The Wolverines took a 10-0 lead in the first half and remained in front for 49 minutes, 3 seconds before Ohio State rallied for a 14-10 win. The Bucks, stepping out of character with the forward pass, used Paul Warfield to score their first touchdown, and the fleet wide receiver also set up the winning touchdown with a fine catch.

Michigan recovered a fumble and cashed in on Timberlake's field goal, then drove 63 yards to score for its 10-0 lead. The Wolverines made a final bid to rescue victory, but the drive stalled on the OSU seven with 1:46 left in the game.

Pete Elliott and his Illinois team defeated Michigan State and then went on to defeat Washington in the Rose Bowl.

Elliott termed the 3-4 record, "a good season. We went out and went after people." Bump saw something in the record others did not, the making of a champion. It was a year late, but sometimes roses bloom a little late.

Bump's Finest Moment

Bump Elliott's five-year plan was running a year late, but the parts were beginning to form into a championship design. He could see it during the 1963 season, the talent, the drive, the attitude of winners.

The heart of Elliott's wing-T was the quarterback position, and Bob Timberlake was no ordinary quarterback. Intelligent, articulate, the 6-foot-4, 215-pounder was almost like using an extra fullback in the lineup. He could run and pass and was an excellent place kicker.

There would be more speed and depth in the backfield than at anytime in Elliott's six years at Michigan. Fast-stepping Carl Ward and Jim Detwiler were two sophomores who would become starters at halfback. Mel Anthony was an ideal fullback.

Linebacker Tom Cecchini, who recovered from a knee injury, and Frank Nunley formed a solid linebacking pair. Bill Yearby on defense and Tom Mack on offense were two of the finest tackles in the Big Ten. The ends were deep and rich, headed by captain Jim Conley, Bill Laskey, and John Henderson. With more freedom to substitute, Elliott and his staff were not lacking in material. Rick Volk, a quarterback, was reassigned to the defensive backfield.

When the Michigan football team reported back for fall practice in 1964, there was only one member of the "family" missing—Henry Hatch. He had been part of the athletic department for 43 years, and most of this time was spent as the Wolverine equipment manager. Tradition is built by people, and

M	YEAR	M		M	YEAR	M
6	1909	6		0	1941	7
10	1910	0		14	1942	16
9	1934			49	1943	6
	1910	0		28	1944	
		7		26	1945	0
		0		21	1946	0
		0		13	1947	6
		0		27	1948	14
		0		14	1949	7
		34		7	1950	7
		26		54	1951	27
		7				
		20				
		7				

Henry Hatch, with the Little Brown Jug, served Michigan forty-three years, mostly as its equipment manager. He was only one of two (former ticket manager Don Weir was the second) Michigan men elected as honorary "M" Club members by both the "M" Club and by the "M" Club managers.

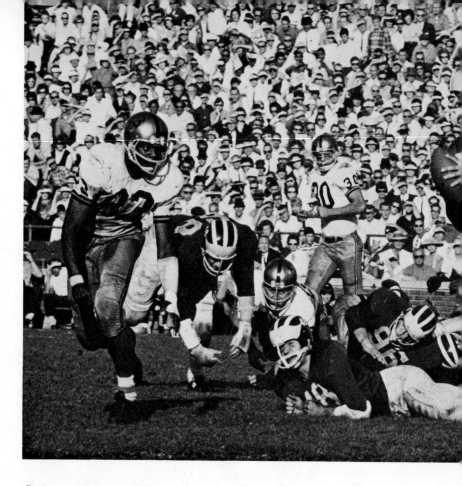

Bob Timberlake (28) led the conference in total offense and became Michigan's first all-American quarterback since Pete Elliott in 1948 as he guided the Wolverines to the 1964 Big Ten

no one symbolized the Michigan tradition more than Henry Hatch. He treated all-Americans and the lowest scrubs the same way—like a father. He sewed, mended, repaired, engineered, and invented football equipment. Every article was for a person, an individual...not just a football player. Henry Hatch had died.

Death came in numbers following the 1963 season: Frank Crawford, who with Mike Murphy was Michigan's first official football coach; Jack Blott, an all-American center and later a line coach under Oosterbaan; and Ralph Aigler, the faculty representative who pushed Michigan back into the Western Conference. Aigler had retired in 1955 and was replaced by Marcus Plant. Plant, like Aigler, became one of the most

312

championship. Here he picks up yardage on an option play against Purdue as the Boilermakers handed Michigan its only loss of the season.

respected faculty men in college athletics.

It was evident early in the season that 1964 could produce something special at Michigan. The defense was deep in numbers and talent. Air Force and Navy were so impressed with the Michigan defense they threw 75 passes in the first two games. Timberlake, who led the Big Ten in rushing in 1963, and Anthony accounted for 250 yards in a 24-7 win over the Air Force. Navy suffered its second shutout in 96 games as Detwiler and Ward combined for 148 yards. Roger Staubach was hobbled by a bruised heel, and the Middies were never a factor in the game, losing 21-0.

The key to the season hinged on the third game against

Rick Sygar takes a five yard pass from Bob Timberlake for a touchdown in top photo, and in bottom photo end John Henderson is catching the winning touchdown pass thrown by Sygar against Michigan State in 1964.

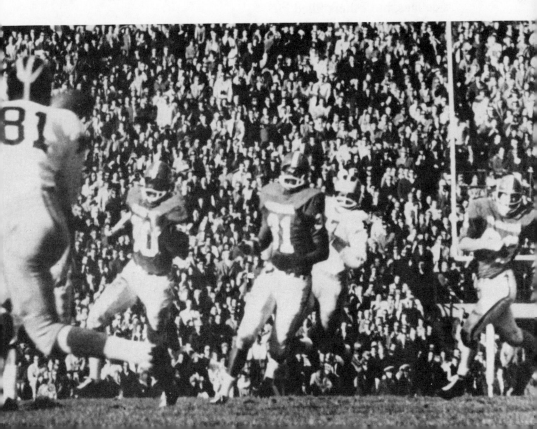

Michigan State, and the Wolverines did it the hard way, scoring two touchdowns in the final period for a 17-0 victory. Rick Sygar, whose career nearly ended when, within a year, his leg was broken twice, caught Timberlake's five-yard touchdown pass. Then Sygar tossed a 31-yard scoring pass to John Henderson to win it in the fourth quarter. The play was used for the first time and involved a pitch from Timberlake to Sygar swinging to his left. Sygar caught three passes as Timberlake hit on 9 of 18 passes for 122 yards.

The victory shot Michigan to fifth place in the polls, before Purdue, still earning its reputation as "Spoilermakers," pulled off a 21-20 upset. Michigan fumbled three times, once in the end zone, yet came back to nearly win the game. Timberlake scored on a 54-yard bootleg play in the fourth period, but when the big quarterback rolled around end on an option run-pass play, looking for two points and victory, he was stopped short.

At midseason injuries began to mount. Several Michigan teams of past years were not able to carry that burden, but this was a special year. Jack Clancy was out for the season, John Rowser, Rich Hahn, and Barry Dehlin followed Clancy to the sidelines, but others filled in.

Michigan almost blew a 19-point lead before outlasting determined Minnesota. A tough, goal line stand saved the Wolverines' first win over the Gophers in five years, 19-12. Northwestern was stopped cold as Timberlake threw two touchdown passes, and Volk fired a third scoring pass in the 35-0 romp. Michigan made it five in a row over Illinois, 21-6, but the nation's top rushing team had to use a fumble and pass interception to start moving. Linebacker Nunley spearheaded a defense that checked the Illini and Jim Grabowski effectively.

Four fumble recoveries and three pass interceptions paved the way for a 34-20 win over Iowa, and the Michigan-Ohio State rerun was on again. Michigan was 5-1 and Ohio 5-0. The Bucks had lost just once, to Penn State, in compiling an overall record of 7-1. Another Big Ten championship and the Rose Bowl trip were on the table.

Elliott could sense that his team was ready. The Michigan campus was ready, staging a pep rally on Friday night to demonstrate it. When the Wolverines came on the field in

Columbus, they were yelling, "Go, Go, Go."

Elliott said, "I think we're ready to play a game."

Captain Jim Conley lost his third coin toss in nine games, but Ohio decided to kick off and take advantage of the gusty, 18-mile per hour wind. These two teams had played nine times with a championship on the line for one or both of them since their game was moved to the final Saturday of the season in 1935. The wind, fumbles, interceptions—coaches call them breaks—figured prominently in many of those decisions. Both Ohio State and Michigan had appeared invulnerable behind their massive, quick defenses, but the break—a fumble—came.

Stan Kemp was averaging 40 yards with his punts, yet late in the second period the specialist from Greenville, Michigan, drove the ball 50 yards to Ohio's Bo Rein. A sophomore sensation for Ohio, Rein had not missed a punt all season, but this one was caught in the fierce winds shooting in from the horseshoe end of the stadium. The ball struck his hands and bounced to the turf. Henderson, sprinting downfield from his end position, dived for it and grabbed the ball on the Ohio 20. Michigan had its break and in two plays had a touchdown on a play drawn up earlier in the week.

The "trailer play" had been designed especially to combat Ohio's quick-reacting linebackers. Michigan unwrapped it for the first time at Ohio's seventeen. Ben Farabee sprinted straight down from his end position as Detwiler trailed him on the play, then cut over the middle. Timberlake rifled the pass to Detwiler on the four, and the powerful halfback scored. There were just 44 seconds left in the half when Timberlake's kick made it 7-0.

The Buckeyes tried to come back in the second half but could not dent the solid defenses of the Wolverines. Rick Volk intercepted two passes and slapped down a third to break up three drives. Ohio gained only 180 yards in total offense. When Timberlake kicked a 27-yard field goal in the fourth period, the game was beyond the capabilities of Ohio.

Elliott said of the 10-0 victory, "This is my happiest moment in football."

317

Rose Bowl IV

The rain and fog of Southern California greeted Michigan's arrival on the coast where a storm of controversy again draped the historic Rose Bowl.

Oregon State and Southern Cal had waged a spirited battle for a berth in the New Year's Day classic. Southern Cal finished its season by upsetting Notre Dame, the nation's top-ranked team, 20-17. The Trojans celebrated for three hours, then the announcement was made: Tommy Prothro's Oregon Staters would play Michigan. USC Athletic Director Jess Hill called the decision, "One of the rankest injustices ever perpetrated in the field in intercollegiate athletics."

Michigan was installed as an eleven-point favorite, and Bump Elliott began to worry. Prothro tabbed Michigan's defense as the best he had seen. Michigan suddenly took on the appearance of a national power, though most West Coast writers were hard-pressed to recognize any of the Wolverines with the exception of Bob Timberlake. The big senior, headed for the ministry, was Michigan's most valuable player. He followed Michigan greats of past years—Friedman, Newman, Harmon, Bump Elliott, Pace—as the Big Ten's most valuable selection in a special poll conducted by the *Chicago Tribune*.

Elliott was quick to point out that Michigan had other players who could hurt a team. He mentioned Mel Anthony, the fullback. He mentioned his defense where tackle Bill Yearby, a junior, was an all-American. He mentioned Michigan's balance.

The Rose Bowl in Pasadena was jammed with 100,423 fans

318

Bill Yearby (75), a two-time all-American tackle at Michigan, watches the 1965 Rose Bowl action from the bench with linebacker Tom Cecchini (53) and end John Henderson (behind Yearby).

on a bright, cool New Year's Day, and it was not long after the kickoff before many of them thought an upset was in the making. Oregon State built a winning record with defense. No team had scored more than two touchdowns on them. When the Beavers scored first, early in the second period, Michigan's fourth straight victory in the bowl was in doubt. Quarterback Paul Brothers completed six straight passes before tossing five yards to Doug McDougal for the touchdown. The doubts lasted only for a few minutes, however.

Timberlake thought he detected an Oregon State linebacker keying on him. When Michigan gained possession of the ball on its 16 midway through the second period, he immediately called a pitch out to his fullback. Anthony took the lateral and blocks by Henderson and Ward shot him past the scrimmage line. He raced 84 yards virtually untouched to score. It was the longest run from scrimmage in the history of the Rose Bowl.

Timberlake missed his first extra point of the season, and Michigan still trailed, 7-6, but later in the period Ward made that misconnection appear unimportant. Timberlake pitched to Ward on the shortside of Michigan's formation, and the little halfback scooted down the sidelines 43 yards to score. Timberlake tried to pick up two extra points with a pass and failed. The half ended with the Big Ten champions leading, 12-7.

Michigan waited until the third period to use a special play Elliott felt could exploit an Oregon State weakness. Assistant coach Bob Hollway while screening films had detected the center lifting the ball just before snapping it on punts. A quick, concentrated three-man rush was mapped out to get a jump on the defense and break one player free. Oregon State had a fourth down on its 39 when guard Bob Mielke roared in to block the punt and set up Anthony's second touchdown. The gates were open, and Michigan touchdowns poured in.

Anthony tallied his third touchdown from seven yards out, then Timberlake dragged a couple of defenders over the goal line on a 24-yard touchdown run. Michigan roared to a 34-7 victory as the Wolverines handed the game ball to their coach.

Anthony was named the outstanding player in the game, another example of Michigan fullbacks appearing to have their finest afternoons in the Rose Bowl. Jack Weisenburger had scored three touchdowns in 1948, and Don Dufek, also the recipient of the Bowl's outstanding player award, scored two in

1951.

The Ohio State victory may have been Elliott's finest moment, but the Rose Bowl of 1965 would remain very special, too.

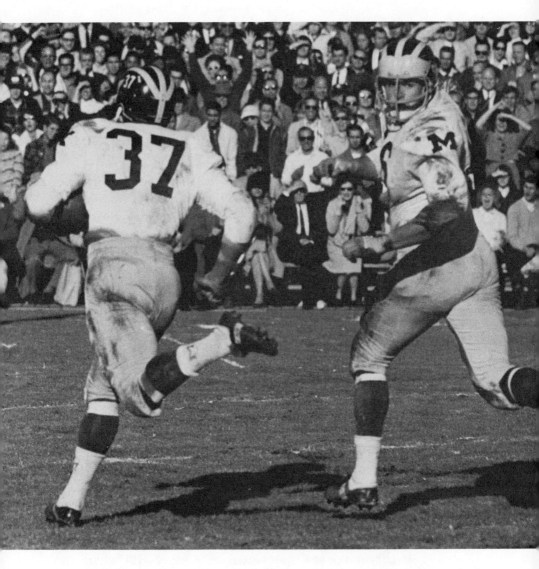

Mel Anthony (37) nears the end zone of his 87-yard touchdown run that set a Rose Bowl record in 1965. Lineman Tom Mack provides the escort.

One Pass Too Many

The Wolverines' 1965 schedule was expanded to ten games for the first time since 1945, and they were favorites to repeat their Big Ten title. But after the first six games, Elliott could only shake his head and say, "I think fate has been more than unkind to these players, and it breaks my heart to see it." Never had a team been hit with more adversity than the Wolverines of 1965. What made it difficult for Elliott to accept was the quality of his players, their dedication, their high hopes of victory, their hopes of repeating as Big Ten champions.

Elliott had twenty-two lettermen returning from his Rose Bowl champions in addition to several key players who missed the title season. Jack Clancy sat out 1964 with a back injury but was back as a wide receiver. John Rowser returned from knee surgery, and Dick Vidmer, who had pressed all-American Bob Timberlake for the starting quarterback job until breaking an ankle, was ready for his first season.

No Big Ten team had repeated as a conference champion in the previous ten years, and there were some concerns that incentive would be lacking because the Wolverines could not return to the Rose Bowl. "We're trying to base our thoughts on being No. 1, winning the national championship," said defensive back Rick Volk.

Michigan opened the season at Chapel Hill where the temperatures were a scorching 100 degrees, and after the 31-24 victory Barry Dehlin, a rugged defensive guard, and hard-luck halfback Jim Detwiler were on crutches. Detwiler came back three weeks later against Michigan State, reinjured his knee, and sat out the rest of the season.

California became Michigan's eighth straight victim, falling 10-7 to Rick Sygar's field goal, but guard Bill Keating was injured and never played again. Then undefeated Georgia upset Michigan, 15-7, the first loss for the Wolverines to a Southern school in twenty-two games. The offense just was not working, and six more fumbles cleared the way for Michigan State to jar the Wolverines, 24-7. Michigan, which fumbled twenty times in its first four games, showed minus rushing yardage as Vidmer was sacked for fifty yards in losses by the Spartans, on their way to a conference title and a Rose Bowl trip.

Elliott inserted Wally Gabler at quarterback, and he nearly engineered a victory over Purdue the following week. Gabler passed forty yards to Clancy for one touchdown and helped set up a field goal by Sygar for a one-point lead. Bob Griese, however, rallied Purdue from a seemingly hopeless position. With four minutes left and operating from his own eleven, Griese passed Purdue into field goal range and personally booted the three-pointer with 55 seconds left for the 17-15 victory. Griese completed 22 out of 38 passes for 273 yards in one of the most spectacular aerial acts ever seen in Michigan Stadium. Clancy caught eight passes for 125 yards for Michigan.

Michigan tried to rebound against Minnesota, but before the game had ended, six Wolverine regulars were on the bench with injuries. Still, Gabler scored a last-minute touchdown to cut the Gopher lead to 14-13. Elliott ordered him to go for victory, but Gabler, trying to pass for two points, missed Clancy in the end zone.

The Wolverines recovered against Wisconsin and won, 50-14, then Carl Ward slashed his way for 139 yards in a 23-3 victory over Illinois. Northwestern blocked a punt and proceeded to roll by Michigan by two touchdowns. Frustrations continued right through the final game with Ohio State. Woody Hayes allowed his team to gamble on a fourth down-and-one situation on the Buckeyes' 17. They made the first down, then drove to a winning field goal with 1:15 left on the clock. Michigan had first downs on Ohio's six and twelve and failed to score in the 9-7 loss.

One of the bright spots of the season was Jack Clancy. He

came to Michigan as a quarterback, switched to halfback, then moved to split end. He had some memorable games in 1965, catching four passes for 104 yards in an easy win over Wisconsin and grabbing eight for 89 yards against Northwestern. In all he caught 52 passes for 762 yards. The 6-foot-1, 192-pounder from Detroit accounted for more than half the receptions and more than half the passing yardage recorded by Michigan.

Clancy was elected captain of the 1966 team, and there was no doubt the Wolverines would improve on their 4-6 record of the previous season. Vidmer was healthy and would join Clancy to form the most productive passing combination in

Jack Clancy, Michigan's all-time pass reception leader, slips away from a Michigan State tackler.

Michigan history. Volk, a nephew of former Michigan all-American Bob Chappuis, and Sygar helped form a solid defensive secondary. Detwiler was ready. The Wolverines rebounded with a fine six-and-four record, but it could have been even better. A strange game with Purdue and a guy named "Silky" Sullivan from Illinois spoiled an otherwise superb season.

Vidmer and Clancy asserted themselves from the opening game. Vidmer passed for 258 yards, and Clancy set records with ten receptions and 197 yards in a 41-0 rout of Oregon State. California was handled, but North Carolina pulled off an upset. Michigan State, recovering from a Rose Bowl loss to UCLA but

heading for its second straight undefeated season, ran Michigan's losing streak to two with a 20-7 win. Vidmer threw forty-two times against the No. 1 ranked Spartans and Clancy caught nine of them for ninety-eight yards. Then came Purdue.

It was an afternoon of pure excitement. Vidmer, battling the clock just before half time, took the Wolverines 80 yards in

Quarterback Dick Vidmer fires a pass against Illinois.

six plays to tie the game at 14-14. Michigan drove 80 yards again to make it 21-14, before a series of misadventures struck. Sygar tried to field a Purdue punt four inches from his goal line, but was tackled for a safety. Then Stan Kemp's punt was blocked by guard Frank Burke, who picked the ball out of the air and scored. Purdue led 22-21.

Michigan did not quit. The Wolverines drove to a first down on the Purdue two but fumbled twice in succession. They came back and launched another last-ditch drive that carried to the Purdue eighteen. On fourth down the decision was made for Sygar to try a field goal. It missed! Elliott said, "I debated a long time on the decision of trying for the first down or field goal. If the same situation came up again, all I can say is I'd debate it again." Sygar kicked seven field goals for Michigan and fifty-two of fifty-three extra point attempts during his career. Bump was never short of confidence in his players.

Michigan's frustrations exploded against Minnesota, and the Vidmer-to-Clancy act was never better. Vidmer connected on 15 of 19 passes for 212 yards and 3 touchdowns. Clancy caught 10 of them for 168 yards, including touchdowns of 24 and 56 yards, in the 49-0 victory.

Wisconsin was beaten, then Sygar very nearly became a Saturday hero the next week when he returned an Illinois punt to give Michigan a 21-14 lead. But Illinois struck back with two touchdowns in the fourth period to win. The second touchdown remains unrivaled in the Michigan record book. The Wolverines drove deep into Illinois territory, and Vidmer attempted to pass for the score. The ball was deflected into the hands of Bruce "Silky" Sullivan and he ran 98 yards for the touchdown.

Michigan completed the 1966 season with victories over Northwestern and Ohio State. Detwiler gained 140 yards against the Bucks as Michigan rushed for 272 yards. Elliott's team won six of ten games and showed a 4-3 mark in the Big Ten. Purdue finished second to undefeated Michigan State and earned the trip to the Rose Bowl on a 6-1 conference record. The Boilermakers edged Southern Cal 14-13 for the roses.

Clancy, who caught 76 passes for 1,079 yards, earned all-American honors. He had 132 receptions for 1,919 yards in his career, both Michigan records. Volk, one of the most punishing tacklers ever to play in the Michigan secondary, was named to the all-American defensive team. Vidmer set school records with his throwing—117 completions for 1,611 yards.

It was the season of the forward pass at Michigan, but a missed field goal and an interception would remain a biting reminder of what could have been.

Ron Johnson . . . Halfback

America's Saturday love affair with college football began more than a century ago. Giant stadiums of steel and concrete in Tuscaloosa, South Bend, Columbus, Austin offered color, drama, the anticipation of victory for millions of fans. These were the showcases for young, talented athletes, and in the fall of 1967 Michigan had one such football player.

Ron Johnson had the necessary equipment of an all-American—size, speed, determination. It was determination that saw him through his sophomore year when he carried the ball just twelve times. When his opportunity came a year later, he was ready. Johnson began modestly in Michigan's first two games in 1967, rushing for 82 yards in a victory over Duke and picking up 48 yards as California won by a point. Then, as so frequently happens on a fall Saturday, college football had a new super star.

A strong Navy team came to Michigan Stadium, and when the Middies left, their coach, Bill Elias, just shook his head and said, "We have never faced a back like Ron Johnson, and hope we do not see one like him again for a long, long time." Navy had won, 26-21, but Johnson's greatness was established. Early in the first quarter he broke off tackle on a power sweep and bolted 62 yards for a touchdown. Navy responded with 10 points, then Johnson raced 51 yards to the Middies' six, and a couple plays later Warren Sipp scored.

Michigan was trailing 20-14 in the fourth period, and Johnson again broke free. This time it was a 72-yard touchdown run. Navy came back to score and win the game, but Wolverine

Bump Elliott with his last and best captain, Ron Johnson.

fans had a new hero. Johnson carried the ball twenty-six times for a remarkable 270 yards. No runner in Big Ten history had gone so far in one afternoon, but this muscular halfback of 192 pounds would reach heights where no player had been.

Johnson, typically, was more concerned with Michigan's loss to Navy than his own performance. "Anyone could gain yards with the type of blocking those guys gave me," he said, pointing to tight end Jim Mandich, guard Ray Phillips, and Garvie Craw, the big, square-jawed fullback.

Johnson was a business administration major. He wanted to go into banking and maintained a "B" average. He never missed a game in two years. Just before his senior season opened, he crashed into the wall in a scrimmage, suffering a dislocated thumb. Asked if the injury would bother him, Johnson said, "I'll just have to carry the ball in the other hand."

Despite Johnson's talents, 1967 was not a good year for Michigan. The Wolverines opened by defeating Duke, then lost five in a row. Johnson hammered Michigan State for 107 yards, but Michigan could not score. Elliott tried to fire up his offense by replacing Dick Vidmer with Dennis Brown against Indiana, and the results were encouraging. Brown passed for 211 yards, ran for 127, and set a Big Ten total offense record with 61 plays. Indiana, offering unpredictable John Isenbarger and quarterback Harry Gonso and on the way to the Rose Bowl, won by a touchdown.

Minnesota made it five straight defeats for the Wolverines before they reached a milestone in college football. Michigan recorded its 500th victory (only four schools, all in the East, had ever reached that level), but it took a massive assault by Johnson to record the 7-3 win over Northwestern. He ran the ball forty-two times. No runner in the Big Ten had been called on that many times before in a single game. Johnson gained 167 yards, and when asked about the endurance record, he said, "Whee, I knew I was tired; but forty-two times, I can't believe it."

Michigan then ran its winning string to three. Tom Curtis' three interceptions helped spill Illinois, and Brown passed for 232 yards as Wisconsin fell.

The season closed on a losing note. Ohio State defeated Michigan for the first time in three years, but Johnson was back in the headlines. He gained 96 yards and became the first runner in Michigan history to gain 1,000 yards in one season. Woody Hayes knew Johnson was close and admitted, "We tried to stop Johnson from going over the 1,000 mark, but he's a big, strong football player with wonderful balance."

Johnson was becoming a target for every defense, and in 1968 their efforts would be intensified. He was voted Michigan's most valuable player as a junior, then became the first black captain in Wolverine football by a vote of his teammates.

Michigan carved out eight victories in ten games during 1968, and much of that success sprang from Johnson's considerable abilities as a player and leader. He evoked a confidence among the players...and coaches. His durability was inspiring.

Johnson and Brown made Michigan's offense explosive. There was a struggle on defense, however, and this shortcoming would cost the Wolverines. Michigan's strength in 1968 was to score quickly, force the other team to pass. And lurking in the defensive backfield were Curtis, George Hoey, Brian Healy, and Jerry Hartman. They would intercept sixteen passes with Curtis at safety picking off ten.

Successful seasons rarely begin with defeat, but Michigan took this route. California used a strong running attack, struck first, and won the opener in Michigan Stadium, 21-7. Michigan then began a string of eight straight victories, routing Duke, 31-10. Johnson gained 205 yards, and sophomore linebacker Marty Huff scored on a 44-yard pass interception. Navy was next as Johnson scored twice, once on a 39-yard run, and Hoey hit the Middies broadside with two long punt returns to set up touchdowns.

Four long years of frustration ended with a 28-14 victory over Michigan State. Johnson's 38-yard scoring run started it, and a 53-yard touchdown pass from Brown to Mandich clinched the decision.

Indiana, with most of its Rose Bowl team back, was geared for victory before a sellout homecoming crowd in Bloomington. The Hoosiers were leading 10-7 in the third period when Hartman picked off Gonso's pass and ran 62 yards to score. The teams traded touchdowns as the offensive fireworks continued. Then Michigan worked out a 27-22 lead late in the fourth period. Michigan faced a fourth down on its 43 with two

Jim Mandich grabs a fourth period pass from Dennis Brown that clinched a victory over Michigan State in 1968. It was the first time in four years that the Wolverines had defeated the Spartans.

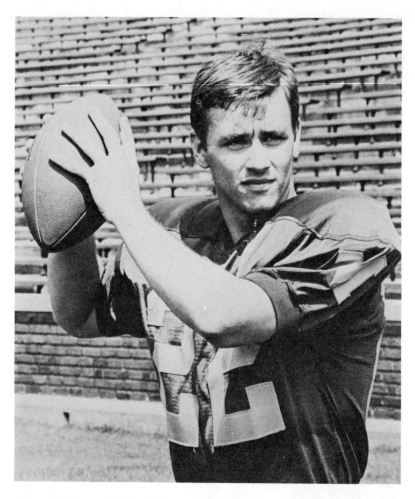

Dennis Brown broke most of Michigan's career passing records in 1967 and 1968. He set a total offense record of sixty-one plays for the Big Ten.

minutes left in the game. Elliott did not want to give the dangerous Hoosiers the ball. Johnson was called on to gain two yards. He made the first down, and the Wolverines ran out the clock. Johnson did inspire confidence.

Michigan continued to roll, shocking Minnesota with 33 points in the first half. Hoey, Curtis, and Healy each intercepted a pass, and Elliott went with his reserves most of the second half as the Gophers made it close, 33-20. The Wolverines struck for three touchdowns in 73 seconds to rout Northwestern and came back to blank Illinois as Brown hit Billy Harris with a 69-yard touchdown pass.

Michigan now was on a direct path to the Rose Bowl. Five straight Big Ten victories were in hand with Wisconsin coming up. Victory was essential, but sometimes an individual, like a Grange or a Harmon, can overshadow victory. Johnson was such a player.

The steady, driving rain held the Michigan Stadium crowd to slightly more than 50,000, but a regional television audience tuned in for the game. Excitement began early as Johnson broke a couple of tackles and powered his way 35 yards to score. Wisconsin fought back to lead, 9-7, at half time. Johnson had Michigan in front early in the third period, running 67 yards. Minutes later he was off again, sprinting 60 yards for a touchdown. After he ran half the length of the field for his fifth touchdown, Elliott pulled his captain from the game, and 20,000 or so fans still remaining rose as one in a thundering ovation. Johnson had gained 347 yards from scrimmage, more than any runner in college history. His five touchdowns established a modern Big Ten record. He broke Harmon's career rushing record. November 16th was a memorable afternoon.

The 34-9 victory sent the Wolverines to Columbus with a chance to capture the Big Ten title. The Rose Bowl was an added prize, and the winner would take it all.

The Buckeyes were favored, but Michigan scored first. Johnson, again the target of Ohio State's strong defenses, broke loose for 39 yards to set Michigan in motion. Brown passed to Mandich for 21, then Johnson scored from the one. Ohio came back with two touchdowns, using raw power on the ground. But Johnson scored again to tie the game at 14-14.

The Bucks continued their assault behind the charges of fullback Jim Otis. They used most of the second period to move 86 yards for a touchdown. They came back in the third period on a long drive that netted a touchdown and a 27-14 lead. The Wolverines were tired. They had lost their big offensive tackle, Dan Dierdorf, early in the first period. Brown had been shaken up by Jack Tatum's crashing tackle. Still, they drove to the Ohio State fourteen, but the season ended there.

Ohio State scored 23 points in the fourth period and

turned the game into a 50-14 rout. The final touchdown came when Otis returned to the game and battered his way into the end zone. An attempt for the *two point* conversion failed. A year later Michigan would remember those fifty points. They would wear red practice jerseys, all with the number "50" across them. But that is another year, another Michigan-Ohio State game.

The decisiveness of the victory earned Ohio State the National Championship, the Big Ten title, and a vote of the conference that sent the Buckeyes to the Rose Bowl where they defeated Southern Cal.

Johnson had completed his Michigan career. He gained 1,391 yards as a senior, and his three-year total stood at 2,440, both Michigan records. He broke seven Big Ten records and tied two more. He was Michigan's most valuable player for the second straight season and received the *Chicago Tribune* silver trophy as the Big Ten's most valuable player. The College Football Writers Association named him to its all-America team.

Honors were only part of Johnson's years at Michigan. Woven in his career were proud moments, ponderous records, and heartbreak. He did everything ever expected of a football player. Elliott said, "He was the best football player and best captain I had during my coaching career."

Johnson was Bump's last captain. A few weeks later Elliott's appointment as Michigan's new associate athletic director was announced. A decade of coaching had passed for Elliott, another layer of Michigan tradition added.

Canham — The Guy From Madison Avenue

Don Canham never thought much about today. He always looked down the road, a year, two years, five years. He knew a balance sheet. You do not build a million dollar business without knowing what the bottom line meant. What he saw, as far as intercollegiate athletics were concerned, was not encouraging.

The cost of Michigan's grant-in-aid program was mushrooming, and there was no relief in sight. If anything, Canham thought, the expense to finance one student-athlete at Michigan would increase by 30 percent in the next five years. Salaries had to go up. And there was the matter of more locker room and training facilities for football. The hockey rink was in its final years and had to be replaced. The problems, all needing financing, seemed to be endless.

Canham knew he had to have sound, imaginative people in administration. It was imperative that unnecessary expenditures be stopped and new sources of revenue be found if Michigan were to modernize its facilities, to remain competitive in athletics. He filled his two administrative positions almost immediately. First, he appointed Dave Strack, a successful basketball coach at Michigan with a master's degree in business administration, as his assistant athletic director. The other position, the vital job of associate director, was held open for Bump Elliott. It remained open for seven months before Elliott accepted.

While Strack started to solve the administrative problems,

337

Elliott began organizing Michigan alumni who were willing to support Michigan athletics financially. Canham then turned his attention to the modernization of Michigan Stadium. An artificial carpet of Tartan Turf was ordered for the field, new twin, electric scoreboards installed, Tartan Turf was put down on Ferry Field, and lights were erected. Canham figured that the green carpet in the stadium would save $10,000 a year in maintenance annually, and within five years every major football power in the nation would have it.

Canham was moving heavily into a job he never really thought much about. Track had been his game. In nineteen years his teams won twelve championships for Michigan. He had started a small sports film business and watched it grow into a million dollar enterprise. When Fritz Crisler retired in 1968, the 49-year-old Canham was asked if he were interested in becoming athletic director. He accepted. It meant putting the company into a trust, but a new opportunity had arisen and he went after it.

He was replacing a giant in Crisler. Fritz had given Michigan a badly needed period of construction, bringing its facilities into the Twentieth Century. He served on the powerful rules committee where his prestige helped bring about the two-point conversion rule and the widening of the goal posts to twenty-four feet.

The silver-haired Crisler had left Michigan with a solid cash surplus. His talents as a businessman were never questioned. He had persuaded Tommy Harmon to enter radio broadcasting the year after he graduated, and later helped negotiate a lucrative contract for the all-American halfback with the Los Angeles Rams. He helped Ron Kramer deal with the Green Bay Packers. Yes, Canham would have money to operate his first year or two, but after that the former track coach would have to insure that the bottom line remained black.

Canham plunged into promotion, hard-sell ticket promotion. There were 100,000 seats in Michigan Stadium, and they had to be filled. He said, "We will make mistakes, but we'll win on the percentage." Canham watched the telephone bills, the light bills. He put athletic operations on a solid business basis. But he knew where to spend money. Michigan's broad athletic program was not neglected. He increased the budget for ticket promo-

Don Canham was appointed athletic director in 1968 and immediately launched a new era in Wolverine athletics.

tion, saying, "If General Motors had no cost of product, how much do you think they would spend on advertising?" His product was an empty seat in the stadium, and Canham brought in a flavor of Madison Avenue. He mailed a million ticket applications for football games, advertised in *Sports Illustrated, Time,* and *Fortune.* He went after young fans, offering every high school and grade school in the state a special $3 ticket. "We have a generation gap in college football and we have to fill it," Canham explained.

There was no doubt football was on the move at Michigan. Canham insisted on it. After Elliott moved from football coach to associate athletic director, Canham had one important decision to make. He could not make a mistake on Bump's replacement.

Hamburgers And Road Maps

Bo Schembechler was hired in 15 minutes. It took Don Canham that long to sense the intensity, the enthusiasm of a man destined to be a winner.

Canham was still in his first year as athletic director at Michigan. His football coach, Bump Elliott, had produced a strong 8-2 record in 1968, but before the season had ended, before the final game had been played, Canham asked Bump if he was interested in becoming the associate athletic director. When Elliott decided to move into administration of athletics after a decade as Michigan's football coach, Canham acted quickly.

He asked Elliott and other football people he respected for recommendations. The name Bo Schembechler, a builder of mid-American football powers at Miami of Ohio, seemed to appear on every list. Elliott phoned Schembechler and asked him if he would be interested in coaching at Michigan. A surprised Schembechler jumped at the opportunity after Elliott explained the changes being made. "They don't call you every day in the week and talk to you about the Michigan coaching job," Bo recalled. "I hoped at the time Bump didn't notice the excitement in my voice."

Schembechler arrived in Ann Arbor a few days before Christmas. He talked to Canham for two hours in the coffee room at the athletic administration building. Marc Plant, the faculty representative, joined them. When Bo was ready to leave, he turned to Canham and said, "Okay, what happens now?"

"I'll call you in a day or two," Canham replied, but he had already determined who the next Michigan football coach would be. "Frankly, I decided to hire him in 15 minutes," Canham revealed. "The first time I met him he came on that way, a man of great enthusiasm. He knew what he wanted, and I could see that he wanted it badly."

The day before Christmas Schembechler's phone in Oxford, Ohio, rang. It was Canham, and he came directly to the point. "Bo, I'm offering you the job at Michigan."

"Good," Bo said. Nothing else, just good.

Canham told him the salary was $21,000, about $1,000 more than Bo would be making the next year at Miami. They

Michigan's thirteenth football coach, Bo Schembechler (left) and the man he succeeded, Bump Elliott, at the news conference announcing Bo's appointment and Bump's new job as associate athletic director.

talked for a few minutes, then Canham asked him how soon he could get back to Ann Arbor.

"How about tomorrow night?" replied Schembechler. He arrived in Ann Arbor the next afternoon at 2 p.m.

Glenn E. Schembechler, Jr., was born to football. He always wanted to be a coach, even during his playing days at Miami. He served as a student assistant under Woody Hayes at Ohio State, coached football in the Army, and accepted his first full-time job in 1954 as line coach at Presbyterian College for $3,400 a year and "cafeteria rights." Then to Bowling Green, to Northwestern under Ara Parseghian, and back to Ohio State and Hayes in 1958. His first head coaching job came in 1963 at Miami, where he spent six seasons, won two championships, and twice was voted Coach of the Year. His Miami teams won forty games, lost seventeen, and tied three.

It was evident from the start of spring practice in 1969 that football at Michigan was changing. The man from Miami brought in his own coaching staff but retained as assistants George Mans and Frank Maloney, two of Elliott's youngest staff members. He brought in a new concept of defense, the five-man angle. He brought in a passion for work, a commitment to winning. He told Canham, "There's no way I'm going to win anything right off the bat. You have to understand that now."

"I know that," Canham said.

"How long do I have?" asked Schembechler.

"You can have five years, take my word for it," Canham said.

Schembechler had a job and five years to do it, but he did not have a written contract. He only had the word of a man he trusted. That was enough.

Schembechler also told Canham there would be a transition between Bump's way of coaching and his and "anything can happen." Schembechler, impulsive, with a quick temper, never let frustrations remain within himself. He was uncompromising in defeat. Once, when Woody Hayes threw a chair at him, Schembechler fired it right back at his boss.

There were flare-ups on the Ferry Field practice field that spring. Schembechler had to establish his methods, his thinking...with players recruited to play for another Michigan

Bo Schembechler was named Michigan's head football coach after the 1968 season. The Miami of Ohio graduate and football coach won a championship his first season at Michigan and was voted national Coach of the Year.

Defensive halfback Tom Curtis (25) picks off one of his 25 career interceptions in 1969 action against Washington. Curtis still holds the NCAA record for most yards returned on interceptions with 440.

coach. It was not easy.

The summer months were long and hot for Schembechler. He criss-crossed the state giving speeches, trying to build a recruiting base. He ate late-night hamburgers and drove his car to Grand Rapids, Flint, St. Joseph...wherever they wanted him. Bennie Oosterbaan talked him into bringing his family to his cottage on Lake Leelanau near Traverse City. After five days Schembechler left for Milwaukee to speak at a clinic. He flew back, spent a couple days more at the cottage with his wife, Millie, and their three boys, then returned to Ann Arbor.

When Schembechler opened practice in the fall, he had a new artificial grass field in Michigan Stadium and a second one under construction on Ferry Field. Canham also began making plans for a sports service building that would include complete facilities for a football team.

That August Schembechler looked over the returning Michigan football players and told the press, "We are not devoid of material. Bump left me with a good football team." He did wonder about replacing all-American tailback Ron Johnson and Dennis Brown, the small quarterback with a sturdy arm who had broken most of Michigan's passing records. The basis for a strong defensive team remained; that was essential to Schembechler. He had a promising quarterback in Don Moorhead, a 6-foot-3 junior who could run and pass.

The incoming sophomores were especially impressive: Reggie McKenzie, Guy Murdock, Paul Seymour along the offensive line; Glenn Doughty, Billy Taylor, and Fritz Seyferth in the backfield; Tom Darden, Fred Grambau, Mike Taylor, Mike Keller, Tom Beckman, and Bruce Elliott on defense. Jim Mandich, the captain, an outstanding tight end, and Tom Curtis at safety were all-American candidates. There were other proven veterans. Schembechler was not convinced he could win in his first year, but he knew Michigan could make a run at the championship.

"The Fire Had Gone Out"

Bo Schembechler's first game as Michigan's football coach gave a High School Band Day crowd of 70,183 a strong indication of what type of football they would be seeing. Vanderbilt was not a national power, but it was the ideal opener for the Wolverines. Don Moorhead gained 103 yards running the option from his quarterback position. Glenn Doughty, the sophomore tailback, showed his high-stepping style of running as he sprinted 80 yards for one touchdown and gained 138 yards. Michigan broke open a close game with 28 points in the final period. A quarterback who can run, a good tailback, and rock-hard defense (Vandy gained just 55 yards on the ground) would be Schembechler's football staples.

Michigan opened up with 23 passes and gained 581 yards in total offense to rout Washington. Missouri was next, and it was an afternoon that Schembechler never forgot. Michigan drove deep into Missouri territory three times in the first quarter and came away with just three points. Three fumbles and a pass interception in the second period helped the Tigers to a 24-3 half time lead. Michigan fought back for two touchdowns in the third period, but Missouri blocked a punt and won easily. The game hinged on turnovers, and it was a lesson well learned by Schembechler's young Wolverines.

Purdue came to Michigan Stadium with a five-game winning streak, but could not contain Moorhead's passing. He connected ten times with Mandich for 156 yards as Michigan moved 247 yards in the air. A 10-point third period broke open a tight game as the Wolverines won 31-20.

Schembechler then received his first introduction to the Michigan-Michigan State rivalry and came off a loser. A fumble and a safety broke the game open for the Spartans. After the 23-12 loss, Schembechler said, "I thought we were three and two for the season, but our alumni told me we were three and three. I didn't know that game counted as two." He would remember how alumni counted in the future.

A defeat of this type early in the season sometimes ruins a season. The players often are slow to respond, and when they do it can be too late. It happens every year in college football, and it almost happened to Michigan. Michigan was a battered club the following Saturday for the Little Brown Jug game in Minnesota. The Gophers promptly grabbed a 9-7 lead at half time, and the season could have collapsed right there. The Wolverines came back in the second half to drive 75 yards, then 66, then 41, and finally 21 yards for touchdowns as Billy Taylor, subbing for the injured Doughty, gained 151 yards. Michigan won it, 35-9.

Taylor, a stubby, deceptively quick runner, came back in his next game to ramble 142 yards in just 15 rushes as Michigan rocked Wisconsin with 35 points in the first half and won, 35-7. Illinois suffered its worst defeat in the 55-year series with Michigan, 57-0. Garvie Craw scored four touchdowns, and the final touchdown came on a pass interception by Bruce Elliott with his father Pete, in the stands watching. Then Iowa fell, 51-6, before Taylor's onslaught of 225 yards from scrimmage. Only Ron Johnson had ever gained more in a single afternoon.

Michigan carried a 5-1 record into the season wrap-up against undefeated Ohio State and came away with a classic upset, a share of the championship, and the trip to the Rose Bowl. The 24-12 victory was carved out in Schembechler style—266 yards rushing and 108 yards in the air, no fumbles, but six interceptions of Ohio State passes.

Immediately after the game, Schembechler launched his recruiting drive and started to make Rose Bowl plans. From November 22 until December 18 when Michigan's United Airlines charter left for California, it would be more hamburgers, more late night trips. The price of victory often is paid in strange currencies.

Two days after arriving in Pasadena, the Michigan football

coach stepped on the scales...the needle shot around to the 220 mark. Schembechler stared at the scales. He could hardly believe it. He had gained 25 pounds since coming to Michigan. He made a mental note to start a regular exercise program when he returned to Ann Arbor, but now there was work to do.

Michigan arrived on the coast with an 8-2 record, and that eighth victory was seen by millions on television. It was an impressive game, but Schembechler knew that the last victory meant nothing unless his team was prepared to play a strong Southern Cal team. His team came back quickly, the enthusiasm was there. Schembechler hoped it had not come too quickly. Then the first misfortune struck. Glenn Doughty, running in practice, injured his knee and immediately underwent surgery. He was one of the most popular players on the Michigan team. He had fought back from an earlier knee injury, and his injury hit the team hard.

The 5 p.m. nightly news conference in the Huntington Hotel was never oversubscribed, but two days before the Rose Bowl game the long, narrow room was jammed with reporters. They waited 15 minutes, 20 minutes, but Schembechler did not arrive. Finally, Jim Young, Bo's defensive coordinator, walked into the room and conferred with his sports information director. "Bo won't be here tonight," Young said softly. "He's got an upset stomach or something." This information was passed along to the press, and some members took the announcement with suspicion. Young filled in for Schembechler at the press conference.

Michigan's team doctors, Jerry O'Connor and Bob Anderson, that evening took Schembechler to a clinic in Pasadena, but an EKG test revealed nothing. Schembechler and his captain, Mandich, went to the annual kickoff luncheon the next day, the day before the game. That night the entire Michigan team and coaching staff were lodged in a monastery in the mountains overlooking Pasadena. It is a custom practiced by most Big Ten teams in order to escape the noise and disturbances on New Year's Eve. The next morning while the players were being taped prior to their short trip to the Rose Bowl, Young came into the room. Some of the players were watching the parade, others the Cotton Bowl. An assistant coach turned off the television sets. Young started to talk. He said Bo had been taken

Glenn Doughty, Michigan's halfback, is helped off the practice field by trainer Lindsy McLean just prior to the 1970 Rose Bowl game. Several other injuries and Bo Schembechler's heart attack preceded a 10-3 loss to Southern Cal.

to the hospital. He had chest pains, and the doctors thought it might be a heart attack.

The players listened. They said nothing. They were stunned and unbelieving at first. Some walked over to the chapel. Frank Gusich, a defensive back, recalls his immediate reaction. "I thought, we'll kick the hell out of them. But it wasn't what I felt. I felt down, cold, like the fire had gone out."

When the Michigan team and coaches ran out on to the grass field of the Rose Bowl, the reaction in the press box was immediate. "Where's Bo?" writers asked. An announcement over the press box address system that Schembechler was sick, possibly suffering from a virus, and would not be at the game, did not satisfy them.

The glamour, the excitement of the Rose Bowl game had vanished for the Michigan team, coaches, officials, and writers. Strangely, the West Coast writers did not attach too much importance to Schembechler's heart attack in their stories the next day. They wrote about a winner, Southern Cal. It was not a spectacular game. Six points were scored in the first half as the teams traded field goals. The Trojans won it in the third quarter when Jimmy Jones hit Bob Chandler on a third down pass at Michigan's 20. Chandler slipped away from a couple of Wolverines and ran unchallenged into the end zone. It was a 33-yard play.

Billy Taylor (42) picks up yardage against the strong Southern Cal defense in this 1970 Rose Bowl action.

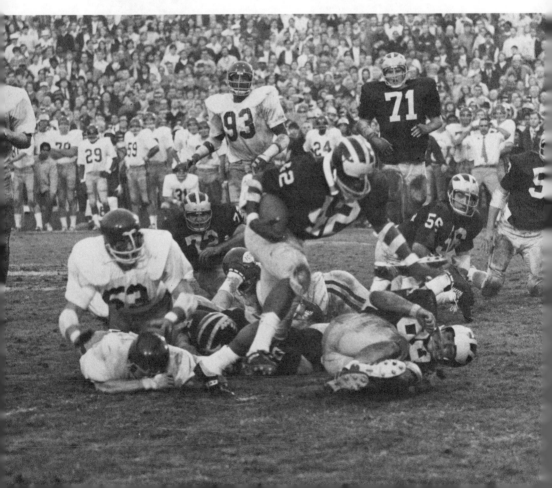

Michigan lacked the fired-on offense, but proved strong defensively in the 1970 Rose Bowl game against Southern Cal. Here Cecil Pryor (55), Tom Darden (35), and Marty Huff (70) stop a Trojan runner in the 10-3 Wolverine loss.

Michigan, coached by Young, had an edge in first downs. USC had more total yards. The 10-3 defeat was the first time a Michigan team had lost in the Rose Bowl after four straight victories. Billy Harris, trying to catch a pass late in the game, injured his knee and was never able to regain his former running abilities.

Michigan's plane left the next day for Detroit. Schembechler remained in a Pasadena hospital. With him were the thoughts of everyone on that plane. They hoped he would come back.

A Winter Of Wondering

Bo Schembechler's second spring practice at Michigan was strange. Watching the once fiery, intense Schembechler move around Ferry Field in a golf cart, silent, just looking at the drills and saying nothing, one writer asked, "Are you sure he'll be coaching in the fall?"

That was a problem for Bo in the months following the Rose Bowl. Coaches from other schools were asking the same question, and the young, talented high school seniors were not sure. Michigan's assistant coaches did a superb job of convincing these prep stars that Bo, indeed, would be back to coach. They brought the youngsters to Schembechler's home. He would dress, meet them in his living room, players like Ed Shuttlesworth, Clint Haslerig, Dave Gallagher. They talked with Bo, and they believed him when he said, "I'll be your coach next fall." Tom Slade, a confident young athlete from Saginaw, called Schembechler on the phone one day and said, "Coach, I know you'll be back, and I'm going to be your quarterback." That was Schembechler's best medicine.

During those long winter months Schembechler wondered. He wondered about his future. Now he had four sons. Glenn E. the III was less than a year old. Schembechler had been voted Coach of the Year by his fellow coaches, and his first serious test came when he was invited to a banquet in Washington, D. C. He could not go, of course, and sent Jim Young to represent him. A telephone hook-up was planned for him to talk to the group of coaches at the gala banquet. "I was nervous as hell,"

Bo recalled. "My heart started to beat, and I wondered if I could handle it. The phone call went well, and then I knew I had taken my first step back."

Schembechler started to exercise, to run, in May of 1970. He ran and observed the diet his doctors ordered. Typically, he never wavered on the diet. There were no hamburgers. When the Wolverines reported to him on August 20th, he weighed 175 pounds. He had lost forty-five pounds and was ready to go after another championship.

Most of the key members of the Rose Bowl team were back for 1970. The biggest losses involved a pair of all-American pass catchers, one on offense and one on defense. Jim Mandich, Michigan's finest tight end since Ron Kramer, caught 50 passes for 676 yards and was voted the team's most valuable player. He had been the captain, and was Bo's type of player. Tom Curtis at safety intercepted 25 passes in his three-year career and returned them for 440 yards, an NCAA record.

Moorhead and Henry Hill, the little middle guard, were the co-captains. The backfield was set with Taylor and Doughty. Very few sophomores expected to start. Still, the season figured to be another Michigan-Ohio State showdown on November 21 in Columbus. That is exactly the way it went.

Schembechler's teams are never impressive early in the season, and that was the case against Arizona in the opener. Dana Coin kicked the longest field goal in modern Michigan history, 42 yards, and Schembechler surprised everybody in the stadium when a screen pass from Don Moorhead to Billy Taylor went for 29 yards and a touchdown. Michigan won, 20-9, and followed that up with a 17-3 win over Washington and quarterback Sonny Sixkiller. The Wolverines had to rally for the second straight week to defeat Texas A&M before the offense finally got untracked and stung Purdue with 29 points.

There were still some doubts about Michigan's abilities when the second largest crowd ever to see a Big Ten football game, 103,508, watched the Wolverines explode for 21 points in the second half to defeat Michigan State. Taylor became the first Michigan player since Bob Chappuis to score three touchdowns on the Spartans, and Glenn Doughty, formerly a tailback, but now playing wingback, provided an insurance tally. Then, Fritz Seyferth accounted for four touchdowns, and

Taylor gained 151 yards as Michigan dumped Minnesota. The following week Moorhead connected on eleven passes in twenty-two attempts for 223 yards in a 29-15 win over Wisconsin. Seyferth scored twice more, one of them coming after a 70-yard pass from Moorhead to Paul Staroba carried to the Badger three. Michigan scored 97 points the next two weeks, shutting out Illinois and Iowa. That sent the undefeated Wolverines into the season finale against an equally undefeated and favored Ohio State team.

A capacity crowd had ideal football weather, and the Buckeyes sent most of the 87,000 fans in motion with the opening kickoff. It sailed deep to Lance Scheffler, who fumbled the ball, and Ohio State recovered. The Bucks settled for a 28-yard field goal, but the tone of the game had been set. Schembechler said, "Breaks will decide the game," and he was right on target.

Michigan tied the game on Coin's 31-yard field goal, then a weird play put the Wolverines in trouble. Staroba boomed a 73-yard punt from deep in Michigan territory just before the half, but it was called back because of a face mask penalty assessed against a Michigan lineman, Reggie McKenzie, charging downfield. Ohio State gained field position with Staroba's second punt, a 42-yarder, and drove in to score. Moorhead fired a touchdown pass to Staroba covering 13 yards, but Coin's extra point attempt was blocked, leaving the Bucks with a 10-9 lead in the third period. Ohio scored ten points in the final period to wrap up the game and a trip to the Rose Bowl. Stanford pulled off a 27-17 upset victory over Rex Kern, Jack Tatum, John Brockington, and company.

Michigan turned in a 9-1 season, and contributed three players to the all-American list: Linebacker Marty Huff, middle guard Henry Hill, and offensive tackle Dan Dierdorf. Hill and Moorhead were voted Michigan's co-most valuable players.

Moorhead in his two years at quarterback broke virtually every Michigan passing record that had been established two years before by Dennis Brown. He threw more passes (425), completed more (200), for more yards (2,550) than any player in Michigan history. He set total offense records for most plays (708) and most yards (3,641).

Schembechler's two year record was a glittering 17-3, and

he was just beginning. There would be no more near misses on championships the next three seasons.

Don Moorhead broke most of Michigan's passing records as he led the Wolverines to seventeen victories in twenty games during the 1969 and 1970 seasons.

The Title Arrives Early

The Big Ten "Skywriters" arrived in Ann Arbor and immediately wanted to know, "Who's the quarterback?"

Roy Damer from Chicago, Gus Schrader of Cedar Rapids, Jim Brahm and Ed Chay from Cleveland, Kaye Kessler of Columbus, thirty-five sportswriters who cover college football were on their charter-plane junket of Big Ten football camps. Their lead stories from Michigan would discuss the quarterback problem, and the replacement for Don Moorhead.

Bo Schembechler told them Kevin Casey, a sophomore from Grand Rapids, was the likely starter, but Tom Slade, also in his first year on the varsity, was pressing for the job. It was certain Michigan would open the 1971 season with an untested, sophomore quarterback.

The rest of the team was established. Seldom had Michigan returned such experience, such depth from a highly successful team. There were fifteen starters back, including all the running backs, four offensive and four defensive linemen, and three members of the defensive secondary. Reggie McKenzie, a 235-pound lightning-quick guard; Mike Taylor, a burly linebacker; Tom Darden, moving from cornerback to safety; and tailback Billy Taylor were all-American candidates.

Michigan's depth was extensive. Runners were stacked three-deep. Schembechler switched Randy Logan from wingback to defensive halfback, a move that eventually would bring him all-American honors. And, again, the team contained two Elliotts. Bump and Pete had played together in 1946 and 1947.

Pete's older son, Bruce, was a starting wideside halfback, while his younger son, Dave, battled for the other defensive halfback position. Bo Rather, a junior with sprinter's speed, switched from defense to split end.

The 1971 schedule was increased to eleven games as colleges desperately sought additional revenue. The Big Ten, moving toward a round-robin, directed that the extra game be played with a conference team. It was spotted as the season opener, and Michigan drew Northwestern. The Wildcats had tied for second the year before and again were considered a factor in the race.

Michigan had trouble with Alex Agase's Northwestern team. Rather scooted 18 yards on an end-around, then figured in the weirdest play in Schembechler's coaching career. Dana Coin, Michigan's superb place kicker, set up for a 42-yard field goal. The Wildcats stationed a defender in front of the goal post. Coin's kick appeared to be short, and the Northwestern defender leaped and batted the ball, which bounced erratically in the end zone. Rather and Guy Murdock were sprinting downfield. Rather caught up to the ball and fell on it, and Murdock fell on him. A three-point field goal attempt turned into seven points with Coin's conversion kick.

Michigan won 21-6, but the game offered a deeper insight into Schembechler, the coach. Michigan pulled the end-around three times during the game, and each time Schembechler waited until a new defensive end entered the game before ordering the play. It was becoming evident that Michigan rarely let opportunity escape.

Power football and defense? Michigan was overstocked. The next three Saturdays the Wolverine victory count read: Virginia, 56-0; UCLA, 38-0; Navy, 46-0. It was awesome. The Cavaliers of Virginia never gained a yard passing and could muster only seventy-eight rushing. Darden returned an interception 92 yards against UCLA, and the Bruins showed just thirty-nine yards on the ground. Navy picked up thirty-four yards rushing. The Wolverines ran the ball for 980 yards in those three victories as a half-dozen different offensive backs scored touchdowns.

There were three key games on Michigan's schedule in 1971, and the first one was coming up against Michigan State in

357

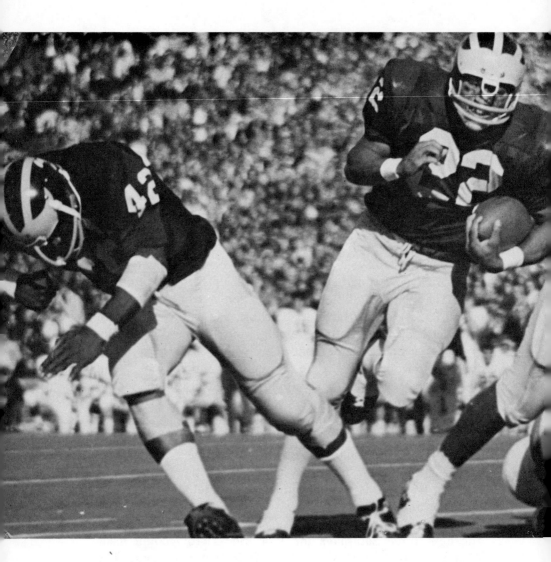

East Lansing. Schembechler made a move for that one. Casey, progressing slowly at quarterback, was hampered by a sore shoulder. Schembechler figured that the game would not be won with passing. Slade, his other quarterback, was a strong, 198-pounder who ran the option well. Slade would start his first varsity game.

A crowd of 80,093 helped fire up the Spartans, but Taylor's 38-yard touchdown run quickly put the Wolverines in front. When Taylor left the game with a shoulder injury, the

Michigan shows its powerful ground offense in 1971 as Glenn Doughty (22) cuts off tackle behind the blocking of Billy Taylor (42) and Reggie McKenzie (65). McKenzie was a consensus all-American guard.

Wolverines' attack sputtered. Their 10-7 lead after three quarters was not imposing. Taylor returned, scored once, and set up another touchdown with a bruising run as Michigan won 24-13. Taylor gained 117 yards, and Slade won the quarterback job.

Michigan's winning streak continued to mount. Slade scored on a 25-yard run, passed 19 yards to Glenn Doughty for a second touchdown, and the Wolverines shook off a sluggish start to rip Illinois 35-6. Minnesota fell and so did Ron

This 21-yard run by Billy Taylor (42) gave Michigan a 10-7 victory over Ohio State and completed a perfect 1971 season for the Wolverines. Reserve quarterback Larry Cipa (13), who

engineered the fourth period drive, throws one key block, and fullback Fritz Seyferth (32) is about to cut down the final Buckeye defender.

361

Johnson's career rushing record. Taylor romped for 166 yards and became Michigan's all-time leading ground gainer in the 35-7 win. The chunky halfback added 172 yards in just eleven carries in a 61-7 rout of Indiana. Iowa gained only eight yards on the ground, while Michigan ran for 493 yards and won by fifty-six points.

Michigan clinched its twenty-third Big Ten title at Lafayette where Purdue, the second key game, was anything but a willing contributor. Dana Coin, whose NCAA extra point record was still running at fifty-three straight, booted a 25-yard field goal with 26 seconds left to win it, 20-17.

The finale with thrice-beaten Ohio State was devoid of the championship element for the first time in four years. It did not matter to the players involved. For the second straight week the Wolverines had to pull it out in the fourth period. Coin's 32-yard field goal provided Michigan with a second period lead, but Tom Campana stung the Wolverines with an 85-yard punt return in the third quarter. Campana was virtually the entire Buckeye offense, gaining 166 yards on five punt returns.

There were just seven minutes to go when the Wolverines, trailing 7-3, took over at their twenty-eight. Larry Cipa replaced the injured Slade at quarterback and directed a classic, pressure drive. With a third down and seven at Michigan's thirty-one, Taylor picked up eight on a draw play. With a third and four Cipa passed twenty-two yards to Rather. With a fourth down and inches to go on Ohio's 24 fullback Fritz Seyferth leaped for the first down. The payoff came on the next play from the twenty-one. Taylor swung wide to the right, and first Cipa, then Seyferth cut down Ohio defenders. Taylor scored easily.

Darden ruined Ohio's final hopes of victory with a leaping pass interception. That play triggered a violent protest from Ohio State and resulted in a wild finish, much like the one these teams produced sixteen years earlier in Michigan Stadium. That ending involved a disputed touchdown by Ohio's Hopalong Cassady as players were ejected, snowballs flew, and penalties called.

Seconds after Darden's interception Woody Hayes stormed onto the field protesting that pass interference should have been called. A penalty was called on Ohio, and a minute later a player ejected. A yard marker was hurled on the field, and

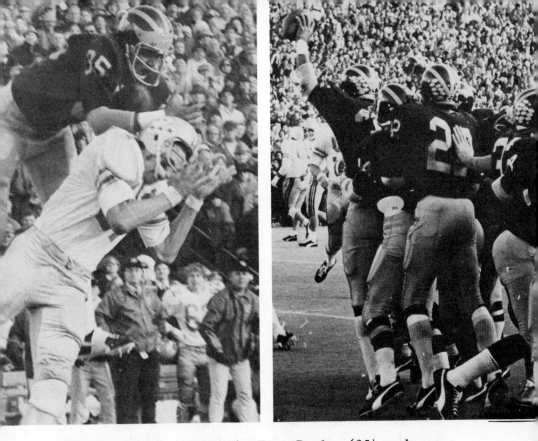

Pictured at left, Michigan's Tom Darden (35) makes an interception against Ohio State in the 1971 game. At right Darden holds up the ball after the interception. The play triggered a protest from Ohio coach Woody Hayes and caused a wild finish in Michigan Stadium. Michigan won the game, 10-7.

Hayes ripped the down marker off its post. Another Michigan-Ohio State game had left sports pages with headlines for days.

Michigan had won eleven straight games. The twelfth was scheduled in Pasadena against Stanford on New Year's Day.

Rain And Roses

California did not provide Bo Schembechler with many fond memories, but the Michigan football coach was not thinking of the past; not the Rose Bowl loss, not his heart attack that followed the 1969 season. "I guess I should have, but I didn't," he said.

Schembechler's problem was rain. When Michigan arrived in Pasadena to prepare for the 1972 Rose Bowl, a light drizzle was falling. When he took his team to a junior college practice field near Pasadena, Schembechler could hardly believe what he saw. The field was soggy, muddy. A groundskeeper had turned on the watering system, and someone forgot to turn it off. The water flowed Friday, Saturday, Sunday. Then the rains came. It poured for five days.

The residents in Southern California said they could not remember when it had rained so much, but that failed to impress Schembechler. His team was not ready to play a football game, and he knew it. On Christmas Day Schembechler toured the entire area, looking for a practice field. Finally, he drove into the mountains, returned that night and announced, "We are leaving for Bakersfield in the morning."

The Wolverines went through a couple of solid, tough workouts at their Bakersfield retreat, but had to leave for the Big Ten banquet in Los Angeles. A report came from the state police that snow had closed the highway leading down the mountain to Pasadena. "The pass is closed," quipped one player. A few minutes later another report was received, and the

Wolverines responded, "The pass is open." Schembechler loaded his team on two buses, when still another report came. "The pass is closed," roared through a team of jovial, laughing Wolverines. The situation was almost comical, but not for Schembechler. He jumped on the bus and said, "The hell with the pass, we're leaving." The pass was open and the Wolverine buses made it, but Schembechler's concern was not lessening.

Michigan returned to the monastery for New Year's Eve, and, for the first time, Schembechler thought of the past. "Everything was the same as it had been two years before," Schembechler recalled. "I had a strange feeling and even pointed out to my coaches the spot where I felt those terrible chest pains. But I weighed 180 pounds now and felt confident about myself."

Schembechler was more concerned about the playing conditions in the Rose Bowl, and before the game he ordered his team to wear long cleats. He thought the field was too soggy and feared his players would slip. "I made a mistake there," Bo admitted. "I guess I was psyched out by the weather." Stanford wore lighter, shorter cleats or artificial turf shoes. "I think we were tired from using the longer cleats by the time the game was over."

The 1972 Rose Bowl was dominated by the defenses. Michigan's powerful running attack rolled up 264 yards, but it took a 30-yard field goal by Dana Coin to gain a 3-0 lead in the second period. Rod Garcia tied it for Stanford in the third period with a 42-yard kick. The Wolverines moved in front in the fourth period when Fritz Seyferth blasted into the end zone from the one. Then the drama began.

Stanford, facing a fourth down situation on its 33-yard line, used a fake punt, and Jackie Brown raced 31 yards. Then Brown broke off tackle for 24 yards and the touchdown that tied the game 10-10.

Later in the period Coin tried a 42-yard field goal. The kick was short. Jim Ferguson caught it on the Stanford three and tried to return it. He retreated a few steps, then Ed Shuttlesworth overpowered the Stanford runner near the goal line. Michigan was awarded a safety and two points.

Leading 12-10, Michigan took Stanford's free kick, but three running plays failed to pick up the vital first down which

Quarterback Tom Slade runs the football in the 1972 Rose Bowl game against Stanford. The Wolverines lost 13-12 on a

last-second field goal.

would have won the game. Barry Dotzauer punted, and Stanford began its clock-fighting drive from the twenty-two. Don Bunce hit on two passes, missed, and completed three more in a row. Two running plays netted three yards and excellent field position. Stanford took time out with 16 seconds left in the game, and Coach John Ralston sent in his little place kicker. Garcia, a soccer style booter, drove the ball on a line 31 yards, straight over the cross bar, and Stanford led for the first time in the game, 13-12. Michigan could do nothing about changing it.

The Rose Bowl defeat was disappointing, but it could not tarnish a regular-season record already on the books. The Wolverines of 1971 won eleven straight games and established team records for first downs, rushing yardage, total offense, and points. The defense yielded just 65.8 yards per game, another record. Most of these standards were set by Michigan's great 1947 team.

Four all-Americans were added to Michigan's total that now stood at an imposing sixty-two—Darden and Mike Taylor on defense, and McKenzie and Billy Taylor on offense. Those four, along with defensive end Mike Keller, were named to the all-Big Ten team. Billy Taylor, voted the Wolverines' most valuable player, ran his career rushing total to 3,072 yards, another record.

Schembechler had taken Bump Elliott's final group of athletes as sophomores, and in three years they won twenty-eight games and lost three in the regular season. They won two Big Ten titles and played in two Rose Bowl games.

Another group of sophomores in 1947 had played on teams which won three conference titles, two national championships, and a Rose Bowl game. The sophomores of 1948 enjoyed another brilliant three-year period with three conference championships, one national title, and a Rose Bowl victory.

Schembechler looked to his 1972 team and the young sophomores coming up. He hoped they would carry on that tradition.

Not Enough Touchdowns

Bo Schembechler made no promises, no guarantees to Dennis Franklin, a willowy, All-State quarterback from Massillon, Ohio, whose football talents had drawn the attention of scores of major colleges. "All he said was I'd get an opportunity to show what I could do," Franklin said. "I believed him."

It was obvious during the spring of 1972 that Franklin needed no promises. He ran like a halfback. His arm was strong, and he knew football. A writer asked him if playing at Michigan before 100,000 fans would bother him. "Gosh, I don't know," Franklin said. "The most I ever played before in Massillon was 20,000 or so."

It was another season for sophomores at Michigan. Gil Chapman, a peppery little speedster from New Jersey; Steve Strinko, a 235-pound linebacker; David Brown, an all-around athlete with size and speed; and Chuck Heater, a slashing, 205 pound tailback—they were part of an exceptional sophomore group that Schembechler greeted with some anticipation.

There were only nine starters returning for the 1972 season. The sophomores, Schembechler thought, would have to make a strong contribution. He did not look for any help from the incoming freshmen, although the Big Ten's new rule allowed first-year students to compete on the varsity level. Paul Seymour, a 6-foot-5, 250-pound senior, moved from tight end to tackle. Michigan could field an extremely experienced offensive line, but the backfield and most of the defense had to be rebuilt.

Franklin became the third sophomore to start at quarterback for Schembechler within a year when Michigan opened against Northwestern. His 21-yard pass to Bo Rather produced the game's only touchdown.

The next game was scheduled in Los Angeles Coliseum against UCLA, and Schembechler's third trip to the coast proved completely satisfying. He put little stock in a jinx. The Wolverines were lodged in their Rose Bowl headquarters, the Huntington Hotel in Pasadena, practiced on the same field they had used before, then ripped the Bruins, 26-9. They powered out drives of 74, 60, 80, and 53 yards to score four times. UCLA's Mark Harmon was injured early in the first quarter as his father, Tom, was broadcasting the game for a television station.

Michigan returned home to face Tulane, and Ed Shuttlesworth, Michigan's 235-pound fullback, scored three times and gained 151 yards in a 41-7 win. Then the sophomore brigade at Michigan began to assert itself. Franklin rifled a pair of touchdown passes, and Dave Brown returned a punt 83 yards in a 35-7 victory over Navy. Chapman surprised Michigan State with a 58-yard touchdown run on an end-around that clinched a rousing defensive contest for Michigan, 10-0. Heater gained 155 yards, Franklin passed for 103, and Chapman returned a punt 73 yards to score against an outmanned Illinois team in Champaign.

Minnesota was never in the game after Shuttlesworth scored four times in the first half. The final score was 42-0.

Michigan's eighth straight victory involved a series of misadventures with Indiana. The Hoosiers lost six fumbles and the Wolverines three. The fired-up Hoosiers battled Michigan to a 7-7 deadlock in the fourth period, but the Wolverines finally pulled it out with two touchdowns.

Iowa was Michigan's fourth shutout victim, 31-0. Then Purdue for the second straight season flirted with an upset before succumbing to another last-minute field goal. Mike Lantry, a Vietnam veteran, kicked one from 30 yards out to win it. Franklin, who engineered Michigan's only touchdown, passed to Rather for 20 yards, to Clint Haslerig for 52, and finally to tight end Paul Seal for 11 yards and the score.

With Michigan State's upset of Ohio State, the Wolverines'

Speedy Gil Chapman breaks into the clear on a 58-yard touchdown end-around run against Michigan State in 1972.

9-6 victory over Purdue assured them of at least a co-championship. They carried an unblemished 10-0 record into the final game with the Buckeyes in Columbus. The Big Ten had repealed the no-repeat rule, allowing any team to make the holiday trip west two, three, four years in succession. The way was cleared for a dynasty to develop.

Fielding Yost had insisted a half-century before, following a dramatic victory over Minnesota, "You don't win football games with first downs, you win them with touchdowns." That philosophy rang bitterly with truth in the climatic game of 1972. Michigan not only had more first downs, a whooping twenty-one to Ohio State's ten, but had more rushing yardage, more passing yardage, one more field goal...more of everything but touchdowns.

Michigan's first touchdown drive was ruined by a penalty. A second threat just before the half ended missed as Heater slipped twice on the wet artificial turf, and Franklin fumbled the center snap on fourth down.

All the scoring came in the second and third periods. Mike Lantry pushed Michigan in front with a 35-yard field goal, but Champ Henson had Ohio ahead, 7-3, at half time with a short plunge. Archie Griffin ran 30 yards for Ohio's second touchdown in the third period. Michigan responded with Shuttlesworth scoring from the one and Franklin passing to Haslerig for two points.

Ohio State held a 14-11 lead when Michigan launched another assault later in the third period that carried to the Buckeye twenty as the clock began its final 15-minute count-down. The Wolverines needed a yard on fourth down. Shuttlesworth, operating on an injured ankle, could not provide it. A minute later Randy Logan intercepted a pass, and Michigan was back on Ohio's five with a first down.

It was eerie, almost like the game played eighteen years earlier in this same stadium, when Michigan's 1954 team had a first and goal on the five; then four running attempts followed, all stopped by the Buckeyes. This time, in the 1972 replay, Harry Banks fought for a yard at right end. Banks ran again for three yards. The little tailback hurled into the line a third time...inches short. It was fourth down, and Franklin tried to squeeze across the goal stripe, but Ohio State held.

There were 8 minutes and 53 seconds left to play.

Ohio State ran the ball out to the nine and punted. Michigan used four plays, then gave up the ball on Ohio's thirty-seven. The Bucks moved to Michigan's thirty and missed

Dennis Franklin sets the Michigan offense in motion. The young sophomore gave the 1972 Wolverines a dangerous option attack.

a field goal. Franklin, starting from his twenty, tried desperately to pass the Wolverines to victory. He hit Rather for nine yards, then for fourteen, again for fourteen, but Michigan ran out of downs on the Ohio forty-one.

The 14-11 victory gave Ohio State a share of the championship with Michigan and the necessary votes for the Rose Bowl, where Southern Cal had the touchdowns, 42-17.

The Michigan-Ohio State game generates controversy. The stakes are high, and every move, every play is magnified accordingly. It was natural in the locker room after the game that writers would question Schembechler's decision to bypass a field goal and a possible tie. A tie, they insisted, would have given his Wolverines an undisputed claim on the conference championship and a Rose Bowl berth. They knew the stakes, but they did not know the Michigan football coach. His team was undefeated, and there was an opportunity to win a national championship. Schembechler had built a powerful, rushing offense. He had confidence in it. He felt his chances were better moving the ball a yard on the ground, than kicking it 18 yards in the air.

Schembechler coached to win...he would not change.

A Long Ride Home

The traffic on interstate 94 was light, even for an early Sunday afternoon. Bo Schembechler was relaxed for the first time in months. His conversation was light, optimistic. He talked of recruiting, the future, the Rose Bowl.

"You know, I'm going to put those guys on their own when we get to California," Schembechler offered. "They'll make their own training rules. I'll let them decide what they want to do. Damn, they're a great bunch of kids." His driver nodded.

Schembechler was talking of the 1974 Rose Bowl game. His Wolverines had just completed an undefeated season, their second one in three years. They had won or shared three straight Big Ten championships, and Schembechler was satisfied. The game the day before, the 10-10 deadlock with Ohio State, however, was frustrating for him. Michigan had come back to tie it in the fourth quarter and nearly won the game. "Six inches, just that far," he held his hands apart showing how close he thought a field goal had come, "and we'd won the damn thing."

The car sped on, past the factories, into the deep highway trenches of Detroit. Schembechler was scheduled at the WWJ-TV studios to tape his television show. Each week he had talked about victory, ten straight victories. The announcement on the selection of the Big Ten Rose Bowl representative was due for 2 p.m. The car radio remained off.

Schembechler talked about the season. It was a special season for him. He talked about his seniors, thirty of them.

Four years earlier they had come to him, to his home, while he was recovering from a heart attack. They had believed him when he said, "I'll be your coach next fall." They were being recruited by other schools, and Schembechler would have understood if they had not believed him.

Schembechler told his team in the fall of 1973, "You are going to win every game; you're going to win the Big Ten championship, and we're going to the Rose Bowl." They believed that, too.

The car swung to the right, made a U-turn, and pulled in next to the curb, a half block from the studio. Schembechler saw a group of people waiting in front of the studio, reporters, cameramen. He got out of the car and started to walk toward the studio. Bill Halls, a sportswriter for the *Detroit News*, was the first to reach Schembechler.

"Have you heard the vote?" Halls asked.

"No," smiled Schembechler, "We were talking and had the radio off. How'd it go?"

"Ohio State," Halls said softly.

"You're kidding." Schembechler's face began to tighten.

Halls said nothing. Schembechler did not wait. He walked past the reporters into the studio. His face reddened, his hands shook. He talked with Michigan's athletic director, Don Canham, on the phone. Canham confirmed the selection. It was a secret vote, but Don Kremer, a sportscaster at WWJ, said it was six-to-four.

"What will I tell those kids? What will I tell those seniors?" Schembechler repeated. He had suffered a heart attack and came back. His teams had lost two Rose Bowl games, and they had come back. He knew there could be no next year for those seniors. "This is the lowest point in my coaching career," Bo said, then turned to Kremer. "I can't do the show today; we'll do it tomorrow." He walked out into the lobby, met the reporters, then began a long ride home to Ann Arbor.

The entire 1973 season for Michigan had built to the climax with Ohio State. They were the two conference favorites, and their November 24th game in Michigan Stadium was to decide the championship. They had shared the title the previous year, and Ohio State went on to the Rose Bowl. Michigan won an undisputed championship in 1971 and

376

The 1973 Wolverine co-captain and MVP, tight end Paul Seal, snares a pass against Navy. Seal maintained the Michigan tradition of excellent tight ends, including Ron Kramer, Jim Mandich, and Paul Seymour.

received the bowl bid.

Schembechler installed a new, option offense which featured his overly talented quarterback, Dennis Franklin. Michigan had lost heavily in the offensive line where Paul Seymour, a giant tackle, had been an all-American. Physically

Michigan all-American safetyman Dave Brown (6) returns a punt 53 yards to score against Michigan State in 1973.

the line was not as powerful, but quicker. Schembechler had to restock his defense. Randy Logan, another all-American and the team's most valuable player in 1972, and four other starters had to be replaced.

The parts all fitted, right from the opener against Iowa. Michigan rushed for 440 yards in the 31-7 victory, then put it all together in a stunning 47-10 triumph over Stanford. Ed Shuttlesworth and Gil Chapman led the rushing attack which produced 240 yards, and Mike Lantry kicked field goals of 50 and 51 yards, the longest in Michigan history.

The only real letdown came in the third game against Navy. Franklin suffered a broken finger, but an improving defense shut out the Middies. Franklin missed the Oregon game, but Larry Cipa again came through, just as he had done against Ohio State two years before. He passed for one touchdown and set up another with an 18-yard strike to freshman Jim Smith. Chapman's 83-yard punt return, a school record, clinched the 24-0 victory.

Chapman ignored a torrential downpour in the game at East Lansing, scoring on a 53-yard run and gaining 117 yards in a 31-0 win over Michigan State. Franklin returned as the starting quarterback and guided the attack flawlessly.

Wisconsin became the first team to score on Michigan in four weeks, and that came on a deflected Badger pass. Franklin unloaded a 46-yard touchdown pass to tight end Paul Seal, and Chapman rushed for 92 yards in the first half. The Wolverines won going away, 35-6. Another big first half pushed Michigan to a 34-7 decision over Minnesota.

The Wolverines were even better against Indiana, hitting the Hoosiers with forty-two points in the first half and finally winning, 49-13. Chuck Heater raced 71 yards to score, Franklin ran 49 yards for a touchdown, and sophomore Gordon Bell 29 yards for a third touchdown.

Illinois surprised Michigan with counter plays in the first half, but the Wolverines adjusted their defenses for the second half and won, 21-6. Chapman continued Michigan's long range scoring, this one from 33 yards out. The ball was bouncing in

Dennis Franklin, returning after suffering a broken finger in the Navy game, fires up the Michigan offense in 1973.

380

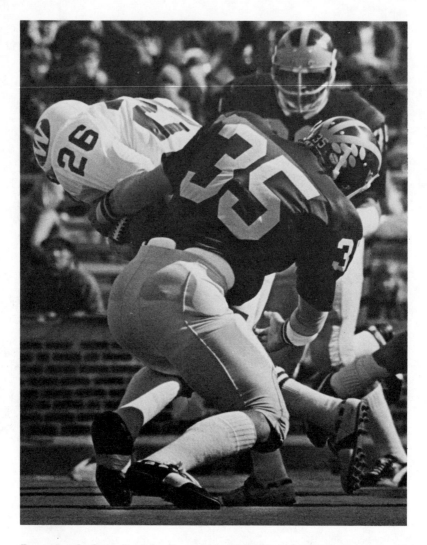

Roverback Don Dufek, Jr., son of Michigan's 1951 Rose Bowl star fullback, stops a Wisconsin runner in this 1973 game.

favor of the Wolverines most of the game. They fumbled six times, but recovered four, including one loose ball that Seal picked up, reversed his field, and ran 20 yards for a touchdown.

Tough Purdue was next, but for the first time in three years the game was close for only a half. Haslerig leaped over a Purdue defender to grab a 41-yard touchdown pass from

Franklin for a 6-3 lead at half time. Michigan scored twice in the third period as a rushing game that netted 310 yards and two key interceptions, by Barry Dotzauer and Don Coleman, provided the edge in a 34-9 victory.

That made it ten victories in a row going into the conference championship match with Ohio State. The Bucks carried a 9-0 mark and were slight favorites on Michigan's home field.

Tailback Chuck Heater shows his slashing running style for Michigan in the 1973 game against Illinois.

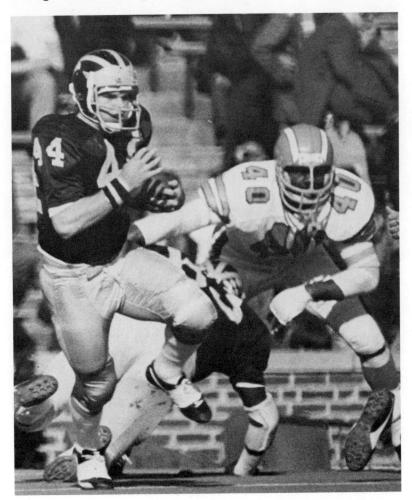

The Tie Game

The setting was ideal, as if it had been programmed by the television network. Michigan vs. Ohio State. Nothing was left out. The conference championship, the Rose Bowl, and a possible National Championship awaited the winner.

The crowd in Michigan Stadium was announced at 105,223. The cameras of ABC had a coast-to-coast audience. This was the first half of a television doubleheader. UCLA and Southern Cal would decide the Rose Bowl question on the West Coast later in the afternoon. Press and radio coverage was enormous, even topping the interest generated for the 1969 game between these two rivals.

Both Ohio State and Michigan had proud, bruising defenses, and they dominated the first quarter. Ohio ran three plays and punted. Michigan ran one play, then fumbled. The Buckeyes gained nine yards in three plays, decided against testing Michigan's defense for the first down, and punted.

Ohio State, unable to register a first down in the entire period, started to move early in the second quarter. Archie Griffin ran 38 yards, nearly breaking away. The Buckeyes moved to Michigan's fourteen but had to settle for a field goal.

Gil Chapman took the ensuing kickoff in the Michigan end zone, headed for the right sidelines, cut back to the middle, and raced to Ohio's twenty-nine. A clipping penalty nullified the seventy-one yard run, however, and Michigan could not move. Ohio had gained vital field position and kept hammering at the Michigan defense. Late in the second quarter the Bucks took

Bo Schembechler on the sideline with the telephone to the press box. His first five years at Michigan produced a remarkable record of 48-6-1, including three co-championships and one outright title. The singular tie occurred in the final game of the 1973 season with Ohio State, 10-10.

Left-footed Mike Lantry missed a 58-yard field goal by less than a foot that would have given Michigan a clear-cut Big Ten championship in its showdown match with Ohio State. Holding is Larry Gustafson.

over on their forty-five and sent Griffin and freshman fullback Pete Johnson into the line eight times. Johnson finally muscled his way across the goal line from the five, and Ohio State had a 10-0 lead at half time.

Michigan came back with the second half kickoff and drove forty yards to Ohio's thirty-two, but Franklin's pass was intercepted by Neal Colzie in the end zone. Late in the period the Wolverines were moving again, and this drive carried to Ohio's thirteen. The Bucks held, and Lantry kicked a 30-yard field goal on the second play of the fourth quarter.

The Wolverines were charged. The momentum had swung. Ohio State gained six yards and punted to Michigan's forty-nine. Ed Shuttlesworth gained five, then Franklin passed 27 yards to Paul Seal. Michigan drove to the ten where Franklin, on fourth down and one, faked the ball to Shuttlesworth and rolled off his right end to score. Lantry's kick tied the game at 10-10.

Michigan launched another drive from its twelve as Franklin completed three straight passes. After the third pass left his hand, Franklin was jarred with a clean, hard tackle. He fell heavily on his shoulder, breaking his collar bone. On fourth down Lantry tried a field goal from Ohio's forty-eight. The powerful left-footed kicker drove the ball on a line; it had the distance and height, but sailed by the upright six inches to the left.

There was a minute left. Woody Hayes was going for victory, but Greg Hare's pass was intercepted by Tom Drake. With seconds left Lantry tried another field goal, this one from forty-four yards out. It missed to the right.

Ohio came back passing, but Hare, who had replaced starter Cornelius Greene, missed on all three attempts as the game ended in a 10-10 tie.

The Big Ten championship was shared by Ohio State and Michigan, but the question of a Rose Bowl representative was left to a vote of the ten athletic directors. Any team could go. Their voting guideline was, "the most representative team in the Big Ten."

The decision was announced in Chicago at the annual basketball press conference the next day. Ohio State was selected. Newspapers reported the vote as six-to-four. An even split in the voting, five-and-five, would have sent Michigan to the Rose Bowl as OSU had been there more recently, the year before. The Bucks ended the Big Ten's four-year losing streak in the Rose Bowl, defeating Southern Cal, 42-17.

It was a near miss for Michigan and for Dave Gallagher, a senior who earned all-American honors as a defensive tackle. He had received Schembechler's last scholarship offer, the thirty-fifth player recruited. It was a near miss for Paul Seal, another senior who was voted Michigan's most valuable player.

For Dave Brown, the all-American safety, there would be another year, another Michigan-Ohio State game in 1974. For Dennis Franklin, an all-Big Ten quarterback, his shoulder would heal and he would return.

Michigan had won thirty-one games, lost one, and tied one during the seasons of 1971-72-73. During Schembechler's five years at Michigan the Wolverines compiled the finest regular record in college football, 48-4-1. Schembechler had never liked tie scores. Now he liked them even less.

Schembechler's Record

AT MIAMI

Year	W	L	T	Pct.	Pts.	Opp.
1963	5	3	2	.625	208	178
1964	6	3	1	.667	209	142
*1965	7	3	0	.700	247	137
*1966	9	1	0	.900	229	76
1967	6	4	0	.600	181	114
1968	7	3	0	.700	240	99
Total	40	17	3	.702	1314	746

AT MICHIGAN

Year	W	L	T	Pct.	Pts.	Opp.
*1969	8	3	0	.727	352	148
1970	9	1	0	.900	288	90
†1971	11	1	0	.917	421	83
*1972	10	1	0	.909	264	57
*1973	10	0	1	1.000	330	68
Total	48	6	1	.889	1655	446
Career Totals	**88**	**23**	**4**	**.792**	**2969**	**1192**

* Cochampionship Season
† Outright Championship

Epilogue

The story of football at Michigan is impossible to bind within the covers of a single book. It is a story, not just of victory and defeat, but of emotion, desire, sacrifice. Without these any decision, even a tie, becomes shallow, meaningless.

Michigan had a fine football record in 1946. Those players had fought a war, and many were playing college football for the first time in three, four, and even five years. They had been shot at, captured, and some dropped bombs on cities. What were they like? Well, one day this group of veterans was staging an ice cream eating contest in the Michigan Union. The winner ate eleven dishes. Fritz Crisler just turned his back and smiled. The war was over.

Bennie Oosterbaan, like Fritz, was a constant and understanding critic as this book was being written. Ben insisted that the storyteller relate the experiences of the football players who came from Wisconsin to Michigan in 1943 under the Navy's V-12 program. "They loved it here, and we loved them," Ben said. "They were accepted by everyone and returned to Wisconsin to play against Michigan."

Oosterbaan offered an endless well of stories. Most of them contained a spirit, a warmth that existed in Michigan football. That was the way he coached.

The story of Michigan football is a story of men, and seventeen-year-old freshmen, too. It is a story of tradition, built by great athletic directors and outstanding coaches; and football players, some great, some good, all committed to excellence.

They did not always succeed, but they tried.

We have endeavored to tell that story. Recalling those early years was difficult at times, expecially when three newspapers each listed a different player scoring the same touchdown. As victory was piled upon victory, championship upon championship, their weight almost obscured the men who made success possible.

The help of Crisler and Oosterbaan, and the players who wrote of their Michigan years, the help of Bill Cusumano, Charles Bloom, and Pat Perry in compiling the story of Michigan football was invaluable. Without them that story would remain buried in dusty scrapbooks, file cabinets, in the thoughts of those who played the game.

Appendix

Michigan's All-Time Football Coaching Records

Years	Coach (School)	Won	Lost	Tied	Pct.
1879-90	No Coaches	23	10	1	.697
1891	Mike Murphy & Frank Crawford	4	5	0	.444
1892-93	Frank E. Barbour (Yale '92)	14	8	0	.632
1894-96	William L. McCauley (Princeton '94)	26	3	1	.896
1897-99	Gustave H. Ferbert (Michigan '97)	24	3	1	.888
1900	Langdon 'Biff' Lea (Princeton)	7	2	1	.778
1901-23 1925-26	Fielding H. Yost (W. Virginia '97)	165	29	10	.845
1924	George Little (Ohio Wesleyan '12)	6	2	0	.750
1927-28	Elton E. 'Tad' Wieman (Mich. '21)	9	6	1	.600
1929-37	Harry G. Kipke (Michigan '24)	46	26	4	.639
1937-47	H. O. 'Fritz' Crisler (Chicago '22)	71	16	3	.816
1948-58	Bennie G. Oosterbaan (Mich. '28)	63	33	4	.656
1959-68	Chalmers W. 'Bump' Elliott (Mich. '48)	51	42	2	.548
1969-	Glenn E. (Bo) Schembechler (Miami of Ohio '51)	48	6	1	.889

(Tie games not figured in percentages)

MICHIGAN'S OPPONENTS THROUGH THE YEARS

TEAM	FIRST GAME	W	L	T
Adrian	1894	1	0	0
Air Force	1964	1	0	0
Albion	1884	16	1	0
American College M. & S.	1904	1	0	0
Ann Arbor	1891	1	0	0
Arizona	1970	1	0	0
Beloit	1898	3	0	0
Buffalo	1900	1	0	0
Butler	1891	1	0	0
California	1940	4	2	0

391

TEAM	FIRST GAME	W	L	T
Camp Grant	1943	1	0	0
Carlisle	1901	1	0	0
Carroll	1916	1	0	0
Case	1894	26	0	1
Central State Teachers	1931	1	0	0
Chicago	1892	19	7	0
Chicago Athletic Assn.	1889	0	1	0
Chicago Athletic Club	1891	0	1	0
Chicago University Club	1884	1	1	0
Cleveland Athletic Assn.	1891	0	1	0
College of P & S	1896	2	0	0
Columbia	1935	3	0	0
Cornell	1889	6	12	0
Dartmouth	1950	1	0	0
Denison	1930	1	0	0
DePauw	1892	3	0	0
Detroit Athletic Club	1890	5	0	0
Detroit Independents	1883	1	0	0
Drake	1903	3	0	0
Duke	1960	4	0	0
Ferris Institute	1903	1	0	0
Georgia	1957	1	1	0
Georgia Tech	1934	1	0	0
Grand Rapids	1896	1	0	0
Great Lakes Training Station	1942	2	0	0
Harvard	1881	4	4	0
Harvard of Chicago	1887	1	0	0
Hillsdale	1899	2	0	0
Illinois	1898	41	18	0
Indiana	1900	24	8	0
Iowa	1900	22	4	3
Iowa Naval Pre-Flight	1942	1	1	0
Kalamazoo	1899	5	0	0
Kansas	1893	2	0	0
Kentucky	1908	1	0	0
Kenyon	1898	1	0	0
Lake Forest	1895	2	0	0
Lawrence	1915	1	0	0
Lehigh	1896	1	0	0
Marietta	1915	2	0	0
Marquette	1909	2	0	0
Miami	1924	1	0	0
Michigan Athletic Assn.	1892	2	0	0
Michigan M.A.	1895	1	0	0
Michigan Normal	1896	5	0	0
Michigan State	1898	41	20	5
Minnesota	1892	40	21	3
Missouri	1955	1	2	0
Mount Union	1913	7	0	0
Nebraska	1905	2	1	1

North Carolina	1965	1	1	0
Northwestern	1892	30	11	2
Notre Dame	1887	9	2	0
Oberlin	1891	9	0	0
Ohio Northern	1903	3	0	0
Ohio State	1897	39	26	5
Ohio Wesleyan	1897	2	1	1
Oklahoma A & M	1926	1	0	0
Olivet	1891	2	0	0
Orchard Lake	1894	1	0	1
Oregon	1948	3	0	0
Oregon State	1959	3	0	0
Pennisulars, Detroit	1885	1	0	0
Pennsylvania	1889	11	8	2
Pittsburgh	1941	2	0	0
Princeton	1881	2	1	0
Purdue	1890	18	7	0
Quantico Marines	1923	1	0	0
Racine College	1879	1	0	0
South Dakota	1912	1	0	0
Southern California	1948	3	1	0
Southern Methodist	1963	1	0	0
Stanford	1901	4	3	0
Stevens Institute	1883	1	0	0
Syracuse	1908	5	4	1
Texas A & M	1970	1	0	0
Toronto	1879	1	0	1
Tulane	1920	3	0	0
UCLA	1956	4	0	0
University of Detroit	1917	1	0	0
U.S. Military Academy (Army)	1945	4	5	0
U.S. Naval Academy (Navy)	1925	8	5	1
Vanderbilt	1905	9	0	1
Virginia	1899	2	0	0
Wabash	1907	1	0	0
Washington	1916	5	0	0
Wesleyan	1883	0	1	0
Western Michigan	1917	2	0	0
Western Reserve	1895	3	0	0
West Virginia	1904	1	0	0
Windsor Club	1885	2	0	0
Wittenberg	1896	2	0	0
Wisconsin	1892	25	7	1
Yale	1881	2	2	0
TOTALS		558	191	29

Michigan's All-Time Football Record

Yr.	Won	Lost	Tied	Mich. Pts.	Opp. Pts.	Captain	Coach
1879	1	0	1	1	0	D. N. Detar	
1880	1	0	0	13	6	John Chase	
1881	0	3	0	4	28	W.S. Horton	
No teams or outside games							
1883	2	3	0	63	83	W.J. Olcott	
1884	2	0	0	36	10	H.G. Prettyman	
1885	3	0	0	82	0	H.G. Prettyman	
1886	2	0	0	74	0	H.G. Prettyman	
1887	3	0	0	66	0	J.L. Duffy	
1888	4	1	0	130	40	J.L. Duffy	
1889	1	2	0	33	80	E.W. McPherran	
1890	4	1	0	129	36	W.C. Malley	
1891	4	5	0	168	114	J. Van Inwagen	Murphy
1892	7	5	0	298	172	G.B. Dygert	Barbour
1893	7	3	0	278	102	G.B. Dygert	Barbour
1894	9	1	1	244	84	James Baird	McCauley
1895	8	1	0	266	14	F. Henninger	McCauley
1896	9	1	0	262	11	H.M. Senter	McCauley
1897	6	1	1	166	46	J.R. Hogg	Ferbert
1898	10	0	0	193	28	J.W. Bennett	Ferbert
1899	8	2	0	176	43	W.C. Steckle	Ferbert
1900	7	2	1	117	55	Neil Snow	Lea
1901	11	0	0	550	0	Hugh White	Yost
1902	11	0	0	644	12	H.S. Weeks	Yost
1903	11	0	1	565	6	C.G. Redden	Yost
1904	10	0	0	567	22	W.M. Heston	Yost
1905	12	1	0	495	2	F.S. Norcross	Yost
1906	4	1	0	72	30	J.S. Curtis	Yost
1907	5	1	0	107	6	P.P. McGoffin	Yost
1908	5	2	1	128	81	A.G. Schultz	Yost
1909	6	1	1	116	34	D.W. Allerdice	Yost
1910	3	0	3	28	9	A.W. Benbrook	Yost
1911	5	1	2	90	38	F.L. Conklin	Yost
1912	5	2	0	158	65	George C. Thomson	Yost
1913	6	1	0	175	21	George Paterson	Yost
1914	6	3	0	233	68	J.W. Raynsford	Yost
1915	4	3	1	130	81	W.D. Cochran	Yost
1916	7	2	0	245	56	J.F. Maultbetsch	Yost
1917	8	2	0	304	53	Cedric C. Smith	Yost
1918	5	0	0	96	6	E.E. Wieman	Yost
1919	3	4	0	93	102	Angus Goetz	Yost
1920	5	2	0	121	21	Angus Goetz	Yost
1921	5	1	1	187	21	R.L. Dunne	Yost
1922	6	0	1	183	13	P.L. Goebel	Yost
1923	8	0	0	150	12	Harry G. Kipke	Yost
1924	6	2	0	155	55	H.F. Steger	Little
1925	7	1	0	227	3	Robert Brown	Yost
1926	7	1	0	191	38	Ben Friedman	Yost
1927	6	2	0	137	39	Bennie Oosterbaan	Wieman
1928	3	4	1	36	62	George Rich	Wieman
1929	5	3	1	109	75	Joe Truskowski	Kipke
1930	8	0	1	111	23	James Simrall	Kipke
1931	8	1	1	181	27	Roy Hudson	Kipke
1932	8	0	0	123	13	Ivan Williamson	Kipke

394

1933	7	0	1	131	18	Stanley Fay	Kipke
1934	1	7	0	21	143	Thomas Austin	Kipke
1935	4	4	0	68	131	William Renner	Kipke
1936	1	7	0	36	127	Matt Patanelli	Kipke
1937	4	4	0	54	110	Joe Rinaldi	Kipke
1938	6	1	1	131	40	Fred Janke	Crisler
1939	6	2	0	219	94	Archie Kodros	Crisler
1940	7	1	0	196	34	Forest Evashevski	Crisler
1941	6	1	1	147	41	Bob Westfall	Crisler
1942	7	3	0	221	134	George Ceithaml	Crisler
1943	8	1	0	302	73	Paul White	Crisler
1944	8	2	0	204	91	Bob Wiese	Crisler
1945	7	3	0	187	99	Joe Ponsetto	Crisler
1946	6	2	1	233	73	Art Renner	Crisler
1947	10	0	0	394	53	Bruce Hilkene	Crisler
1948	9	0	0	252	44	Dominic Tomasi	Oosterbaan
1949	6	2	1	135	85	Alvin Wistert	Oosterbaan
1950	6	3	1	150	114	Al Wahl	Oosterbaan
1951	4	5	0	135	122	Bill Putich	Oosterbaan
1952	5	4	0	207	134	Merritt Green	Oosterbaan
1953	6	3	0	163	101	D.OShaughnessy	Oosterbaan
1954	6	3	0	139	87	Ted Cachey	Oosterbaan
1955	7	2	0	179	94	Ed Meads	Oosterbaan
1956	7	2	0	233	123	Tom Maentz	Oosterbaan
1957	5	3	1	187	147	Jim Orwig	Oosterbaan
1958	2	6	1	132	211	John Herrnstein	Oosterbaan
1959	4	5	0	122	161	George Genyk	Elliott
1960	5	5	0	133	84	Gerald Smith	Elliott
1961	6	3	0	212	163	George Mans	Elliott
1962	2	7	0	70	214	Bob Brown	Elliott
1963	3	4	2	131	127	Joe O'Donnell	Elliott
1964	9	1	0	235	83	Jim Conley	Elliott
1965	4	6	0	185	161	Tom Cecchini	Elliott
1966	6	4	0	236	138	Jack Clancy	Elliott
1967	4	6	0	144	179	Joe Dayton	Elliott
1968	8	2	0	217	155	Ron Johnson	Elliott
1969	8	3	0	352	148	Jim Mandich	Schembechler
1970	9	1	0	288	90	Don Moorhead & Henry Hill	Schembechler
1971	11	1	0	421	83	Frank Gusich & Guy Murdock	Schembechler
1972	10	1	0	264	57	Tom Coyle & Randy Logan	Schembechler
1973	10	0	1	330	68	Dave Gallagher & Paul Seal	Schembechler

395

Les Etter served twenty-three years as Michigan's sports information director.

Dr. A. W. Coxon was Michigan's team physician from 1940 until retiring in 1964.

Jim Hunt was nationally respected as Michigan's trainer during the 1950s and 1960s. He was named to the Helms Foundation Hall of Fame.

The Victors and The Yellow and Blue—Louis Elbel, left, who wrote "The Victors," and Fred Lawton, who wrote "The Yellow and Blue," attending "M" Day at the Michigan Golf Course.

Frank Royce (left) buys his 1971 season tickets from former Michigan ticket manager Don Weir. Royce has attended every Michigan home game since 1901, including the clash with Carlisle for which he is holding a ticket.

Football Scores By Years

May 30, 1879
Michigan.........1; Racine College.. 0
Fall, 1879
Michigan..........0; Toronto........ 0
Season Summary
Games won, 1; Lost 0; Tied, 1.
Points for Michigan, 1; For Opponents, 0.
1880
Michigan.........13; Toronto........ 6
Season Summary
Games won, 1; Lost 0; Tied 0.
Points for Michigan, 13; For Opponents, 6.
1881
Michigan..........0; Harvard........ 4
Michigan..........0; Yale.......... 11
Michigan..........4; Princeton......13
Season Summary
Games won, 0; Lost 3; Tied 0.
Points for Michigan, 4; For Opponents, 28.
1882
No regular team or outside games.
1883
Michigan..........0; Yale.......... 46
Michigan..........0; Harvard........ 3
Michigan..........6; Wesleyan......14
Michigan..........5; Stevens Institute.1
Michigan.........40; Detroit Ind...... 5
Season Summary
Games won, 2; Lost 3; Tied. 0.
Points for Michigan, 51; For Opponents, 69
1844
Michigan.........18; Albion......... 0
Michigan.........18; Chicago U Club. 10
Season Summary
Games won 2; Lost 0; Tied, 0.
Points for Michigan, 36; For Opponents 10.
1885
Michigan.........10; Windsor Club... 0
Michigan.........30; Windsor Club... 0
Michigan.........42; Peninsulars, Det. 0
Season Summary
Games won, 3; Lost 0; Tied, 0.
Points for Michigan, 82; For opponents, 0.
1886
Michigan.........50; Albion......... 0
Michigan.........24; Albion......... 0
Season Summary
Games won, 2; Lost, 0; Tied, 0.
Points for Michigan, 74; For Opponents, 0.
1887
Michigan.........32; Albion......... 0
Michigan..........8; Notre Dame..... 0
Michigan.........26; Harvard of Chic.. 0
Season Summary
Games won, 3; Lost, 0; Ties, 0.
Points for Michigan, 66; For Opponents 0.
1888
Michigan..........4; Chicago U Club. 26
Michigan.........26; Notre Dame..... 6
Michigan.........10; Notre Dame..... 4
Michigan.........14; Detroit A.C..... 6
Michigan.........76; Albion......... 4
Season Summary
Games won, 4; Lost, 1; Tied, 0.
Points for Michigan, 130; For Opponents 46
1889
Michigan.........33; Albion......... 4
Michigan..........0; Cornell........56
Michigan..........0; Chicago A.A....20
Season Summary
Games won, 1; Lost 2; Tied, 0.
Points for Michigan, 33; For Opponents, 80

1890
Michigan.........56; Albion........ 10
Michigan.........16; Albion........ 0
Michigan.........18; D.A.C........ 0
Michigan.........34; Purdue........ 6
Michigan..........5; Cornell........20
Season Summary
Games won, 5; Lost, 1; Tied, 0.
Points for Michigan, 129; For Opponents 36
1891
Michigan.........26; Oberlin......... 6
Michigan.........18; Olivet......... 6
Michigan..........4; Albion........ 10
Michigan.........12; Cornell........58
Michigan..........0; Chicago A.C....10
Michigan.........42; Butler......... 6
Michigan..........0; Cornell........10
Michigan..........4; Cleveland A.A... 8
Michigan.........62; Ann Arbor High.. 0
Season Summary
Games won, 4; Lost, 5; Tied, 0.
Points for Michigan, 172; Opponents, 114.
1892
Michigan.........74; Michigan A.A....0
Michigan.........68; Michigan A.A....0
Michigan.........10; Wisconsin..... 6
Michigan..........6; Minnesota.....14
Michigan.........18; DePauw........ 0
Michigan..........8; Northwestern... 10
Michigan..........0; Purdue........ 24
Michigan.........60; Albion........ 8
Michigan..........0; Cornell........44
Michigan.........10; Cornell........30
Michigan.........18; Chicago.......10
Michigan.........26; Oberlin........24
Season Summary
Games won, 7; Lost, 5; Tied, 0.
Points for Michigan, 296; Opponents, 170.
1893
Michigan..........6; D.A.C......... 0
Michigan.........26; D.A.C......... 0
Michigan..........6; Chicago.......10
Michigan.........20; Minnesota.....20
Michigan.........18; Wisconsin.....34
Michigan.........46; Purdue........ 8
Michigan.........34; DePauw........ 0
Michigan.........72; Northwestern... 6
Michigan.........22; Kansas........0
Michigan.........28; Chicago.......10
Season Summary
Games won, 7; Lost 3; Tied 0.
Points for Michigan, 278; Opponents 102.
1894
Michigan.........12; Orchard Lake...12
Michigan.........26; Albion........ 10
Michigan.........48; Olivet......... 0
Michigan.........40; Orchard Lake....6
Michigan.........46; Adrian......... 0
Michigan.........18; Case......... 8
Michigan..........0; Cornell........22
Michigan.........22; Kansas........12
Michigan.........14; Oberlin......... 6
Michigan.........12; Cornell........ 4
Michigan..........6; Chicago........ 4
Season Summary
Games won, 9; Lost 1; Tied, 1.
Points for Michigan, 244; For Opponents 84
1895
Michigan.........34; M.M.A......... 0
Michigan.........42; D.A.C......... 0
Michigan.........64; Adelbert.......0
Michigan.........40; Lake Forest..... 0

398

Michigan........42; Oberlin.........0
Michigan.........0; Harvard.........4
Michigan........12; Purdue.........10
Michigan........20; Minnesota......0
Michigan........12; Chicago.........0
Season Summary
Games won, 8; Lost 1; Tied 0.
Points for Michigan, 266; For Opponents 14
1896
Michigan........18; Normal.........0
Michigan........44; Grand Rapids...0
Michigan........28; C. of P & S....0
Michigan........66; Lake Forest.....0
Michigan........16; Purdue.........0
Michigan........40; Lehigh.........0
Michigan.........6; Minnesota.....4
Michigan........10; Oberlin........0
Michigan........28; Wittenberg....0
Michigan.........6; Chicago.......7
Season Summary
Games won, 9; Lost, 1; Tied 0.
Points for Michigan, 262; For Opponents 11
1897
Michigan........24; Normal.........0
Michigan.........0; Ohio Wesleyan..0
Michigan........36; O.S.U.........6
Michigan........16; Oberlin.........0
Michigan........34; Purdue........4
Michigan........14; Minnesota......0
Michigan........12; Chicago.......21
*Michigan........0; Varsity Alumni. 15
Season Summary
Games won, 6; Lost 1; Tied, 1.
Points for Michigan, 168; For Opponents 31
1898
Michigan........21; Normal.........0
Michigan........29; Kenyon........0
Michigan........39; M.A.C.........0
Michigan........18; Western Reserve.0
Michigan........23; Case..........5
Michigan........23; Notre Dame.....0
Michigan.........6; Northwestern...5
Michigan........12; Illinois........5
Michigan........22; Beloit.........0
Michigan........12; Chicago......11
*Michigan........11; Varsity Alumni. 2
Season Summary
Games won, 10; Lost, 0; Tied, 0;
Points for Michigan, 205; For Opponents 26
1899
Michigan........11; Hillsdale........0
Michigan........26; Albion.........0
Michigan........17; Western Reserve.0
Michigan........12; Notre Dame.....0
Michigan.........5; Illinois.........0
Michigan........38; Virginia.........0
Michigan........10; Pennsylvania..11
Michigan........28; Case..........6
Michigan........24; Kalamazoo.....9
Michigan.........5; Wisconsin....17
*Michigan........0; Varsity Alumni. 0
Season Summary
Games won, 8; Lost, 2; Tied, 0.
Points for Michigan, 176; For Opponents 43
1900
Michigan........29; Hillsdale.......0
Michigan........11; Kalamazoo.....0
Michigan........24; Case..........6
Michigan........11; Purdue.........6
Michigan........12; Illinois.........0
Michigan........12; Indiana.........0
Michigan.........5; Iowa..........28
Michigan.........7; Notre Dame.....0
Michigan.........0; Ohio State......0
Michigan.........6; Chicago.......15
Season Summary
Games won, 7; Lost, 2; Tied, 1.
Points for Michigan, 117; For Opponents 55

*Exhibition
**First Rose Bowl Game.

1901
Michigan........50; Albion..........0
Michigan........57; Case...........0
Michigan........33; Indiana........0
Michigan........29; Northwestern...0
Michigan.......128; Buffalo........0
Michigan........22; Carlisle........0
Michigan........21; O.S.U.........0
Michigan........22; Chicago........0
Michigan........89; Beloit.........0
Michigan........50; Iowa..........0
**Michigan.......49; Leland Sanford Jr.0
Season Summary
Games won, 11; Lost 0; Tied 0.
Points for Michigan, 550; For Opponents 0.
1902
Michigan........88; Albion.........0
Michigan........48; Case...........6
Michigan.......119; M.A.C.........0
Michigan........60; Indiana........0
Michigan........23; Notre Dame....0
Michigan........86; O.S.U.........0
Michigan.........6; Wisconsin......0
Michigan.......107; Iowa..........0
Michigan........21; Chicago........0
Michigan........63; Oberlin........0
Michigan........23; Minnesota.....6
Season Summary
Games won, 11; Lost, 0; Tied, 0.
Points for Michigan, 644; For Opponents 12
1903
Michigan........31; Case..........0
Michigan........79; Bleoit.........0
Michigan........65; Ohio Northern..0
Michigan........51; Indiana.........0
Michigan........88; Ferris Institute..0
Michigan........47; Drake..........0
Michigan........76; Albion.........0
Michigan.........6; Minnesota.....6
Michigan........36; O.S.U.........0
Michigan........16; Wisconsin......0
Michigan........42; Oberlin........0
Michigan........28; Chicago........0
Season Summary
Games won, 11; Lost, 0; Tied, 1.
Points for Michigan, 565; For Opponents 6.
1904
Michigan........33; Case..........0
Michigan........48; Ohio Northern...0
Michigan........95; Kalamazoo.....0
Michigan........72; P. & S.........0
Michigan........31; O.S.U.........6
Michigan........72; Am. Col M. ?S...0
Michigan.......130; West Virginia....0
Michigan........28; Wisconsin......0
Michigan........36; Drake.........4
Michigan........22; Chicago......12
Season Summary
Games won, 10; Lost 0; Tied, 0.
Points for Michigan, 567; For Opponents 22
1905
Michigan........65; Ohio Wesleyan..0
Michigan........44; Kalamazoo.....0
Michigan........36; Case..........0
Michigan........23; Ohio Northern...0
Michigan........18; Vanderbilt......0
Michigan........31; Nebraska......0
Michigan........70; Albion.........0
Michigan........48; Drake..........0
Michigan........33; Illinois.........0
Michigan........40; O.S.U.........0
Michigan........12; Wisconsin......0
Michigan........75; Oberlin........0
Michigan.........0; Chicago.......2
Season Summary
Games won, 12; Lost, 1; Tied, 0.
Points for Michigan, 495; For Opponents 2.

1906

Michigan........28; Case..........0
Michigan.........6; O.S.U.........0
Michigan........28; Illinois.........9
Michigan........10; Vanderbilt......4
Michigan.........0; Pennsylvania...18
*Michigan.........0; Varsity Alumni..0

Season Summary
Games won, 4; Lost 1; Tied, 0.
Points for Michigan, 72; For Opponents 30.

1907

Michigan.........9; Case...........0
Michigan........46; M.A.C..........0
Michigan........22; Wabash.........0
Michigan........22; O.S.U..........0
Michigan.........8; Vanderbilt......0
Michigan.........0; Pennsylvania...6

Season Summary
Games won, 5; Lost 1; Tied, 0.
Points for Michigan, 107; For Opponents 6.

1908

Michigan........16; Case...........6
Michigan.........0; M.A.C..........0
Michigan........12; Notre Dame.....6
Michigan........10; O.S.U..........6
Michigan........24; Vanderbilt......6
Michigan........62; Kentucky........0
Michigan.........0; Pennsylvania...29
Michigan.........4; Syracuse......28

Season Summary
Games won, 5; Lost, 2; Tied, 1.
Points for Michigan 128; For Opponents 81.

1909

Michigan.........3; Case...........0
Michigan........33; O.S.U..........6
Michigan.........6; Marquette.......5
Michigan........44; Syracuse.......0
Michigan.........3; Notre Dame....11
Michigan........12; Pennsylvania...6
Michigan........15; Minnesota......6

Season Summary
Games won, 6; Lost, 1; Tied, 0.
Points for Michigan, 116; For Opponents 34

1910

Michigan.........3; Case...........3
Michigan.........6; M.A.C..........3
Michigan.........3; O.S.U..........3
Michigan........11; Syracuse.......0
Michigan.........0; Pennsylvania...0
Michigan.........6; Minnesota......0

Season Summary
Games won, 3; Lost, 0; Tied, 3.
Points for Michigan, 20; For Opponents, 9.

1911

Michigan........24; Case...........0
Michigan........15; M.A.C..........3
Michigan........19; O.S.U..........0
Michigan.........9; Vanderbilt......8
Michigan.........6; Syracuse.......6
Michigan.........0; Cornell.........6
Michigan........11; Pennsylvania...9
Michigan.........6; Nebraska.......6

Season Summary
Games won, 5; Lost, 1; Tied, 2.
Points for Michigan, 90; For Opponents 38.

1912

Michigan........34; Case...........0
Michigan........55; M.A.C..........7
Michigan........14; O.S.U..........0
Michigan.........7; Syracuse......18
Michigan.........7; South Dakota..6
Michigan........21; Pennsylvania...27
Michigan........20; Cornell.........7

Season Summary
Games won, 5; Lost, 2; Tied, 0.
Points for Michigan, 158; For Opponents 65

1913

Michigan........48; Case...........0
Michigan........14; Mount Union....0

Michigan.........7; M.A.C.........12
Michigan........33; Vanderbilt......2
Michigan........43; Syracuse.......7
Michigan........17; Cornell.........0
Michigan........13; Pennsylvania....0

Season Summary
Games won, 6; Lost, 1; Tied 0.
Points for Michigan, 175; For Opponents 21

1914

Michigan........58; DePauw........0
Michigan........69; Case..........0
Michigan........27; Mount Union...7
Michigan........23; Vanderbilt....3
Michigan.........3; M.A.C.........0
Michigan.........6; Syracuse......20
Michigan.........0; Harvard.......7
Michigan........34; Pennsylvania...3
Michigan........13; Cornell........28

Season Summary
Games won, 6; Lost, 3; Tied, 0.
Points for Michigan 233; For Opponents 68.

1915

Michigan........39; Lawrence.......0
Michigan........35; Mt. Union......0
Michigan........28; Marietta........6
Michigan........14; Case...........3
Michigan.........0; M.A.C.........24
Michigan.........7; Syracuse......14
Michigan.........7; Cornell........34
Michigan.........0; Pennsylvania....0

Season Summary
Games won, 4; Lost, 3; Tied, 1.
Points for Michigan, 130; Opponents 81.

1916

Michigan........30; Marietta........0
Michigan........19; Case...........3
Michigan........54; Carroll.........0
Michigan........26; Mt. Union......0
Michigan.........9; M.A.C..........0
Michigan........14; Syracuse......13
Michigan........66; Washington U...7
Michigan........20; Cornell........23
Michigan.........7; Pennsylvania...10

Season Summary
Games won, 7; Lost, 2; Ties, 0.
Points for Michigan, 245; For Opponents 56

1917

Michigan........41; Case...........0
Michigan........17; Western State..13
Michigan........69; Mt. Union......0
Michigan........14; Univ. of Detroit..3
Michigan........27; M.A.C..........0
Michigan........20; Nebraska.......0
Michigan........62; Kalamazoo C....0
Michigan........42; Cornell.........0
Michigan.........0; Pennsylvania...16
Michigan........12; Northwestern...21

Season Summary
Games won, 8; Lost, 2; Tied, 0.
Points for Michigan, 304, For Opponents 53

1918

Michigan........33; Case...........0
Michigan........13; Chicago........0
Michigan........14; Syracuse.......0
Michigan........21; M.A.C..........6
Michigan........14; Ohio State......0

Season Summary
Games won, 5; Lost, 0; Tied, 0.
Points for Michigan, 96; For Opponents, 6.

1919

Michigan........34; Case...........0
Michigan........26; M.A.C..........0
Michigan.........3; Ohio State.....13
Michigan........16; Northwestern...13
Michigan.........0; Chicago.......13
Michigan.........7; Illinois........29
Michigan.........7; Minnesota.....34

Season Summary
Games won, 3; Lost, 4; Tied, 0.
Points for Michigan, 93; For Opponents 102

1920

Michigan	35; Case	0
Michigan	35; M.A.C.	0
Michigan	6; Illinois	7
Michigan	21; Tulane	0
Michigan	7; Ohio State	14
Michigan	14; Chicago	0
Michigan	3; Minnesota	0

Season Summary

Games won, 5; Lost 2; Tied 0.
Points for Michigan 121; For Opponents 21.

1921

Michigan	44; Mount Union	0
Michigan	65; Case	0
Michigan	30; M.A.C.	0
Michigan	0; Ohio State	14
Michigan	3; Illinois	0
Michigan	7; Wisconsin	7
Michigan	38; Minnesota	0

Season Summary

Games won, 5; Lost, 1; Tied, 1.
Points for Michigan, 187; For Opponents 21

1922

Michigan	48; Case	0
Michigan	0; Vanderbilt	0
Michigan	19; Ohio State	0
Michigan	24; Illinois	0
Michigan	63; M.A.C.	0
Michigan	13; Wisconsin	6
Michigan	16; Minnesota	7

Season Summary

Games won, 6; Lost, 0; Tied, 1.
Points for Michigan, 183; For Opponents 13

1923

Michigan	36; Case	0
Michigan	3; Vanderbilt	0
Michigan	23; Ohio State	0
Michigan	37; M.A.C.	0
Michigan	9; Iowa	3
Michigan	26; Quantico Mar.	6
Michigan	6; Wisconsin	3
Michigan	10; Minnesota	0

Season Summary

Games won, 8; Lost, 0; Tied, 0.
Points for Michigan, 150; For Opponents 12

1924

Michigan	55; Miami	0
Michigan	7; M.A.C.	0
Michigan	14; Illinois	39
Michigan	21; Wisconsin	0
Michigan	13; Minnesota	0
Michigan	27; Northwestern	0
Michigan	16; Ohio State	6
Michigan	2; Iowa	9

Season Summary

Games won, 6; Lost, 2; Tied, 0.
Points for Michigan, 155; For Opponents 54

1925

Michigan	39; M.A.C.	0
Michigan	63; Indiana	0
Michigan	21; Wisconsin	0
Michigan	3; Illinois	0
Michigan	54; U.S.N.A.	0
Michigan	2; Northwestern	3
Michigan	10; Ohio State	0
Michigan	35; Minnesota	0

Season Summary

Games won, 7; Lost, 1; Tied, 0.
Points for Michigan, 227; For Opponents 3.

1926

Michigan	42; Okla. A&M	3
Michigan	55; M.S.C.	3
Michigan	20; Minnesota	0
Michigan	13; Illinois	0
Michigan	0; U.S. Navy	10
Michigan	37; Wisconsin	0
Michigan	17; Ohio State	16
Michigan	7; Minnesota	6

Season Summary

Games won, 7; Lost, 1; Tied, 0.
Points for Michigan, 191; For Opponents 38

1927

Michigan	33; Ohio Wesleyan	0
Michigan	21; M.S.C.	0
Michigan	14; Wisconsin	0
Michigan	21; Ohio State	0
Michigan	0; Illinois	14
Michigan	13; Chicago	0
Michigan	27; Navy	12
Michigan	7; Minnesota	13

Season Summary

Games won, 6; Lost, 2; Tied, 0.
Points for Michigan, 137; For Opponents 39

1928

Michigan	7; Ohio Wesleyan	17
Michigan	0; Indiana	6
Michigan	7; Ohio State	19
Michigan	0; Wisconsin	7
Michigan	3; Illinois	0
Michigan	6; U.S. Navy	6
Michigan	3; M.S.C.	0
Michigan	10; Iowa	7

Season Summary

Games won, 3; Lost, 4; Tied, 1.
Points for Michigan, 36; For Opponents 62.

1929

Michigan	39; Albion	0
Michigan	16; Mt. Union	6
Michigan	17; M.S.C.	0
Michigan	16; Purdue	30
Michigan	0; Ohio State	7
Michigan	0; Illinois	14
Michigan	14; Harvard	12
Michigan	7; Minnesota	6
Michigan	0; Iowa	0

Season Summary

Games won, 5; Lost, 3, Tied, 1.
Points for Michigan, 109; For Opponents 75

1930

Michigan	33; Denison	0
Michigan	27; Cen. St. Teachers	0
Michigan	34; Mich. St. Norm.	0
Michigan	14; Purdue	13
Michigan	13; Ohio State	0
Michigan	15; Illinois	7
Michigan	6; Harvard	3
Michigan	7; Minnesota	0
Michigan	16; Chicago	0

Tied with Northwestern for the Big Ten Championship.

Season Summary

Games won, 8; Lost 0; Tied, 1.
Points for Michigan, 111; For Opponents 23

1931

Michigan	27; Cen. St. Teachers	0
Michigan	34; Mich. St. Norm.	0
Michigan	13; Chicago	7
Michigan	7; Ohio State	20
Michigan	35; Illinois	0
Michigan	21; Princeton	0
Michigan	22; Indiana	0
Michigan	0; Michigan State	0
Michigan	6; Minnesota	0
Michigan	16; Wisconsin	0

Tied with Northwestern and Purdue for Big Ten Championship.

Season Summary

Games won, 8; Lost, 1; Tied, 1.
Points for Michigan, 181; For Opponents 27

1932

Michigan	26; Michigan State	0
Michigan	13; Northwestern	6
Michigan	14; Ohio State	0
Michigan	32; Illinois	0
Michigan	14; Princeton	7

401

Michigan.........7; Indiana.........0
Michigan........12; Chicago.........0
Michigan.........3; Minnesota......0
Big Ten and National Champions.

Season Summary
Games won, 8; Lost, 0; Tied, 0.
Points for Michigan, 123; For Opponents 13

1933
Michigan........20; Michigan State.. 6
Michigan........40; Cornell.........0
Michigan........13; Ohio State......0
Michigan........28; Chicago.........0
Michigan.........7; Illinois.........6
Michigan........10; Iowa...........6
Michigan.........0; Minnesota......0
Michigan........13; Northwestern... 0
Won Big Ten and National Championship.

Season Summary
Games won, 7; Lost, 0; Tied, 1.
Points for Michigan, 131; For Opponents 18

1934
Michigan.........0; Michigan State. 16
Michigan.........0; Chicago.......27
Michigan.........9; Georgia Tech....2
Michigan.........6; Illinois.........7
Michigan.........0; Minnesota.....34
Michigan.........0; Wisconsin.....10
Michigan.........0; Ohio State.....34
Michigan.........6; Northwestern.. 13

Season Summary
Games won, 1; Lost, 7; Tied, 0.
Points for Michigan, 21; For Opponents 143

1935
Michigan.........6; Michigan State. 25
Michigan.........7; Indiana.........0
Michigan........20; Wisconsin.....12
Michigan........19; Columbia......7
Michigan........16; Pennsylvania...6
Michigan.........0; Illinois.........3
Michigan.........0; Minnesota.....40
Michigan.........0; Ohio State.....38

Season Summary
Games won, 4; Lost, 4; Tied, 0.
Points for Michigan, 68; For Opponents 131

1936
Michigan.........7; Michigan State. 21
Michigan.........3; Indiana........14
Michigan.........0; Minnesota.....26
Michigan........13; Columbia......0
Michigan.........6; Illinois.........9
Michigan.........7; Pennsylvania...27
Michigan.........0; Northwestern... 9
Michigan.........0; Ohio State.....21

Season Summary
Games won, 1; Lost, 7; Tied, 0.
Points for Michigan, 36; For Opponents 127

1937
Michigan........14; Michigan State. 19
Michaigan.......0; Northwestern... 7
Michigan.........6; Minnesota.....39
Michigan.........7; Iowa...........6
Michigan.........7; Illinois.........6
Michigan........13; Chicago.......12
Michigan.........7; Pennsylvania...0
Michigan.........0; Ohio State..... 21

Season Summary
Games won, 4; Lost, 4; Tied, 0.
Points for Michigan, 54; For Opponents 110

1938
Michigan........14; Michigan State.. 0
Michigan........45; Chicago.......7
Michigan.........6; Minnesota......7
Michigan........15; Yale..........13
Michigan........14; Illinois.........0
Michigan........19; Pennsylvania..13
Michigan.........0; Northwestern... 0
Michigan........18; Ohio State......0

Season Summary
Games won, 6; Lost, 1; Tied, 1.
Points for Michigan, 131; For Opponents 40

1939
Michigan........26; Michigan State. 13
Michigan........27; Iowa...........7
Michigan........85; Chicago.......0
Michigan........27; Yale...........7
Michigan.........7; Illinois........16
Michigan.........7; Minnesota..... 20
Michigan........19; Pennsylvania...17
Michigan........21; Ohio State.... 14

Season Summary
Games won, 6; Lost, 2; Tied, 0.
Points for Michigan, 219; For Opponents 94

1940
Michigan........41; California.......0
Michigan........21; Michigan State. 14
Michigan........26; Harvard........ 0
Michigan........28; Illinois.........0
Michigan........14; Pennsylvania...9
Michigan.........6; Minnesota......7
Michigan........20; Northwestern.. 13
Michigan........40; Ohio State.....0

Season Summary
Games won, 7; Lost, 1; Tied, 0.
Points for Michigan, 196; For Opponents 34

1941
Michigan........19; Michigan State.. 7
Michigan.........6; Iowa...........0
Michigan........40; Pittsburgh......0
Michigan........14; Northwestern... 7
Michigan.........0; Minnesota......7
Michigan........20; Illinois.........0
Michigan........28; Columbia......0
Michigan........20; Ohio State..... 20

Season Summary
Games won, 6; Lost 1; Tied, 1.
Points for Michigan, 147; For Opponents 41

1942
Michigan.........9; Great Lakes.....0
Michigan........20; Michigan State.. 0
Michigan........14; Iow Pre Flight.. 26
Michigan........34; Northwestern.. 16
Michigan........14; Minnesota.....16
Michigan........28; Illinois........14
Michigan........35; Harvard........7
Michigan........32; Notre Dame... 20
Michigan.........7; Ohio State..... 21
Michigan........28; Iowa..........14

Season Summary
Games won, 7; Lost, 3; Tied, 0.
Points for Michigan, 221; Opponents 134.

1943
Michigan........26; Camp Grant.....0
Michigan........57; Western Mich...6
Michigan........21; Northwestern...7
Michigan........12; Notre Dame... 35
Michigan........49; Minnesota......6
Michigan........42; Illinois........ 6
Michigan........23; Indiana.........6
Michigan........27; Wisconsin......0
Michigan........45; Ohio State..... 7

Season Summary
Games won, 8; Lost, 1; Tied, 0.
Points for Michigan, 302; For Opponents 73

1944
Michigan........12; Iowa Pre-Flight.. 7
Michigan........14; Marquette......0
Michigan.........0; Indiana.......20
Michigan........28; Minnesota.....13
Michigan........27; Northwestern... 0
Michigan........40; Purdue........14
Michigan........41; Pennsylvania..19
Michigan........14; Illinois.........0
Michigan........14; Wisconsin......0
Michigan........14; Ohio State.....18

Season Summary
Games won, 8; Lost, 2; Tied, 0.
Points for Michigan, 204; For Opponents 91

1945
Michigan........27; Great Lakes.....2
Michigan.........7; Indiana........13

402

Michigan........40; Michigan State.. 0
Michigan........20; Northwestern.. 7
Michigan........7; Army......... 28
Michigan........19; Illinois......... 0
Michigan........26; Minnesota..... 0
Michigan........7; Navy......... 33
Michigan........27; Purdue....... 13
Michigan........7; Ohio State.... 3

Season Summary
Games won, 7; Lost, 3; Tied, 0.
Points for Michigan, 187; For Opponents 99

1946
Michigan........21; Indiana........0
Michigan........14; Iowa.......... 7
Michigan........13; Army......... 20
Michigan........14; Northwestern. 14
Michigan........9; Illinois........ 13
Michigan........21; Minnesota..... 0
Michigan........55; Michigan State. 7
Michigan........28; Wisconsin..... 6
Michigan........58; Ohio State..... 6

Season Summary
Games won, 6; Lost, 2; Tied, 1.
Points for Michigan, 233; For Opponents 73

1947
Michigan........55; Michigan State.. 0
Michigan........49; Stanford........13
Michigan........69; Pittsburgh..... 13
Michigan........49; Northwestern.. 21
Michigan........13; Minnesota..... 6
Michigan........14; Illinois......... 7
Michigan........35; Indiana........ 0
Michigan........40; Wisconsin..... 6
Michigan........21; Ohio State..... 0

Season Summary
Games won, 9; Lost, 0; Tied, 0.
Points for Michigan, 345; For Opponents 53

1948 ROSE BOWL GAME
Michigan........49; Southern Cal... 0

1948
Michigan........13; Michigan State.. 7
Michigan........14; Oregon......... 0
Michigan........40; Purdue......... 0
Michigan........28; Northwestern... 0
Michigan........27; Minnesota..... 14
Michigan........28; Illinois......... 20
Michigan........35; Navy.......... 0
Michigan........54; Indiana........ 0
Michigan........13; Ohio State..... 3

Season Summary
Games won, 9; Lost, 0; Tied, 0.
Points for Michigan, 252; For Opponents 44

1949
Michigan........7; Michigan State.. 3
Michigan........27; Stanford........ 7
Michigan........7; Army......... 21
Michigan........20; Northwestern.. 21
Michigan........14; Minnesota..... 7
Michigan........13; Illinois......... 0
Michigan........20; Purdue........ 12
Michigan........20; Indiana........ 7
Michigan........7; Ohio State..... 7

Season Summary
Games won, 6; Lost, 2; Tied, 1.
Points for Michigan, 135; For Opponents 85

1950
Michigan........7; Michigan State. 14
Michigan........27; Dartmouth...... 7
Michigan........6; Army......... 27
Michigan........26; Wisconsin..... 13
Michigan........7; Minnesota..... 7
Michigan........0; Illinois......... 7
Michigan........20; Indiana........ 7
Michigan........34; Northwestern.. 23
Michigan........9; Ohio State..... 3

Season Summary
Games won, 5; Lost, 3; Tied, 1.
Points for Michigan, 136; Opponents, 108.

1951 ROSE BOWL GAME
Michigan........14; California....... 6

1951
Michigan........0; Michigan State. 25
Michigan........13; Stanford.......23
Michigan........33; Indiana........14
Michigan........21; Iowa.......... 0
Michigan........54; Minnesota..... 27
Michigan........0; Illinois......... 7
Michigan........7; Cornell....... 20
Michigan........0; Northwestern.. 6
Michigan........7; Ohio State..... 0

Season Summary
Games won, 4; Lost, 5; Tied, 0.
Points for Michigan, 135; Opponents 122.

1952
Michigan........13; Michigan State. 27
Michigan........7; Stanford.......14
Michigan........28; Indiana........13
Michigan........48; Northwestern.. 14
Michigan........21; Minnesota..... 0
Michigan........13; Illinois........ 22
Michigan........49; Cornell....... 7
Michigan........21; Purdue....... 10
Michigan........7; Ohio State..... 27

Season Summary
Games won, 5; Lost, 4; Tied, 0.
Points for Michigan, 207; Opponents 134.

1953
Michigan........50; Washington.....0
Michigan........26; Tulane......... 7
Michigan........14; Iowa.......... 13
Michigan........20; Northwestern.. 12
Michigan........0; Minnesota..... 22
Michigan........24; Pennsylvania..14
Michigan........3; Illinois........ 19
Michigan........6; Michigan State. 14
Michigan........20; Ohio State..... 0

Season Summary
Games won, 6; Lost, 3; Tied, 0.
Points for Michigan, 163; Opponents, 101.

1954
Michigan........14; Washington.....0
Michigan........7; Army......... 26
Michigan........14; Iowa.......... 13
Michigan........7; Northwestern.. 0
Michigan........34; Minnesota..... 0
Michigan........9; Indiana........ 13
Michigan........14; Illinois......... 7
Michigan........33; Michigan State. 7
Michigan........7; Ohio State..... 21

Season Summary
Games won, 6; Lost, 3; Tied, 0.
Points for Michigan, 139; For Opponents 87

1955
Michigan........42; Missouri....... 7
Michigan........14; Michigan State.. 7
Michigan........26; Army.......... 2
Michigan........14; Northwestern.. 2
Michigan........14; Minnesota..... 13
Michigan........33; Iowa.......... 21
Michigan........6; Illinois........ 25
Michigan........30; Indiana........ 0
Michigan........0; Ohio State.....17

Season Summary
Games won, 7; Lost, 2; Tied, 0.
Points for Michigan, 179; For Opponents 94

1956
Michigan........42; U.C.L.A. 13
Michigan........0; Michigan State.. 9
Michigan........48; Army......... 14
Michigan........34; Northwestern. 20
Michigan........7; Minnesota..... 20
Michigan........17; Iowa.......... 14
Michigan........17; Illinois......... 7
Michigan........49; Indiana........26
Michigan........19; Ohio State..... 0

Season Summary
Games won, 7; Lost, 2; Tied, 0.
Points for Michigan, 233; Opponents, 123.

1957
Michigan........16; Southern Cal.... 6

403

Michigan........26; Georgia.........0
Michigan.........6; Michigan State. 35
Michigan........34; Northwestern.. 14
Michigan........24; Minnesota..... 7
Michigan........21; Iowa........... 21
Michigan........19; Illinois........ 20
Michigan........27; Indiana........13
Michigan........14; Ohio State..... 31

Season Summary
Games won, 5; Lost, 3; Tied, 1.
Points for Michigan, 187; Opponents, 147.

1958
Michigan........20; U.S.C......... 19
Michigan........12; M.S.U......... 12
Michigan........14; Navy.......... 20
Michigan........24; Northwestern.. 55
Michigan........20; Minnesota..... 19
Michigan........14; Iowa.......... 37
Michigan.........8; Illinois........ 21
Michigan.........6; Indiana.........8
Michigan........14; Ohio State.... 20

Season Summary
Games won 2; Lost 6; Tied, 1.
Points for Michigan, 132; Opponents, 211.

1959
Michigan........15; Missouri...... 20
Michigan.........8; Michigan State. 34
Michigan........18; Oregon State... 7
Michigan.........7; Northwestern... 20
Michigan........14; Minnesota..... 6
Michigan........10; Wisconsin..... 19
Michigan........20; Illinois........ 15
Michigan.........7; Indiana........26
Michigan........23; Ohio State..... 14

Season Summary
Games won, 4; Lost, 5; Tied, 0.
Points for Michigan, 122; Opponents, 161.

1960
Michigan........21; Univ. of Oregon..0
Michigan........17; Michigan State. 24
Michigan........31; Duke.......... 6
Michigan........14; Northwestern... 7
Michigan.........0; Minnesota..... 10
Michigan........13; Wisconsin..... 16
Michigan.........8; Illinois.......... 7
Michigan........29; Indiana........ 7
Michigan.........0; Ohio State.... 7

Season Summary
Games won, 5; Lost, 4; Tied, 0.
Points for Michigan, 133; For Opponents 84

1961
Michigan........29; UCLA.......... 6
Michigan........38; Army.......... 8
Michigan.........0; Michigan State. 28
Michigan........16; Purdue........ 14
Michigan........20; Minnesota..... 23
Michigan........28; Duke..........14
Michigan........38; Illinois......... 6
Michigan........23; Iowa.......... 14
Michigan........20; Ohio State..... 50

Season Summary
Games won 6; Lost, 3; Tied, 0.
Points for Michigan 212; Opponents, 163.

1962
Michigan........13; Nebraska...... 25
Michigan........17; Army.......... 7
Michigan.........0; Michigan State. 28
Michigan.........0; Purdue........ 37
Michigan.........0; Minnesota..... 17
Michigan........12; Wisconsin..... 34
Michigan........14; Illinois........ 10
Michigan........14; Iowa.......... 28
Michigan.........0; Ohio State..... 28

Season Summary
Games won 2; Lost, 7; Tied, 0.
Points for Michigan 70; Opponents, 214.

1963
Michigan........27; S. Methodist... 16
Michigan........13; Navy.......... 26
Michigan.........7; Michigan State.. 7

Michigan........12; Purdue........ 23
Michigan.........0; Minnesota..... 6
Michigan........27; Northwestern... 6
Michigan........14; Illinois......... 8
Michigan........21; Iowa.......... 21
Michigan........10; Ohio State..... 14

Season Summary
Games won, 3; Lost, 4; Tied, 2.
Points for Michigan, 131; Opponents, 127.

1964
Michigan........24; Air Force....... 7
Michigan........21; Navy.......... 0
Michigan........17; Michigan State. 10
Michigan........20; Purdue........ 21
Michigan........19; Minnesota..... 12
Michigan........35; Northwestern... 0
Michigan........21; Illinois......... 6
Michigan........34; Iowa.......... 20
Michigan........10; Ohio State..... 0

Season Summary
Games won, 8; Lost, 1; Tied, 0.
Points for Michigan, 235; For Opponents 83

1965 ROSE BOWL GAME
Michigan........34; Oregon State.... 7

1965
Michigan........31; North Carolina. 24
Michigan........10; California....... 7
Michigan.........7; Georgia........ 15
Michigan.........7; Michigan State. 24
Michigan........15; Purdue........ 17
Michigan........13; Minnesota..... 14
Michigan........50; Wisconsin..... 14
Michigan........23; Illinois......... 3
Michigan........22; Northwestern.. 34
Michigan.........7; Ohio State...... 9

Season Summary
Games won, 4; Lost, 6; Tied, 0.
Points for Michigan, 185; Opponents, 161.

1966
Michigan........41; Oregon State.... 0
Michigan........17; California....... 7
Michigan.........7; North Carolina. 21
Michigan.........7; Michigan State. 20
Michigan........21; Purdue........ 22
Michigan........49; Minnesota..... 0
Michigan........28; Wisconsin..... 17
Michigan........21; Illinois........ 28
Michigan........28; Northwestern.. 20
Michigan........17; Ohio State..... 3

Season Summary
Games won, 6; Lost, 4; Tied, 0.
Points for Michigan, 236; Opponents, 138.

1967
Michigan........10; Duke........... 7
Michigan.........9; California....... 10
Michigan........21; Navy.......... 26
Michigan.........0; Michigan State. 34
Michigan........20; Indiana........ 27
Michigan........15; Minnesota..... 20
Michigan.........7; Northwestern... 3
Michigan........21; Illinois........ 14
Michigan........27; Wisconsin..... 14
Michigan........14; Ohio State..... 24

Season Summary
Games won, 4; Lost, 6; Tied, 0.
Points for Michigan, 144; Opponents, 179.

1968
Michigan.........7; California...... 21
Michigan........31; Duke.......... 10
Michigan........32; Navy.......... 9
Michigan........28; Michigan State. 14
Michigan........27; Indiana........ 22
Michigan........33; Minnesota..... 20
Michigan........35; Northwestern... 0
Michigan........36; Illinois......... 0
Michigan........34; Wisconsin..... 9
Michigan........14; Ohio State..... 50

Season Summary
Games won, 8; Lost, 2; Tied, 0.
Points for Michigan 277; Opponents, 155.

1969

Michigan	42;	Vanderbilt..... 14
Michigan	45;	Washington..... 7
Michigan	17;	Missouri...... 40
Michigan	31;	Purdue........ 20
Michigan	12;	Michigan State. 23
Michigan	35;	Minnesota...... 9
Michigan	35;	Wisconsin..... 7
Michigan	57;	Illinois.......... 0
Michigan	51;	Iowa.......... 6
Michigan	24;	Ohio State..... 12

Season Summary
Games won, 8; Lost, 2; Tied, 0.
Points for Michigan, 340; Opponents, 138.

1970 ROSE BOWL GAME
Michigan..........3; Southern Cal... 10

1970

Michigan	20;	Arizona...... 9
Michigan	17;	Washington..... 3
Michigan	14;	Texas A&M.... 10
Michigan	29;	Purdue..........0
Michigan	34;	Michigan State. 20
Michigan	39;	Minnesota..... 13
Michigan	29;	Wisconsin..... 15
Michigan	42;	Illinois.......... 0
Michigan	55;	Iowa.......... 0
Michigan	9;	Ohio State..... 20

Season Summary
Games won 9; Lost 1; Tied 0.
Points for Michigan 288; For Opponents 90.

1971

Michigan	21;	Northwestern... 6
Michigan	56;	Virginia........ 0
Michigan	38;	UCLA.......... 0
Michigan	46;	Navy.......... 0
Michigan	24;	Michigan State. 13
Michigan	35;	Illinois.......... 6
Michigan	35;	Minnesota..... 7
Michigan	61;	Indiana........ 7

Michigan	63;	Iowa.......... 7
Michigan	20;	Purdue........ 17
Michigan	10;	Ohio State..... 7

Season Summary
Games won 11; Lost, 0; Tied 0.
Points for Michigan 409; For Opponents 70.

1972 ROSE BOWL GAME
Michigan..........12; Stanford.......13

1972

Michigan	7;	Northwestern... 0
Michigan	26;	UCLA.......... 9
Michigan	41;	Tulane......... 7
Michigan	35;	Navy.......... 7
Michigan	10;	Michigan State.. 0
Michigan	31;	Illinois.......... 7
Michigan	42;	Minnesota..... 0
Michigan	21;	Indiana......... 7
Michigan	31;	Iowa.......... 0
Michigan	9;	Purdue........ 6
Michigan	11;	Ohio State..... 14

Season Summary
Games won 10; Lost, 1; Tied, 0.
Points for Michigan 264; For Opponents 57.

1973

Michigan	31;	Iowa.......... 7
Michigan	47;	Stanford.......10
Michigan	14;	Navy.......... 0
Michigan	24;	Oregon........ 0
Michigan	31;	Michigan State. 0
Michigan	35;	Wisconsin...... 6
Michigan	34;	Minnesota..... 7
Michigan	49;	Indiana........ 13
Michigan	21;	Illinois......... 6
Michigan	34;	Purdue......... 9
Michigan	10;	Ohio State..... 10

Season Summary
Games won, 10; Lost, 0; Tied, 1.
Points for Michigan, 330; For Opponents 68

Michigan Wolverine

All-Time Michigan Marks

CONSECUTIVE GAME STREAKS

Games Unbeaten	56	(55-0-1, 1901-05)
	25	(25-0-0, 1946-49)
	19	(18-0-1, 1921-24)
Home Games Unbeaten	* 29	(28-0-1, 1969-73)
	14	(13-0-1, 1931-33)
	14	(14-0-0, 1946-50)
Conference Games Unbeaten	17	(16-0-1, 1901-05)
	16	(15-0-1, 1931-33)
	15	(15-0-0, 1946-48)
Home Conference Games Unbeaten	* 23	(22-0-1, 1968-73)
	17	(17-0-0, 1946-51)
Games Won	29	(1901-03)
	26	(1903-05)
	25	(1946-49)
Home Games Won	28	(1969-73)
	14	(1946-50)
Conference Games Won	15	(1946-48)
	14	(1931-33)
	11	(1969-70)
Home Conference Games Won	22	(1968-73)
	17	(1946-51)

*Current Streak

HIGHEST SCORING MICHIGAN VICTORIES

130-0 over West Virginia....................................1904
128-0 over Buffalo...1901
119-0 over Michigan Agricultural College...................1902
(Michigan's most recent, highest scoring victory by more than 40 points was 63-7 over Iowa, 1971)

LARGEST MICHIGAN DEFEATS

56-0 to Cornell...1889
40-0 to Minnesota..1935
50-14 to Ohio State.......................................1968

LOWEST SCORING MICHIGAN VICTORY

1-0 over Racine College..................................1879
3-0 Michigan has won eight games by 3-0 score
Most recent victory over Minnesota....................1932

LOWEST SCORING MICHIGAN DEFEAT

2-0 Chicago...1905
3-2 Northwestern 1925

CONSECUTIVE SHUTOUT VICTORIES

Twelve... 1901-02, 1905

Michigan's All-Americans (66)

FULLBACKS
Cedric Smith 1917
Frank Steketee 1918
Robert Westfall 1941
William Daley 1943

HALFBACKS
William Heston 1903-04
James Craig 1913
John Maulbetsch 1914
Harry Kipke 1922
Thomas Harmon 1939-40
Robert Chappuis 1947
Chalmers Elliott 1947
James Pace 1957
Richard Volk 1966
Ron Johnson 1968
Tom Curtis 1969
Billy Taylor 1971
Tom Darden 1971
Randy Logan 1972
Dave Brown 1973

QUARTERBACKS
Benny Friedman 1925-26
Harry Newman 1932
Pete Elliott 1948
Robert Timberlake 1964

LINEBACKERS
Marty Huff 1970
Mike Taylor 1971

CENTERS
William Cunningham 1898
Alolph Schulz 1907
Henry Vick 1921
Jack Blott 1923
Robert Brown 1925
Maynard Morrison 1931
Charles Bernard 1932-33

ENDS
Neil Snow 1901
Stanfield Wells 1910
Paul Goebel 1922
Bennie Oosterbaan 1925-26-27
Ted Petoskey 1931-33
Edward Frutig 1940
Elmer Madar 1946
Richard Rifenburg 1948
Lowell Perry 1951
Ronald Kramer 1955-56
John Clancy 1966
Jim Mandich 1969

TACKLES
Miller Pontius 1913
Tom Edwards 1925
Otto Pommerening 1928
Francis Wistert 1933
Albert Wistert 1942
Mervin Pregulman 1943
Alvin Wistert 1948-49
Allen Wahl 1949-50
Arthur Walker 1954
William Yearby 1964-65
Dan Dierdorf 1970
Paul Seymour 1972
Dave Gallagher 1973

GUARDS
Albert Benbrook 1909-10
Ernest Allmendinger 1917
Frank Culver 1917
E.R. Slaughter 1924
Harry Hawkins 1925
Ralph Heikkinen 1938
Julius Franks 1942
Henry Hill 1970
Reggie McKenzie 1971

(This revised list of Michigan All-Americans conforms with
the official Big Ten list)

Michigan in the Rose Bowl

(Won 4, Lost 2)

1902	MICHIGAN	49	Stanford	0
1948	MICHIGAN	49	Southern Cal.	0
1951	MICHIGAN	14	California	6
1965	MICHIGAN	34	Oregon State	7
1970	Michigan	3	SOUTHERN CAL.	10
1972	Michigan	12	STANFORD	13
	Totals Michigan	161	Opponents	36

Big Ten All-Time Football Records

(All games through 1973)

TEAM	Yrs.	No. of Games	Won	Lost	Tied	Pct.
MICHIGAN 94		778	558	191	29	.744
OHIO STATE........85		734	475	205	46	.690
MINNESOTA........89		717	450	290	38	.662
MICHIGAN STATE....77		667	406	224	36	.643
WISCONSIN 85		700	380	275	45	.580
PURDUE 86		697	375	281	41	.571
ILLINOIS 84		725	385	299	41	.562
IOWA 84		698	337	329	32	.506
NORTHWESTERN 83		702	324	335	39	.488
INDIANA 86		688	285	364	39	.439

Michigan — "Champions of the West"

25 Big Ten Titles

Year	Conference Record	Coach	Year	Conference Record	Coach
1898	3-0-0	Ferbert	*1943	6-0-0	Crisler
*1901	4-0-0	Yost	1947	6-0-0	Crisler
1902	5-0-0	Yost	1948	6-0-0	Oosterbaan
*1903	3-0-1	Yost	*1949	4-1-1	Oosterbaan
*1904	2-0-0	Yost	1950	4-1-1	Oosterbaan
*1906	1-0-0	Yost	1964	6-1-0	Elliott
*1918	2-0-0	Yost	*1969	6-1-0	Schembechler
*1922	4-0-0	Yost	1971	8-0-0	Schembechler
*1923	4-0-0	Yost	*1972	7-1-0	Schembechler
1925	5-1-0	Yost	*1973	7-0-1	Schembechler
*1926	5-0-0	Yost			
*1930	5-0-0	Kipke			
*1931	5-1-0	Kipke			
*1932	6-0-0	Kipke			
1933	5-0-1	Kipke			

* shared conference title

National Titles

1901 — Yost   1904 — Yost   1947 — Crisler
1902 — Yost   1932 — Kipke   1948 — Oosterbaan
1903 — Yost   1933 — Kipke

UNIVERSITY OF MICHIGAN FOOTBALL LETTERMEN

A

Abbott, Howard T., '89, '90, '91
Abrahams, Morris M., '69
Adams, Dr. Theodore W., '18
Aldrich, William I., '93
Aliber, James A., '43, '44
Alix, Dennis R., '63
Allen, Frank G., '78, '79, '80, '81
Allerdice, David W., '07, '08, '09
Allis, Dr. Harry D., '48, '49, '50
Allmendinger, Ernest J., '11, '12, '13
Amrine, Robert Y., '34
Amstutz, Ralph H., '42, '43
Anthony, Melvin, '62, '63, '64
Armour, James, '73
Atchison, James L., '48, '49
Auer, Howard J., '29, '30, '31
Aug, Vincent J., '34, '35
Austin, Thomas D., '32, '33, '34
Ayers, Norwood B., '96, '97
Ayres, John, '81

B

Babcock, Richard G., '23, '24, '25
Babcock, R. S., '87
Babcock, Samuel, '25
Baer, Frederick N., '52, '53, '54
Baer, Raymond, '25, '26, '27
Bahlow, Edward H., '46
Bailey, Donald A., '64, '65, '66
Baird, James, '93, '94, '95
Baker, Fred L., '95, '96
Baker, William P., '97, '98
Baldacci, Louis G., '53, '54, '55
Ball, William D., '88, '89
Ballou, Robert M., '46
Balog, James T., '51, '52, '53
Balzhiser, Richard E., '52, '53
Banar, James F., '68, '69
Bank, Theodore P., '20, '21
Banks, Charles N., '85, '86

Banks, Harry, '71, '72
Barabe, Clifford A., '97, '98
Barclay, William C., '35, '36, '37
Barlow, Alfred H., '05
Barmore, Edmund H., '78, '79, '80
Barr, Terry A., '54, '55, '56
Bartell, A. C., '93
Bartholomew, Dr. Bruce A., '51
Bartlett, Dr. William H., '48, '49
Barton, Charles P., Jr., '12
Bass, Michael T., '64, '65, '66
Bastian, Clyde E., '14, '15
Bates, James V., '52, '54, '55
Batsakes, John J., '58
Bauman, Clement L., '43, '44
Baumgartner, Robert A., '67, '68, '69
Beach, Elmer E., '82, '83
Beach, Raymond W., '82, '83, '84, '85
Beard, Chester C., '33, '34
Beaumont, J. A., '77
Beckman, Thomas C., '69, '70, '71
Begle, Ned G., '00
Beison, Dr. Richard A., '51, '52, '53
Bell, Gordon G., '73
Belsky, Jerome, '36, '37
Bennett, Donald C., '51, '52, '53
Bennett, Edwin J., '98
Bennett, John W. F., '96, '97, '98
Benton, Leland H., '13, '14, '15
Benton, Lou N., '14
Bentz, Warren W., '44, '45
Berger, Thomas E., '56, '57
Berline, James H., '67
Bernard, J. Charles, '31, '32, '33
Berutti, William J., '69, '70
Betts, N. James, '68, '69, '70
Bickle, Douglas G., '61
Billings, Bill E., '51, '52
Bird, James P., '92
Bishop, Harry S., '06
Bissell, Frank S., '34, '35

Bitner, Harry, '81, '82
Blanchard, Donald R., '62
Bloomingston, John A., '95
Blott, Jack L. '22, '23
Bochnowski, Alexander H., '56, '57
Boden, Marshall H., '28
Bogle, Thomas A., '10, '11
Bolas, George A., '34
Boor, Donald P., '41, '42
Borden, Hugh P., '82, '83
Borgmann, William F., '33, '34
Borleske, Stanley E., '10, '11
Boshoven, Robert J., '57
Boutwell, Benjamin J., '89
Bovard, Alan J., '27, '28, '29
Boville, Dr. Edwin G., '18
Bowers, David C., '56, '57
Bowman, James N., '55
Boyd, Alan W., '16, '17
Boyle, Michael H., '12
Bradford, Wesley E., '50, '51
Brandon, David A., '73
Brandstatter, James P., '69, '70, '71
Branoff, Tony D., '52, '53, '54, '55
Brennan, John C., '36, '37, '38
Brielmaier, Gerald E., '44
Brieske, James, '42, '46, '47
Brigstock, Thomas S., '65
Broadnax, Stanley E., '67, '68
Brock, Henry, '84
Brooks, Charles E., '54, '55, '56
Brown, David S., '72, '73
Brown, Dennis M., '67, '68
Brown, Henry R., '98, '00
Brown, Randolph W., '80
Brown, Rick W., '69
Brown, Robert J., '23, '24, '25
Brown, Robert M., '61, '62
Bryan, Fred J., '43
Burg, George R. U., '44, '46
Burks, Roy, '72, '73
Bushnell, Thomas H., '12, '13, '14
Bushong, Jared L., '57, '58, '59

Bushong, Reid J., '58, '59, '60
Butler, David C., '64
Butler, W. Jack, '40
Buzynski, John J., '66
Byers, James A., '56, '57, '58

C

Cable, Ben T., '74
Cachey, Theodore J., '52, '53, '54
Caldarazzo, Richard, '68, '69
Caley, William H., '98
Call, Norman D., '40
Callahan, Alexander J., '57, '58, '59
Callahan, Robert F., '45, '46
Campbell, Charles H., '78, '79
Campbell, Robert D., '35, '37
Cantrill, Cecil, '31, '32
Cappon, Franklin, '20, '21, '22
Carpenter, Alden J., '69, '70, '71
Carpenter, Jack C., '46
Carpell, Otto C., '11, '12
Carr, Bert M., '95, '96, '97
Carter, Charles B., '02, '04
Cartwright, Oscar, '17
Cary, John C., '19
Casey, Kevin B., '71
Casey, William M., '07, '08, '09
Catlett, James B., '13, '14, '15
Cecchini, Thomas A., '63, '64, '65
Cederberg, Jon C., '73
Ceithaml, George F., '40, '41, '42
Chadbourne, Thomas, '90
Chandler, M. Robert, '61, '62, '63
Chapman, Gil, '72, '73
Chapman, Harvey E., Jr., '61, '62, '63
Chapman, Harvey E., Sr., '32, '33
Chappuis, Robert R., '42, '46, '47
Chase, John, '78, '79, '80
Cherry, John A., '73
Chiames, George, '45
Chubb, Ralph L., '44, '46
Cipa, Lawrence A., '71, '72, '73
Clancy, John D., '63, '65, '66

Clark, Fay G., '09
Clark, Dr. Oswald V., Jr.,'48,'49,'50
Clark, William D., '04, '05
Clement, Carl H., '06
Cline, Dr. J. Daniel, '52, '53, '54
Coakley, Gary R., '71, '72
Cochran, William D., '13, '14, '15
Cohn, Abe J., '17, '18, '20
Coin, Dana S., '69, '70, '71
Colby, Branch H., '76
Cole, Harry N., '12
Cole, Walter M., '13
Cole, Wheaton D., '10
Coleman, Donald A., '72, '73
Collette, William H., '12
Conklin, Dr. Fredric L.,'09,'10,'11
Conley, James P., '62, '63, '64
Coode, James E., '71, '72, '73
Cooper, Robert E., '36
Copeland, Dr. Ernest, '76
Corey, George R., '54, '55
Cornwell, Arthur, '10
Cornwell, Francis M., '28, '29, '30
Corona, Clement L., '55, '56
Cowan, Keith E., '59, '60
Cox, Roderick H., '30, '32
Coyle, Thomas J., '70, '71, '72
Cragin, Raymond A., '28
Craig, James B., '11, '12, '13
Crandell, John S., '43
Crane, Fenwick J., '43, '46
Craw, Garvie T., '67, '68, '69
Cress, Elmer W., '19
Crumpacker, Maurice, '08
Cruse, William R., '17, '18, '19
Culligan, William L., '44, '46
Culver, Frank W., '17, '19
Cunningham, Dr. Leo P., '41
Cunningham, Dr. William R., '96,
    '97, '98, '99
Curran, Louis B., '21, '22, '23
Curtis, Guy P., '59, '60, '61
Curtis, John S., '03, '04, '05, '06

Curtis, Thomas N., '67, '68, '69
Czak, Edward W., '39, '40
Czirr, James C., '73
Czysz, Dr. Frank, '18, '19

D

Dahlem, Alvin G., '28, '29
Daley, William E., '43
Damm, Russell M., '32
Danhof, Jerome A., '66
Daniels, John W., '70, '72
Daniels, Norman J., '29, '30, '31
Darden, Thomas V., '69, '70, '71
Davies, James H., '55, '56, '57
Davis, Timothy F., '73
Davison, Samuel, '08
Day, Floyd A., '65
Day, Michael J., '73
Dayton, Joseph D., '65, '66, '67
Deacon, Andrew S., '76, '77, '78
Dean, Walter C., '21
DeBaker, Charles E., '30, '31, '32
DeHaven, George W., '87, '88, '89
Dehlin, Charles B., Jr., '63, '64,
    '66
DeMassa, Thomas A., '59
DenBoer, Gregory L., '72, '73
Denby, Edwin, '95
Dendrinos, Peter D., '47
Denzin, John D., '68
DePont, Edward P., '91, '92
DePuy, Richard G., '78, '79, '80,
    '81, '82
DePuy, William O., '81
D'Eramo, Paul J., '65, '66
Derricotte, Dr. Gene, '44, '46,
    '47, '48
Derleth, Robert J., '42, '43, '45,
    '46
Deskins, Donald R., Jr., '58, '59
DeStefano, Guy J., '60
Detwiler, James R., '64, '65, '66
Dewey, R. Sydney, '24, '25, '26

Dickey, James A., '56, '57, '58
Dierdorf, Daniel L., '68, '69, '70
Dingman, Robert W., '51, '52
Doane, Thomas E., '68
Dodd, William A., '62, '63
Domhoff, Victor E., '24, '26, '27
Dorn, Edward L., '84
Dott, Richard M., '80, '83
Doty, Alfred L., Jr., '67
Dotzauer, Barry S., '71, '72, '73
Dougall, William R., Jr., '61
Douglass, Leslie H., '30, '31
Douglass, Prentiss, '08
Doughty, Glenn M., '69, '70, '71
Drake, Thomas E., '71, '73
Draveling, Leo F., '28, '29, '30
Drehmann, Peter C., '67, '68
Dreyer, Walter O., '43
Drumheller, Thomas J., '95, '96
Dufek, Donald E., '48, '49, '50
Dufek, Donald P., '73
Duff, William J., '84
Duffy, Ignatius, '96
Duffy, James E., '85
Duffy, John L., '85, '86, '87, '88
Duffy, Mark F., '71
Dugger, Donald R., '51, '52, '53
Dunleavy, George, '22
Dunn, John F., '20
Dunn, Roland G., '16, '19
Dunne, Maurice F., '14, '15, '16
Dunne, Robert J., '18, '19, '20, '21
Dutcher, Gerald E., '70
Dutter, George S., '52, '53
Dworsky, Daniel L., '45, '46, '47, '48
Dyer, Horace L., '93, '94
Dygert, George, '91, '92, '93, '94

E
Eastman, Harry, Jr., '30
Eaton, Donald R., '70, '71, '73
Edmunds, Dr. William P., '09, '10

Edwards, Thomas L., '24, '25
Edwards, Thomas R., '77, '78, '79
Egan, John E., '95
Eldred, Dale L., '55
Elliott, Bruce N., '69, '70, '71
Elliott, Chalmers, '46, '47
Elliott, David L., '71, '73
Elliott, Peter R., '45, '46, '47, '48
Ellis, Gregory A., '70, '71, '72
Ellis, Joseph O., '34
Embs, William J., '07, '08
Erben, Robert F., '48, '49
Evashevski, Forest J., Jr., '62, '63, '64
Evashevski, Forest J., Sr., '38, '39, '40
Everhardus, Chris, '34, '35
Everhardus, Herman, '31, '32, '33
Eyke, Walter L., '06

F
Farabee, Ben G., '62, '63, '64
Farabee, David A., '68
Farmer, Douglas A., '37
Farnham, Thaddeus, '95, '96
Farrand, Dr. Royal, '87
Farrer, Richard D., '48, '49, '50
Faul, Lawrence J., '55, '56, '57
Fay, Stanley E., '31, '32, '33
Federico, Eric D., '68, '69
Fediuk, Arthur W., '73
Felver, Howard, '96, '97
Ferbert, Gustave, '93, '94, '95, '96
Fillichio, Michael E., '57, '58, '59
Finkbeiner, Donald A., '19
Fischer, Robert H., '43
Fisher, David R., '64, '65, '66
Fitch, Alan D., '49
Flanagan, Dennis, '65
Flora, Robert L., '39, '40, '41
Flora, Dr. William R., '24, '25, '26
Foltz, James, '45
Fonde, Henry, '45, '46, '47

412

Ford, Gerald R., Jr., '32, '33, '34
Ford, Leonard G., '45, '46, '47
Fortune, William P., '17, '18, '19
Fox, James W., '53, '54, '55
France, Richard R., '98, '99
Francis, Alan J., '68, '69
Franklin, Dennis E., '72, '73
Franks, Dennis J., '72, '73
Franks, Dr. Julius, '41, '42
Fraumann, Harlin E., '40, '41
Freehan, William W., '60
Freeman, J. Paul, '18
Freeney, Charles, '09
Freihofer, Cecil, '44, '45
Freihofer, Walter B., '42
Freund, Dr. Raynor, '92, '93, '94, '95
Friedman, Benjamin, '24, '25, '26
Fritz, Ralph A., '38, '39, '40
Froemke, Gerald W., '17, '19
Frutig, Edward C., '38, '39, '40
Frysinger, Terry R., '68
Fuller, Frederic W., Jr., '25, '27
Fuog, Russell J., '32, '33, '34

G

Gabel, Norman, '25, '26, '27
Gabler, John H., '67, '68, '69
Gabler, Wallace F. III, '65
Gallagher, David D., '71, '72, '73
Gallagher, John M., Jr., '43
Galt, Martin H., '13
Garber, Jesse G., '35, '36
Garfield, Stephen M., '22
Garrels, Allen E., '11
Garrels, John C., '05, '06
Gedeon, Elmer J., '36, '37, '38
Geistert, Walter E., '28
Gembis, Joseph, '27, '28, '29
Gemmell, Robert, '82, '83
Genebach, Lowell B., '17
Genyk, George W., '57, '58, '59
Geyer, H. Ronald, '52, '53, '54

Ghindia, John V., Jr., '48, '49
Gilbert, Louis M., '25, '26, '27
Gill, David D., '99
Gilmore, Thomas W., '81, '82, '83
Glidden, Dr. Stephen, '89
Glinka, David J., '60, '61, '62
Goebel, Jerome P., '54, '55, '57
Goebel, Paul G., '20, '21, '22
Goetz, Dr. Angus G., '17, '18, '19, '20
Goldsmith, DuVal P., '31
Gooding, Cecil, '03
Goodsell, Dr. John O., '16, '17
Gorte, C. Michael, '64
Goss, Thomas A., '66, '67, '68
Gottschalk, Luther, '85
Gracey, Clifford, '16
Graham, Walter, '04, '05, '06, '07
Grambau, Frederick E., '69, '71, '72
Grant, Todd T., '59, '60, '61
Graver, Herbert, '01, '02, '03
Gray, James P., '58
Green, Donald W., '09, '10
Green, James R., '62, '63
Green, Merritt W., '50, '51, '52
Greene, John J., '43
Greenleaf, Dr. George F., '93, '94, '95, '96
Greenwald, Harold T., '26
Greenwood, John C., '55, '56
Greer, Edward R., Jr., '44
Gregory, Bruce, '24, '25
Gregory, George, '01, '02, '03
Griffin, Charles T., '91, '92, '93
Grinnell, Henry S., '26, '27
Groce, Alvin V., '57, '58
Grosh, Dr. Lawrence C., '90, '91, '92, '93
Grube, Charles W., '23, '24, '25
Gusich, Frank J., '69, '70, '71
Gustafson, Lawrence J., '71, '72, '73

413

H

Hadden, Harry G., '94
Hagle, Anson, '88, '89
Hahn, Richard P., '62, '63, '64
Hainrihar, Gary C., '72, '73
Hall, Benjamin L., '59, '60, '61
Hall, Forrest M., '95
Hall, Werner W., '68, '69, '70
Halstead, John C., '58, '59, '60
Hammels, James V., '19
Hammond, Harry S., '04, '05,
    '06, '07
Hammond, Thomas, '03, '04, '05
Hanish, Joseph A., '16, '17
Hankwitz, G. Michael, '67, '68, '69
Hanna, Henry D., '65
Hannah, Donald W., '59, '60
Hannan, Frederic C., '97
Hanshue, Cloyce E., '34, '35
Hanzlik, Robert L., '43
Harden, Linwood, '72
Harding, Frank F., '92, '93
Hardy, William C., '65, '66
Harless, William W., '86, '87, '90
Harmon, Thomas D., '38, '39, '40
Harper, Darrell L., '57, '58, '59
Harpring, John J., '68, '69, '70
Harrigan, Frank A., '27
Harris, William J., '68, '69, '70
Harrison, Gregory W., '70
Hart, William J., '70, '71, '72
Hartman, Gerald E., '66, '67, '68
Haslerig, Clinton E., '71, '72, '73
Hatheway, Dr. E. P., '80
Hawkins, Harry, '23, '24, '25
Hayden, Edward W., '29
Hayes, Ralph W., '91
Hayman, Wayne, 1873
Healy, Brian E., '67, '68, '69
Heater, Charles E., '72, '73
Heath, William H., '26
Heffelfinger, Jon P., '67
Heikkinen, Ralph I., '37, '38

Hendershot, Fred, '16, '17, '18
Henderson, John W., Jr., '63, '64
Henderson, William P., '19
Hendricks, Thomas, Jr., '54, '55
Heneveld, Lloyd A., '47, '48, '49
Henning, Charles, '77
Henninger, Frederick, '93, '94,
    '95, '96
Henry, Preston, '69, '70
Herrnstein, A. E., '01, '02
Herrnstein, John E., '56, '57, '58
Herrnstein, William H., Jr., '23,
    '24, '25
Hershberger, Donavan P., '45,
    '46, '47, '48
Hess, Dr. John H., Jr., '49, '50
Heston, John P., '31, '32, '33
Heston, LeRoy G., '26, '27
Heston, William M., Jr., '29, '30
Heston, William M., Sr., '01, '02,
    '03, '04
Hetzler, Howard, '85
Hewitt, William E., '29, '30, '31
Heynen, Richard B., '55, '56, '57
Hickey, Edward L., '53, '54, '55
Higgins, Francis, '85, '86
Hildebrand, Willard H., '32, '33,
    '34
Hildebrand, Willard R., '58, '59,
    '60
Hilkene, Bruce L., '44, '46, '47
Hill, David J., '54, '55
Hill, Henry W., '68, '69, '70
Hill, Richard F., '54, '55, '56
Hinton, Gene, '45, '49
Hirsch, Elroy L., '43
Hoban, Michael A., '71, '72, '73
Hoban, William P., '72, '73
Hoey, George W., '67, '68
Hoffman, Leo W., '26, '27
Hogg, James R., '96, '97
Holden, George S., '90
Holgate, James G., '43

Hollis, Peter J., '65
Hollister, John W., '93, '95
Hollway, Robert C., '47, '48, '49
Holmes, Daniel W., '28
Hood, E. Edward, '61, '62
Hook, R. Wallace, Jr., '36, '38
Hooper, James H., '95
Horton, Walter, '80, '81
Houtman, John L., '60, '61, '63
Howell, Dr. Frank, '50, '51, '52
Hoyne, Jeffrey B., '63, '64, '65
Hozer, Stanley J., '28, '30, '31
Hribal, James F., '66
Hudson, M. Roy, '29, '30, '31
Huebel, Herbert H., '11, '12
Huff, R. Martin, '68, '69, '70
Hughitt, Ernest F., '13, '14, '15
Huiskens, Thomas A., '70
Hulbert, Bruce W., '28
Hulke, Scott E., '71
Hull, Dr. G. M., '88
Humphries, Derrick A., '66
Hurley, Robert S., '52, '53
Hutchinson, Loomis, '97

I

Imsland, Jerry L., '68, '69
Ingalls, Donald R., '39, '40, '41

J

Jackson, Allen M., '48, '49, '50
Jackson, Norman E., '50
Jacobson, Tage, '33, '34
James, Efton M., '13
James, Hugh H., '03
James, John H., '03
Janke, Frederick C., '36, '37, '38
Jaycox, John M., '84, '85, '86
Jefferis, A. W., '91, '92
Jennings, G. Ferris, '34
Jensen, Thomas P., '73
Jilek, Daniel D., '73
Jobson, Tommy E., '58, '59, '60

Johns, James E., '20, '21, '22
Johnson, Earl, Jr., '55
Johnson, Ernest C., '35
Johnson, Farnham, '43
Johnson, George H., '45, '47
Johnson, Keith A., '73
Johnson, Larry L., '73
Johnson, Paul J., '65, '67
Johnson, Dr. Robert S., '58, '59, '60
Johnson, Ronald A., '66, '67, '68
Johnson, Roy W., '19
Johnson, Thomas, '49, '50, '51
Johnson, Walter N., '56, '57, '58
Johnston, Dr. Collins H., '78, '81
Johnston, James D., '72
Jones, Dennis B., '62
Jones, Joseph M., '69
Jones, Paul, '02
Jordan, Forrest R., '39
Jordan, John D., Jr., '36
Julian, Alfred J., '57, '58, '59
Juttner, Charles F., '97, '99

K

Kamhout, Carl R., '55
Kampe, Kurt W., Jr., '47
Kane, Gary F., '58, '59
Karpus, Arthur J., '18
Karwales, John J., '41, '42
Kayner, Howard S., '11
Keating, Thomas A., '61, '62, '63
Keating, William L., '64, '65
Kee, Thomas G., '70, '71, '72
Keefer, Jackson M., '22
Keena, Leo J., '97, '99
Keller, Michael F., '69, '70, '71
Kelsey, Ray T., Jr., '49, '50, '51
Kelto, Reuben W., '39, '40, '41
Kemp, Stanley S., '64, '65, '66
Kempthorn, Richard J., '47, '48, '49
Kenaga, Raymond K., '53

Kennedy, Charles F., Jr., '42
Kennedy, Robert W., '43
Kennedy, J. Edward, Jr., '40, '41
Kern, Frank J., '43
Kerr, Thomas G., '60
Ketteman, Richard L., '57
Kiesel, George C. F., Jr., '47
Kieta, Robert J., '68
Killian, Timothy J., '68, '69, '70
Killilea, Henry J., '84
Kines, Charles G., '64, '65
King, R. Steven, '73
Kinyon, Peter C., '50, '51
Kipke, Harry G., '21, '22, '23
Kirby, Craig W., '63, '64, '65
Kirk, Bernard C., '21, '22
Kiskadden, Dr. Alexander C., '86
Knickerbocker, Stanley P., '52,
    '54, '55
Knode, Dr. Kenneth T., '18, '19
Knode, Robert T., '21
Knutson, Eugene P., '51, '52, '53
Kocan, Ronald R., '62
Koceski, Leo R., '48, '49, '50
Kodros, Archie J., '37, '38, '39
Kohl, Harry E., '40
Kohl, Ralph W., '47, '48
Kolesar, Dr. Robert C., '40, '41,
    '42
Kolesar, William P., '53, '54, '55
Korowin, James F., '59, '61
Koss, Gregory A., '72, '73
Kovacevich, David A., '62, '63
Kowalik, John F., Jr., '62
Kowalik, John F., Sr., '31, '32, '33
Kraeger, George W., '43, '46
Kramer, Jon E., '66, '67
Kramer, Melvin G., '35
Kramer, Ronald J., '54, '55, '56
Kreager, Carl A., '49, '50
Krejsa, Robert C., '40
Kress, Edward S., '52, '53
Kromer, Paul S., '38, '39, '40

Krueger, Frederick L., '57
Kuick, Don D., '47
Kunow, Walter, '23, '24
Kunsa, Joseph J., '68
Kupec, C. J., '72
Kurtz, David W., '61, '62, '63
Kuzma, Thomas G., '41, '42

L

Laine, John T., '41
LaJeunesse, Omer J., '30, '31
Lambert, Oscar P., '17
Landsittel, Thomas A., '66
Lantry, Michael W., '72, '73
Laskey, William G., '62, '63, '64
Lavine, Louis, '36, '37, '38
Lawrence, James E., '02
Lawton, George M., '10
Lazetich, Milan, '44
LeClaire, Laurence E., '50, '51, '52
Lee, Louis R., '64, '65, '66
Lehr, John J., '61
Leith, Jerry C., '59
Lentz, Charles W., Jr., '48, '49
Leonard, Heman, '92, '93, '94
LeRoux, Arthur N., '44
Lewis, Kirk J., '73
Lightner, Henry W., '13
Lincoln, James H., '35, '36
Linthicum, Frank, '08, '09, '10
Lintol, John F., '44, '45, '46
Lockard, Harold C., '40, '41
Loell, John L., '06, '07
Logan, Randolph, '71, '72
Longman, Frank C., '03, '04, '05
Loucks, Alvin E., '19
Lousma, Jack R., '56
Lovette, John H., '25, '26
Luby, Earle B., '35, '36, '37
Lukz, Joseph E., '69
Lund, Donald A., '42, '43, '44
Lyall, James M., '73
Lynch, John A., '68

Lyons, John J., '13, '14

M

Mace, William H., '82
Mack, Hugh R., Jr., '43
Mack, Thomas L., '64, '65
MacPhee, William D., '58
MacPherran, Edgar W., '87, '88, '89
Madar, Elmer F., '41, '42, '46
Maddock, James A., '54, '55, '56
Maddock, Joseph H., '02, '03
Mader, Gerald H., '62, '63, '64
Madsen, Edgar, '24
Maentz, D. Scott, '59, '60, '61
Maentz, Thomas S., '54, '55, '56
Magidsohn, Joe, '09, '10
Magoffin, Paul P., '05, '06, '07
Mair, Peter K., '66, '67
Maloney, Frank M., '61
Mandich, James M., '67, '68, '69
Mann, Robert, '46, '47
Mans, George W., '59, '60, '61
Marciniak, Gerald P., '56, '57, '58
Marcovsky, Abraham S., '32
Marcum, John F., Jr., '62, '63, '64
Marion, Phillip E., '23, '24
Marion, Robert L., '54, '55
Marks, Thomas R., '00
Martens, Albert C., '16
Marzonie, George A., '36, '37
Matheson, Robert K., '51, '52
Maulbetsch, John F., '14, '15, '16
Maves, Earl E., '43
McBride, John R., '70
McClelland, Donald B., '47, '48, '49
McCoy, C. Richard, Jr., '68, '69, '70
McCoy, Ernest H., '57
McDonald, Charles G., '98, '99
McDonald, Duncan B., '51, '52, '53, '54

McGugin, Dan E., '01, '02
McHale, Frank M., '13, '14
McIntyre, Kent C., '26
McKena, Thomas L., '90
McKenzie, Reginald, '69, '70, '71
McLean, John F., '98, '99
McLenna, Bruce O., '61
McMillan, Neil, Jr., '10, '11
McNeil, Tom H., '83, '84, '85
McNeill, Edward D., '45, '46, '47, '48
McNitt, Gary D., '58, '59, '60
McPherson, James N., '59
McRae, Benjamin P., '59, '60, '61
McWilliams, Richard H., '49, '50
Meads, G. Edgar II, '53, '54, '55
Meek, Richard C., '11
Mehaffey, Dr. Howard H., '38, '44
Melchiori, Wayne F., '52
Melzow, William, '39, '40, '41
Metz, David F., '72, '73
Meyer, Jack O., '38
Meyers, Earl J., '35
Middlebrook, John F., '71
Mielke, Robert W., '64, '65, '66
Miklos, Gerald W., '66, '67, '68
Miller, James F., Jr., '25, '26, '27
Miller, James J., '07, '09
Miller, James K., Jr., '23, '24
Miller, Wallace B., '30
Minko, John P., '60, '61, '62
Mitchell, Charles S., '78, '79
Molenda, John J., '25, '26
Momsen, Anton, Jr., '45, '46, '49, '50
Monthei, Dennis B., '67
Moore, Dr. Albert, '83
Moore, Edward M., '68, '69, '70
Moorhead, Donald W., '68, '69, '70
Morgan, Dennis T., '65, '66, '67
Morgan, Robert O., '30
Morrison, Chester C., '17, '18
Morrison, Maynard D., '29, '30, '31
Morrow, Gordon H., '57

417

Morrow, John M., Jr., '53, '54, '55
Morrow, William M., '85, '86
Mowrey, Harry J., '91
Mroz, Vincent P., '43
Muelder, Wesley W., '45
Muir, William T., '62, '64
Muirhead, Stanley, '21, '22, '23
Murdock, Guy B., '69, '70, '71
Musser, James C., '12, '13
Mutch, Craig A., '72, '73
Myers, Bradley J., '57, '58, '59
Myll, Clifton A., Jr., '43

N

Naab, Fred W., '43
Negus, Fred W., '43
Neisch, LeRoy E., '21, '22, '23
Nelson, David, '40, '41
Nelson, Douglas F., '67
Nelson, Viggo, '20
Newell, Peter J., '68, '69, '70
Newman, Harry L., Jr., '58, '59
Newman, Harry L., Sr., '30, '31, '32
Newton, Fred B., '06
Nicholson, John E., Jr., '37, '38, '39
Nielsen, Paul, '39
Nieman, Thomas S., '70
Niemann, Walter A., '15, '16
Ninde, Daniel B., '94
Nolan, Delbert L., '61
Norcross, Fred S., '03, '04, '05
Norton, John K., '15
Noskin, Stanton C., '57, '58, '59
Nunley, Frank H., '64, '65, '66
Nussbaumer, Robert J., '43, '44, '45
Nyland, Herman Z., Jr., '26, '27
Nyren, Marvin R., '55, '56, '57

O

Oade, James E., '25

O'Donnell, Joseph R., '60, '62, '63
Ohlenroth, William G., '48, '49, '50
Olcott, William J., '81
Oldham, Donald L., '50, '51, '52
Oldham, Michael, '69, '70, '71
Olds, Fredric C., '37, '38, '39
Oliver, Russell D., '32, '33, '34
Olshanski, Henry S., '43
Oosterbaan, Bennie G., '25, '26, '27
Oppman, Douglas K., '58
Ortmann, Charles H., '48, '49, '50
Orwig, Dr. James B., '55, '56, '57
Orwig, James W., '28
O'Shaughnessy, Richard E., '51, '52, '53
Osterman, Russell J., '50, '51

P

Pace, James E., '55, '56, '57
Padjen, John, Jr., '50
Palmaroli, John M., '26, '27
Palmer, Paul D., '59
Palmer, Peter N., '50
Palomaki, David J., '60
Parker, H. Fred, '24, '25
Parker, Ray F., '29
Parkhill, Thomas H., '65
Parks, Daniel E., '68, '69
Patanelli, Matthew L., '34, '35, '36
Patchen, Brian P., '63, '64
Paterson, George C., '11, '12, '13
Patrick, Dr. Harry, '05, '06
Pattengill, Victor, '09, '10
Paul, Louis P., '92, '93
Pavloff, Louis, '59, '62
Peach, Willard L., '16, '19
Pearson, Dr. William W., '91, '92, '93
Peckham, H. John, Jr., '53, '54, '55
Pederson, Dr. Bernhardt L., '51, '52

418

Pederson, Ernest A., '35, '37
Penksa, Robert A., '67, '68
Perlinger, Jeffrey L., '73
Perrin, John S., '20
Perry, Lowell W., '50, '51, '52
Peterson, Dr. Donald W., '49, '50, '51
Peterson, Dr. Thomas R., '44, '47, '48, '49
Petoskey, E. Jack, '43
Petoskey, Fred L., '31, '32, '33
Petro, Charles C., '21
Phillips, Edward J., Jr., '36, '38
Phillips, Raymond, '65, '66, '67
Picard, Frank A., '10, '11
Pickard, Frederick R., '50, '51
Pierson, Barry F., '67, '68, '69
Pighee, John A., '72
Poe, Howard W., '27, '28, '29
Pommerening, Otto P., '27, '28
Pond, Irving K., '79
Ponsetto, Dr. Joseph L., '43, '44, '45
Pontius, Miller H., '11, '12, '13
Poorman, Edwin B., '28, '29
Poplawski, Thomas, '71, '72
Popp, Herbert L., '49, '50
Porter, David S., '66, '67
Poulos, Paul K., '58, '59, '60
Powers, Hiram, '91, '92, '93
Powers, John E., '49, '50
Prahst, Gary K., '56, '57, '58
Prashaw, Milton M., '45
Pregulman, Mervin, '41, '42, '43
Prettyman, Horace G., '82, '83, '85, '86, '88, '89, '90
Pritchard, Thomas B., '61, '62, '63
Pritula, William, '42, '46, '47
Pryor, Cecil L., '68, '69
Przygodski, George M., '73
Ptacek, Robert J., '56, '57, '58
Puckelwartz, William H., '25, '27
Pullen, Thomas R., '65

Purdum, Claire E., '30
Purucker, Norman B., '37, '38
Putich, William, '49, '50, '51

Q

Quinn, Clement P., '10, '11, '12
Quinn, Cyril J., '12, '13

R

Radigan, Timothy J., '65
Raeder, James P., '59, '60, '61
Raimey, David E., '60, '61, '62
Ranney, Leroy W., '08, '09
Rather, David E., '70, '71, '72
Raymond, Philip, '16
Raynsford, James W., '12, '13, '14
Redden, Curtis G., '01, '02, '03
Redner, Arthur E., '00, '01
Reed, Frank F., '78, '79
Regeczi, John M., '32, '33, '34
Rehor, Fred L., '15, '16
Reimann, Lewis C., '14, '15
Remias, Steve, '34, '35
Renda, Hercules, '37, '38, '39
Rennebohm, Robert B., '43
Renner, Arthur W., '43, '44, '45, '46
Renner, William W., '33, '35
Rentschler, David F., '55, '56
Rescarla, Russell G., '51, '52
Reynick, Charles J., '77, '78
Reynolds, John C., '66
Rheinschild, Walter M., '05, '07
Rich, George E., '26, '27, '28
Richards, J. D., '94, '95, '96, '97
Richardson, A. E., '99
Ries, Richard G., '63
Rifenburg, Richard G., '46, '47, '48
Riley, Thomas J., '08
Rinaldi, Joseph M., '35, '36, '37
Rindfuss, Richard M., '62, '63, '64
Rio, Anthony P., '57, '59

419

Ritchie, C. Stark, '35, '36, '37
Ritley, Robert M., '69
Ritter, Charles A., '54
Roach, Thomas G., '29
Roberts, Willis R., '76
Robinson, Don W., '41, '42, '46
Roby, Douglas F., '21, '22
Rockwell, F. A. '23, '24
Roehm, Laurence, '15
Rogers, Joe C., '39, '40, '41
Root, Edgar D., '74
Rosatti, Rudolph F., '22
Rosema, Robert J., '71
Roseman, Roger W., '65, '66, '67
Rotunno, Michael J., '54, '55, '56
Rowser, John F., '63, '65, '66
Rumney, Mason P., '06, '07
Rundell, Warren S., '93, '94
Russ, J. Carlton, '72, '73
Ruzicka, Charles W., '63, '65
Rye, Harold, '17, '19

S

Safley, Ben, 1872, '76
Sample, Frederick, '68
Samuels, Tom C., '30, '31
Sanderson, Edmond L., '92, '93
Sarantos, Peter A., '69
Sansom, Elijah T., '68
Savage, Carl M., '32, '33
Savage, Michael S., '33, '34, '35
Savilla, Roland, '37, '38, '39
Scheffler, Lance G., '68, '69, '70
Schick, Gary J., '65
Schlicht, Leo R., '51
Schmidt, Paul R., '61
Schoenfeld, Dr. John, '26, '27
Schopf, Jon B., '59, '60, '61
Schram, Richard G., '62
Schulte, Henry F., '03, '04, '05
Schulz, Adolph G., '04, '05, '07, '08
Schumacher, Gerald F., '70, '71, '72

Schuman, Stanton J., '35
Scott, S. Spencer, '13
Seal, Paul N., '71, '72, '73
Searle, John G., '21
Sears, Harold W., Jr., '34
Senter, Henry M., '93
Sexton, Walter E., '71, '72
Seyferth, John F., Jr., '69, '70, '71
Seymour, Paul C., '70, '71, '72
Seymour, Philip H., '67, '68, '70
Shannon, Edward J., Jr., '54, '55, '56
Sharpe, Ernest M., '65, '66, '67
Sharpe, Philip E., '41, '42
Shatusky, Michael R., '56, '57
Shaw, Walter W., '00
Sherman, Roger, '91, '93
Sherman, Samuel S., Sr., '89, '90
Shields, Edmund C., '95
Shorts, Bruce, '00, '02
Shuttlesworth, E. Ed, '71, '72, '73
Sickels, Quentin B., '44, '46, '47, '48
Siegel, Donald J., '36, '37, '38
Siegmund, Dr. Rudolph, '99
Sigler, William K., '43
Sigman, Leonel A., '55, '56
Sikkenga, Jay H., '31
Simkus, Arnold, '62, '64
Simrall, Dr. James, '28, '29, '30
Singer, Oscar A., '32, '33
Sipp, Warren D., '66, '67, '68
Sirosky, Dennis B., '68
Sisinyak, Eugene T., '56, '57, '58
Skinner, James L., '85
Slade, Thomas A., '71, '72, '73
Slaughter, E. R., '22, '23, '24
Slezak, David R., '61
Smeja, Rudy M., '41, '42, '43
Smick, Daniel, '36, '37, '38
Smith, Andrew W., '09

420

Smith, Cedric D., '15, '16, '17
Smith, Frederic L., '88, '89
Smith, Gerald, '58, '59, '60
Smith, James A., '73
Smith, Jeffrey A., '61
Smith, John E., '45
Smith, Steven C., '63, '64, '65
Smith, Tony L., '70, '71, '72
Smith, William A., '37, '38, '39
Smith, Willie, '56, '57, '58
Smithers, John A., '35, '36
Snider, Eugene M., '54, '56, '57
Snover, Edward J., '76
Snow, Muir B., '96, '97
Snow, Neil W., '98, '99, '00, '01
Soboleski, Joseph R., '45, '46, '47, '48
Sobsey, Solomon, '35
Sorensen, T. C. '29
Spacht, Ronald L., '61
Sparkman, R. Wayne, '62, '63
Sparks, Clifford M., '16, '17, '19
Spearman, Clinton, '70, '71, '72
Spencer, Royce E., '67
Spidel, John W., '56, '57, '58
Splawn, Laurence L., '14
Sprague, Ernest M., '87, '88
Squier, George G., '26, '28
Staatz, Dr. Karl S., '14, '15
Stabb, Chester C., '36
Stamman, Carl P., '24, '25
Stamos, John E., '59, '60, '61
Stanford, Dr. Thad C., '51, '52, '53
Stanton, Edward C., Jr., '36, '37
Staroba, Paul, '68, '69, '70
Stawski, Dr. Willard S., '61
Steckle, Allen, '97, '98, '99
Steele, Harold O., '22, '23, '24
Steger, Geoffrey C., '71, '73
Steger, Herbert F., '22, '23, '24
Steinke, Alfred E., '28, '29
Steketee, Frank W., '18, '20, '21
Stenberg, Robert P., '42, '43

Stetten, Dr. Maynard L., '58
Stieler, Stephen O., '59
Stincic, Thomas O., '66, '67, '68
Stine, Dr. William R., '58, '59, '60
Straffon, Dr. Ralph A., '49, '50
Straub, Harvey G., '28
Street, Dr. Charles E., '98, '99
Stribe, Ralph C., Jr., '50, '51, '52
Strinko, Steve D., '72, '73
Strobel, Jack A., '60, '61, '62
Strong, David A., '38, '39
Strozewski, Richard J., '50, '52, '53
Stuart, Theodore M., '04, '05
Sukup, Milo F., '38, '39, '40
Sullivan, John T., '07, '08
Sutherland, Dr. C. J., '89, '90
Sutherland, George S., '49
Sutton, John R., '89
Swan, Donald M., '21, '24
Sweeley, Everett M., '99, '00, '01, '02
Sweet, Cedric C., '34, '35, '36
Swift, Thomas P., '44
Sygar, Richard S., '64, '65, '66
Syring, Richard E., '58, '60
Sytek, James H., '58
Szydlowski, Ronald E., '73
Szymanski, Richard P., '61, '62, '63

T

Talcott, William W., '98
Takach, Thomas J., '69
Taylor, LeVerne H., '27
Taylor, Michael, '69, '70, '71
Taylor, William L., '69, '70, '71
Teetzel, Clayton T., '97
Teninga, Walter H., '45, '47, '48, '49
Tessmer, Estel S., '30, '31, '33
Teuscher, Charles G., '57
Thisted, Carl E., '25
Thomas, John E., '73

421

Thomas, John R., Jr., '68
Thomas, Joseph M., '96
Thomson, George C., '10, '11, '12
Thornbladh, Robert N., '71, '72,
   '73
Timberlake, Robert W., '62, '63,
   '64
Timm, Robert F., '50, '51, '52
Tinker, Horace C., '38, '39
Tinkham, David J., '50, '51, '52
Titas, Francis G., '67, '68, '69
Tomasi, Dominic P., '45, '46, '47,
   '48
Topor, Ted P., '50, '51, '52
Torbet, Roy H., '11, '12, '13
Topp, Dr. Eugene R., '52, '53
Totzke, John H., '28
Townsend, Frederic, '81
Trainer, David, '89, '90
Traphagan, Roice A., '13
Triplehorn, Howard, '34
Trosko, Fred, '37, '38, '39
Troszak, Douglas A., '71, '72, '73
Trowbridge, W. R., '86
Trump, Jack A., '43
Truske, Joseph E., '26, '28, '29
Tucker, Curtis J., '71, '72, '73
Tumpane, Patrick W., '73
Tunnicliff, William H., '59, '60,
   '61
Tupper, Dr. Virgil, '92
Tureaud, Kenneth E., '59, '60, '61
Tyng, Alexander, 1870

U
Ulevitch, Dr. Herman, '37
Usher, Edward T., '18, '20, '21
Utz, Irwin C., '21, '22, '23

V
Valek, Vincent, '38
Valpey, Arthur, Jr., '35, '36, '37
VanDervoort, Edward R., '22, '23

VandeWater, Clarence H., '36, '37
VanDyne, Rudd D., '59, '60
VanOrden, William J., '20, '21,
   '22
VanPelt, James S., Jr., '55, '56,
   '57
VanSummern, Robert W., '48, '49
Vercel, Jovan, '73
Vernier, Robert W., '42, '46
Veselenak, John J., '53, '54
Vick, Henry A., '18, '19, '20, '21
Vick, Richard, '23
Vidmer, Richard F., '65, '66, '67
Viergever, John D., '33, '34, '35
Villa, Giovanni, '93, '94, '95, '96
Volk, Richard C., '64, '65, '66

W
Wade, Mulford, '87
Wadhams, Timothy, '69
Wahl, Charles F., '44
Wahl, Robert A., Jr., '48, '49, '50
Walker, Alan G., '71
Walker, Arthur D., '52, '53, '54
Walker, Harlan N., '18
Walker, John C., '58, '60, '61
Walls, Grant W., Jr., '60
Wambacker, J. W., '96
Ward, Carl D., '64, '65, '66
Ward, James A., '60, '61, '62
Ward, Willis F., '32, '33, '34
Wardley, Frank L., '42
Warner, Donald R., '73
Washington, Martin I., '68
Wasmund, William S., '07, '08, '09
Watkins, James K., '07, '09
Watson, Dr. R. William, '14, '15
Watts, Harold M., '43, '44, '45, '46
Weber, Walter J., '25, '26
Wedge, Robert E., '66, '67, '68
Weeks, Dr. Alanson, '98
Weeks, Harold J., '07
Weeks, Harrison, '99, '00, '01, '02

Weinmann, Thomas R., '67

Weisenburger, John E., '44, '45, '46, '47

Wells, Rex C., '43

Wells, Richard C., '63, '64, '65

Wells, Stanfield, '09, '10, '11

Welton, Arthur D., '86

Werner, Mark W., '68, '69

Weske, Richard F., '15, '16, '17

Westfall, Robert B., '39, '40, '41

Weston, Archie B., '17, '19

Westover, Louis W., '31, '32, '33

Weyers, John W., '44

Whalen, James L., '15

Wheeler, Clare J., Jr., '28, '29, '30

White, Howell S., '22, '23

White, Hugh, '98, '00, '01

White, John T., '46, '47

White, Paul G., '41, '42, '43, '46

White, Robert E., '69

Whittle, John D., '27

Widman, Charles H., '98

Wieman, Elton E., '16, '17, '20

Wiese, Robert L., '42, '43, '44, '46

Wikel, Howard L., '43, '47

Wilhite, Clayton E., '64, '65, '66

Wilhite, James R., '67, '68

Wilkins, F. Stuart, '45, '46, '47, '48

Williams, Gerald H., '53, '54

Williams, Richard J., '28

Williams, Ronald M., '52, '53

Williamson, Ivan B., '30, '31, '32

Williamson, Richard P., '66, '67

Williamson, Walter L., '72, '73

Wilson, Donald L., '29

Wilson, Ebin, '01

Wilson, Hugh E., '19, '20, '21

Wine, Raymond L., '56, '57

Wink, Jack S., '43

Wise, Clifford C., '40, '42

Wisniewski, Irvin C., '47, '48, '49

Wistert, Albert A., '40, '41, '42

Wistert, Alvin L., '47, '48, '49

Wistert, Francis M., '31, '32, '33

Witherspoon, Thomas W., '50, '51, '52

Wolter, James R., '49, '50, '51

Wombacher, John, '95, '96

Wood, George H., '87

Woodruff, P. G., '81

Woodward, Paul W., '62, '63

Woodworth, Paul, '91, '92

Woolley, Edwin L., '68

Workman, Harry A., '06

Wormwood, Frank F., '81, '82

Wright, Dr. Charles D., '85, '86, '87

Wright, Harry T., '35

Wright, Kenneth J., '65, '66

Y

Yanz, John A., '62, '64

Yanz, Richard C., '67

Yearby, William M., '63, '64, '65

Yerges, Howard F., '44, '45, '46, '47

Yont, J. G., '94, '95

Yost, Field H., Jr., '31

Z

Zacharty, John J., '58

ZanFagna, Donald M., '51

Zatkoff, Roger, '50, '51, '52

Zeiger, Harold M., '16

Ziem, Frederick C., '36

Zimmerman, Robert A., '39

Zubkus, E. James, '59, '61

Zuccarelli, David C., '71, '72

Zuganelis, George M., '69